Interpersonal Divide

Interpersonal Divide in the Age of the Machine

Second Edition

MICHAEL BUGEJA, PhD

IOWA STATE UNIVERSITY,
GREENLEE SCHOOL OF JOURNALISM
AND COMMUNICATION

New York   Oxford

OXFORD UNIVERSITY PRESS

Oxford University Press is a department of the University of Oxford.
It furthers the University's objective of excellence in research, scholarship, and
education by publishing worldwide. Oxford is a registered trademark
of Oxford University Press in the UK and certain other countries.

Published in the United States of America by Oxford University Press
198 Madison Avenue, New York, NY 10016, United States of America.

For titles covered by Section 112 of the US Higher Education Opportunity
Act, please visit www.oup.com/us/he for the latest information about pricing
and alternate formats.

Library of Congress Cataloging-in-Publication Data
Names: Bugeja, Michael J., author.
Title: Interpersonal divide in the age of the machine / Michael Bugeja, Ph.D.,
    Iowa State University, Greenlee School of Journalism and Communication.
Description: Second Edition. | New York : Oxford University Press, [2017]
    Revised edition of the author's Interpersonal divide, c2005. |
    Includes bibliographical references and index.
Identifiers: LCCN 2017023649| ISBN 9780190600990 (pbk.) |
    ISBN 9780190601003 (ebook)
Subjects: LCSH: Interpersonal relations. | Mass media—Social aspects. |
    Technology—Social aspects. | Communities. | Social perception.
Classification: LCC HM846 .B84 2017 | DDC 302—dc23
LC record available at https://lccn.loc.gov/2017023649

9 8 7 6 5 4 3 2 1

Printed by Webcom, Inc. in Canada.

For Shane Michael and Diane

CONTENTS

....

ABOUT THE AUTHOR

....

Michael J. Bugeja is an ethicist and author of twenty-three books, including *Living Ethics Across Media Platforms* and *Vanishing Act: The Erosion of Online Footnotes and Implications for Scholarship in the Digital Age. Living Ethics*, along with the first edition of *Interpersonal Divide: The Search for Community in a Technological Age*, won the prestigious Clifford G. Christians award for research in media ethics. Dr. Bugeja directed the Greenlee School of Journalism and Communication at Iowa State University of Science and Technology.

Dr. Bugeja is a frequent source for insights about media, technology and ethics, interviewed by the *New Yorker*, the *New York Times*, the *Washington Post*, the *Christian Science Monitor, USA Today, International Herald Tribune, Newsday, American Journalism Review, Columbia Journalism Review, Chronicle of Higher Education* and other media outlets. His creative and scholarly works have appeared in a variety of publications, including *Harper's*, the *Chronicle Review, Journalism and Mass Communication Educator, Journal of Mass Media Ethics, New Media and Society* and *Journalism Quarterly*, among others. His awards include a National Endowment for the Arts fellowship, a National Endowment for the Humanities grant and an Ohio Arts Council fellowship. He received the Iowa Newspaper Association's highest honor, the Distinguished Service Award. Dr. Bugeja also has received several teaching honors, including an AMOCO Foundation Outstanding Teacher Award and the University Professor Teaching Award, both bestowed by student bodies of major research institutions. He also won the Iowa State University Outstanding Administrator Award and the Scripps Howard Administrator of the Year Award. He was elected to the Accrediting Council on Education in Journalism and Mass Communications. Before entering academe, Dr. Bugeja worked as a state editor and national correspondent for United Press International.

ACKNOWLEDGMENTS
....

The author wishes to acknowledge colleagues who have deepened his conscience and expanded his consciousness during research and preparation of the second edition of *Interpersonal Divide*, including Jan Lauren Bowles, Eric Abbott and Melissa Garrett. He especially thanks his editor Toni Magyar, editorial assistant Allegra Howard, copyeditor Elizabeth Nelson Bortka and project manager Elizabeth Kelly. No book reaches its potential without constructive criticism. Comments and suggestions by external reviewers—Anthony Spina (Fairleigh Dickinson University), Edward Lee Lamoureux (Bradley University), Neil M. Alperstein (Loyola University Maryland), Mark Brown (California State University–Sacramento), Daniel de Roulet (Irvine Valley College), Victoria Holtz-Wodzak (Viterbo University), Glenn Geiser-Getz (East Stroudsburg University), Michael Larkin (University of California–Berkeley), Paul Mihailidis (Emerson College), Ben S. Bunting Jr. (Oregon Institute of Technology), Christopher J. Finlay (Loyola Marymount University), James W. Miller (Dominican University), Chandra Commuri (California State University–Bakersfield), Calvin L. Troup (Duquesne University), Samantha Phillips (University of Miami), Timothy J. Pasch (University of North Dakota), Janet McMullen (University of North Alabama)—are deeply appreciated. He dedicates this book to his son, Shane Michael, a soil scientist, and to his beautiful spouse,

Diane Bugeja, who teaches photojournalism at the Greenlee School, Iowa State. Finally, the author is especially grateful for the support and guidance of Oxford University Press, whose employees and sales personnel ensure the success of editorial projects, even ones that go against the grain of conventional thinking, such as the work you are reading.

PREFACE

....

When the first edition of this book was published in 2005, the title— *Interpersonal Divide*—alluded to the work of Pippa Norris, a Harvard University political scientist, who defined the popular phrase "digital divide" as having three distinct components: the *global* divide associated with Internet access between industrialized and developing nations; the *social* divide between those with and without access in each nation; and the *democratic* divide between those who do and who do not use communication technology to participate in public life.[1] Those divides existed then, deserving attention; however, as governments and corporations collaborated to bridge those divides, for the common good and/or for profit, another more ominous void developed, eroding relationships at home, school and work. Then as now, the phrase—"interpersonal divide"—concerns the social gap that develops when individuals misperceive reality because of media overconsumption and misinterpret others because of technology overuse.

In 2005, *Interpersonal Divide* was a warning. In 2017, it is an alarm. We are literally hyperventilating on media and mobile technologies. As early as 2006, the Associated Press reported, "Americans spend more time watching TV, listening to the radio, surfing the Internet, and reading newspapers than anything else except breathing."[2] At the time, the website "The Future of Journalism" reported that the average consumer spent 65 days per year watching television, up from 61 in 2000; 41 days listening to the radio, up from 39 days in 2000; 8.1 days on the Internet, up from 4.3 days in 2000; 7.3 days reading newspapers, down from

xiii

8.4 days in 2000; and 9.5 days reading books and magazines, down from 10 days in 2000.[3] By 2014, those figures changed drastically, documenting just how much consumers relied on digital information and social media. Mobile technology then was forecast to grow by 23 percent, with the average consumer spending 5 hours and 46 minutes per day using all manner of digital devices, or more than 87.7 days per year, or a total 155.6 days when television viewing was added.[4] Americans average about 6.8 hours of sleep per night, or 103.4 days per year.[5] Deduct that from 365 days in a year, and the typical consumer spends 70 percent of waking hours looking at a screen.

The first edition of *Interpersonal Divide* was researched between 1999 and 2004; hence, those early 2000 statistics were pertinent in advancing the theory that media saturation and technology overuse were creating fewer opportunities for face-to-face communication. The goal of this edition is much different. What happens to basic human morality when 70 percent of waking hours are spent watching a screen? What happens to our humanity when machines take over everyday tasks in the age of big data? What happens to the future of today's college students and their children, nieces and nephews when machines provide answers to problems large and small without addressing why those problems occurred in the first place? Machines can correlate instantaneously informing us what happened where, when, how and to whom. But they cannot think critically or find solutions the way people have for millennia, by illogical, creative responses to obstacles and challenges, including discoveries by accident. Do universal principles such as truth-telling, nonviolence and dignity—cornerstones of philosophy rooted in time, culture and place since Confucius in Asia and Socrates in Greece—change as we shift from using technology for part of our day to consuming it for most of our day, to wearing it during our day and, finally, to embedding it in our bodies now and in the near future?

The first edition of *Interpersonal Divide* was alarming enough for its time, based in part on the philosophy of Jacques Ellul—that technology changes everything it touches without itself being changed much at all. To understand the power of machines, we must contemplate and re-evaluate Ellul without clinging to the entrepreneurial hype of commercial value in the new era of analytics, as we shall explore in the second edition. For Ellul, technology is touted by one criterion: efficiency; its laws are irreversible. When they cause problems, they either cease to operate or require more technology to do tasks. Soon machines must communicate with each other through large networks of technology. When that happens, every aspect of human discourse and activity becomes subject and subservient to the machine: economic problems require political solutions, political solutions require business adaptation; business adaption requires government surveillance, and so on. As C. George Benello writes in "Technology and Power: Technique as a Mode of Understanding Modernity," concerning Ellul:

> Technique has become a universal language, a universal determinant of human culture. And it has become autonomous, a closed system determining the conditions of social, political, and economic change rather than being guided by imperatives developed independently of it [6]

The second edition of *Interpersonal Divide* takes that precept to a new level, asking, *What happens to ethical norms of a society monitored every moment by the technology users access, wear and rely on so that people no longer question the operating systems that control them? Does that fact of modern life change humane values and universal principles to such an extent that we abandon them and adopt the values and technological principles of the machine?* According to computer scientist and philosopher Jaron Lanier in *Who Owns the Future*, "Given both the momentum to screw up the human world and the capability to vastly improve it, how will people behave?"[7]

The goal here is to investigate that troubling question as controversial in 2017 as the thesis of the first edition was in 2005, prophesying that technology had changed our interpersonal relationships. Now everyone acknowledges that. This edition challenges us to scrutinize data science and take inventory of ourselves through the lens of the human condition, from which media and technology offer escape. We must assess the impact of the machine on the conscience and address basic moral and social conundrums, from the disenfranchisement of the lower classes to the degradation of the environment. On a personal level, we must begin by documenting the interpersonal void in homes, schools and workplaces. As such, *Interpersonal Divide* will:

- Update and document how other generations coped with great technological change.
- Illustrate how each medium changes the message, resulting in cultural upheaval that also causes deep rifts in personal and professional relationships.

- Discuss media and civic issues from an applied and virtue ethics perspective.
- Address the impact on society of machines in the age of big data.
- Focus steadfastly on the importance of community in our lifelong quest to harmonize consciousness (awareness of how our actions impact others) and conscience (innate knowledge of right and wrong).

To be sure, other authors have made similar arguments since the initial publication of *Interpersonal Divide*, including Sherry Turkle in *Alone Together: Why We Expect More from Technology and Less from Each Other*. In that regard, the *Huffington Post* noted that *Interpersonal Divide's* "classic and prescient study of technology and social capital made points very similar to those of *Alone Together* seven years earlier."[8] Indeed, the first edition of this book documented the existence of an interpersonal divide, now part of our technical lexicon. The second edition posits a greater divide, one that removes us from the circle of human beings and places us within the circuitry of the machine.

The approach here remains general. As the sociologist Manuel Castells writes in *The Power of Identity*, a topic as broad and inter-disciplinary as the topic of *Interpersonal Divide*, "*This is not a book about books*. Thus, we will not discuss existing theories on each topic, or cite every possible source on issues presented here."[9] Such an approach, writes Castells, would be pretentious and superficial. The intent in any multidisciplinary work is to explain complex truths in plain language rather than to validate those truths via complex language. Journalist James Howard Kunstler emphasizes the importance of this in his watershed book on the erosion of community in our time, *Home from Nowhere*, arguing that "so many problems with our everyday environment are caused by the over-specialization of trained specialists unwilling to look at the bigger picture beyond the narrow purview of their specialty."[10] Also, concepts expressed here have been thoroughly researched but are presented without an abundance of statistics, tables, or numerical data that make universal ideas seem topical or obsolete. Jargon is eschewed for the same reason. Lexicons of media and technology change as rapidly as gadgets do. That is why, whenever possible, topics are defined generally rather than academically, engaging as many as possible in the conversation for as long a time as possible.

For instance, the phrase "media and technology" means different things to different people, depending on lifestyles and professions. Online gamers have their own views and vocabularies, as do consumer information advocates and data scientists. Thus, common meanings will be emphasized whenever possible in *Interpersonal Divide*. The word *media* means the channels through which messages are delivered. *Technology* means the mechanism delivering those messages. Media here means "the mass, the globalized, the regional, the national, the local, the personal media; the broadcast and interactive media; the audio and audio-visual and the printed media; the electronic and the mechanical, the digital and analogue media; the big screen and the small screen media; the dominant and alternative media; the fixed and the mobile, the convergent and the stand-alone media."[11] Beginning with the ancient Greeks, technology finds it roots in the word "techne," or skill in the arts. The genre as envisioned by Plato and Plotinus featured an ascending scale from crafts to the sciences and from there to the physical and intellectual, with technical arts relegated to the middle of the trajectory.[12] What has changed in our time is the elevation of technical arts to the top of the totem with machines supplying the intellectual through correlation without causation (understanding what occurred but failing to understand why).

The focus here is on the use and marketing of technology and media, rather than byzantine analyses on the infrastructure of communication systems or computer networks. Technology so saturates our civilization that libraries, bookstores and e-book vendors do not know how to categorize it. While you can find a section on the history of science, you must look for technology books "through many departments, including sociology cultural studies, women's studies, history, media, anthropology, transportation, and do-it-yourself."[13] In sum, *Interpersonal Divide in the Age of the Machine* discusses the evolution of current media and technology that will be with us in format for some time to come: computers, Internet, mobile devices, wearable and bodily embedded technologies, and so on. The impact of those technologies will not change, even though the equipment that delivers them will.

Moreover, a broad, interdisciplinary approach allows for *synthesis*—the process of combining concepts usually not associated with each other, to envision deeper truths. That is why *Interpersonal Divide* brings together a number of intellectual strands that do not usually turn up in discussions of technology and media consumption. The objective is to assemble a new mosaic of the modern era that synthesizes such literatures as media studies, psychology, sociology, information technology, computer science, applied ethics, and science and technology studies. *Interpersonal Divide* postulates that media and technology are affecting millions and their morality in similar, transformative ways. If so, those ways should be extant in a variety of activities and disciplines, primarily ones impacting communities and the people who dwell therein. This methodology proved effective in Robert Putnam's best-selling book, *Bowling Alone: The Collapse and Revival of American Community*, in which he sought "as diverse a range of evidence as possible on continuities and change in American social life," theorizing that if "the transformation that I discern is as broad and deep as I believe it to be, it ought to show up in many different places, so I have cast a broad net."[14]

The "net" here also is broad, but the focus is narrow—an exploration of and response to our predicament of lost community in a mediated society. While other digital divides have closed in North America, Europe, parts of Africa and much of Asia, because of increased access, with multiple televisions, personal computers and smartphones accumulating in households of every social bracket, the long-term interpersonal impact of these devices has yet to be fully assessed, especially as it pertains to universal principles, even though warnings surfaced as early as 1970. In his visionary book, *The Information Machines*, journalist and educator Ben Bagdikian wrote:

> It has taken two hundred years of the Industrial Revolution for men to realize that they are not very good at predicting the consequences of their inventions: to the surprise of almost everyone, automobiles changed sex habits. Information devices are no exception: machines for mass communications produce unexpected changes in the relationship of the individual to his society.[15]

Interpersonal Divide documents and assesses changes resulting from the Technology Revolution of the 1990s that continued unabated into the twenty-first century. There was a similar assessment of television in the 1970s. In her popular 1977 book about TV's impact on society, *The Plug-In Drug*, Marie Winn asserts, "I am not an enemy of the medium nor do I believe it is devoid of value. My aim, instead, is to promote a new way of thinking about TV."[16] That is the aim here, too, concerning media and technology and their impact on community and the values and principles that once defined those environs. Neither is this book a work of social panic, in which proponents of traditional media argue fervently against technological innovation the way that newspaper publishers argued against the telegraph and later as telegraph companies argued against the telephone. "It is not surprising that the Internet is feared for its ability to remove individuals psychologically from their social settings (even though the phone, the television, the book, and other media-based techno-cultures share this trait),"[17] writes educator Lelia Green in *Communication, Technology and Society*. However, what Green and other communication scholars fail to assess is the *cumulative* impact on society of media and technology proliferation and the escalating psychological impact of a techno-culture that has identified digital gadgetry as the means to economic prosperity, social happiness and civic harmony.

The philosophical analysis of that impact in *Interpersonal Divide* is an act of criticism and, as such, is covered by fair use standards of U.S. copyright law. Although the works of several scholars are cited here, only as much content as necessary has been used to make a point or clarify an issue. Online citations have been accessed during a period between 2011 and 2016 and included in endnotes. Links associated with some citations may cease to work in the future because domains lapse or web page formats change—issues associated with the very subject of this book, a medium that endures digitally in libraries, once the onsite intellectual hub of American communities.[18] (In those few cases, the reader is encouraged to use Wayback Machine [www.archive.org] to retrieve the content if the original citation is desired.) In her book *Cyberliteracy*, a rhetorical analysis of the Internet, Laura J. Gurak articulates a similar methodology. She quotes from books to make an observation or embellish an argument and cites works according to fair use.[19] "If anything," she writes, "examples used in this book bring positive value to the original by pointing readers to these sources."[20] Because hers also is an act of criticism, Gurak has not chosen to seek permissions, especially on use of web material:

> For one, the Web pages contained herein are used for criticism. In addition, when a person or organization makes a website available to the world, that person or organization knows full well that the resulting Web page will be uploaded onto thousands of computer screens,

linked to by other websites, and printed out on desktop laser printers. None of these uses require written permission, and a book, especially an act of criticism, is hardly different.[21]

That is also the case in *Interpersonal Divide*.

This book hopes to inspire dialogue and introspection with journal exercises and discussion topics which, if pertinent, can also yield paper ideas. Ideally, those reading this work should report the results of their journal exercises and experiments in blogs, using technology to criticize and evaluate technology. Exercises, discussion and ideas are meant to develop awareness about the import of personal ethics and interpersonal communication in the high-tech media age. Certainly, the topic merits such attention, for media and technology are here to stay and will determine how we will live, interact, learn and create in the future. Conversely our search for community is universal and unique to our species—the very notion being threatened by digital saturation. Face-to-face interaction—at home, school and work, and in public— remains a powerful mode of communication. As society examines the long-term impact of the interpersonal divide, seeking resolutions, people will influence the future direction of media and technology as much as both will influence people. That relationship must be dual and beneficial, however. *Interpersonal Divide* will make that case in the chapters to follow.

The Need to Belong

*When Americans, depressed by the scary places where they
work and dwell, contemplate some antidote, they often conjure
up the image of the American small town. . . . For the idea of a
small town represents a whole menu of human values that the gi-
gantism of corporate enterprise has either obliterated or mocked.*

—JAMES HOWARD KUNSTLER,
The Geography of Nowhere

....

Thought, Word and Deed

We crave one thing, regardless of race, sex, culture or social class: *acceptance.* The need to belong is powerful because, introvert or extrovert, we
are social creatures with a conscience—the ethical inkblot upon which
others and we make indelible marks. We etch more than outcomes and
consequences of our actions there, involving others; we imprint our
thoughts about actions before even taking them. From karma to Christ,
this universal concept of conscience implores us to be mindful about
our every *thought, word and deed.* The conscience is the psyche's "inner
ear" and vibrates with emotion—at times pleasant, at times horrifically
unpleasant—in response to thoughts, words and deeds before they
are uttered or acted on and then afterward, so we can assess outcome,
impact and possible motive. When we concede, *We know in our hearts
that we are right (or wrong),* we refer to this inner compass. When we
acknowledge, *We have lost our way,* we mean that we have not followed
this compass. Although others may influence us, the way artists are influenced by masters (role models) or by dilettantes (idols), we are the
primary sculptors of conscience; through it, we create magna opera or
rock piles of our lives.

According to pop philosophy, "We come into the world alone and we leave it alone." Birth and death are bookmarks of the human condition. While entrances and exits on earth may be solitary, our time on the planet is social and physical, from the paths that we travel in our search for acceptance to the communities that we call home. Communities provide opportunities for acceptance, serving as "gathering place" or "proving ground." We meet friends, partners, merchants and neighbors there. Through our interactions, we learn "people" skills and develop values and character.

We thrive in real habitats. Social activist Parker J. Palmer wrote that the most public place is the street, for there we meet strangers with whom we may interact, even when nobody speaks. People send a message through the channel of their bodies in real place, acknowledging that "we occupy the same territory, belong to the same human community."[1] Throughout human history, children have played in neighborhoods, adults have interacted with others there, and entrepreneurs have done business nearby. True, suburban sprawl may have changed the nature of games, interactions and commerce. Recreation centers may have replaced public parks; developments, homogenized housing; and mega malls, dislodged Main Streets. However, our relationships in these places for the most part remained social and genuine because we still had to communicate with strangers face to face. That fact remains pivotal when contemplating ramifications not only of the interpersonal divide but of the greater gulf being created by digital saturation. Even Palmer in his enlightened 1981 book, *The Company of Strangers*, could not foresee the erosion of community beyond the concourses of the mega mall which, he believed, had replaced public streets, deemed unsafe. When people perceive real habitat to be unsafe, Palmer warned, they withdraw from it, and it becomes unsafe. "Space is kept secure not primarily by good lighting or police power but by the presence of a healthy public life,"[2] he writes. The mall may not be the best public space in which to interact authentically with strangers, but usually it is more meaningful than doing so online, shopping the digital malls of Amazon and eBay or posting how we feel every minute on Twitter, our status on Facebook, our whereabouts on Foursquare and our selfies on Instagram.

The selfie, in fact, is an iconic sign of the times, owing itself largely to the front-facing camera introduced in the iPhone 4. Marshall McLuhan, known for his famous declaration, *the medium is the message*—believing that technology (chiefly television) would create a global village—did not foresee "the self is the message and the selfie is the medium," eloquently described by *New Yorker* writer Kate Losse.[3] The selfie is a sign of one's social media prowess with the solitary ego as cultural centerpiece. People have died taking selfies, losing footing on ledges; some have shot themselves, taking selfies; and some risked their lives, taking selfies with grizzly bears in the background.[4] We so trust our machines and their virtual environments that we are oblivious to dangers of physical environments. The more machines document and surveil every moment of our lives, the more they have metamorphosed into lives of their own, with users unable to assess where the gadgets end and their real existence begins.

Increasingly in this manner, we have transcended the initial observation of *Interpersonal Divide* in 2005: "In light of mobile devices and universal access, media and technology displace many of us from physical to virtual environs, blurring boundaries and identities and occupying so much of our time that we have little left at day's end to devote to hometowns and each other." In 2017, the "other" is significantly less important than the self because technology mines the self's demographics and psychographics readily shared with the world 24/7 via smartphones and omnipresent access to social networks and favorite websites.

Yet the need to belong is as urgent as ever, if not more so. According to Palmer, "More than ever we need the process of public life to renew our sense of belonging to one another," without which we pay a terrible price, losing "our sense of comfort and at-homeness in the world."[5] As a result, we yearn for acceptance and routinely look to media and technology to bridge the interpersonal void. Digital, instantaneous communication promised to enhance relationships with family and friends, to revitalize our schools, increase productivity at work, and to provide us with more leisure time at home; instead, our personal, educational and professional relationships often falter because communication systems alter *value* systems, with the primary emphasis on corporate profit and boredom-killing entertainment. Those were never core values of personal and educational growth or cornerstones of a professional work ethic. No wonder, then, that the search for acceptance is apt to be done sitting down in front of screens and monitors for most of our waking hours. Or walking the digital streets, texting someone somewhere else or tweeting (in characters, not words) our every thought and deed, however mundane, so as to be liked or friended by digital others. That undermines the vitality of community where social norms—from civility to trustworthiness—are developed through face-to-face interaction, for even networks of honorable individuals, when isolated, cannot easily advance civic virtue.[6] People deprived of interpersonal contact eventually suspect rather than trust others because their perception of reality has been skewed, prompting misinterpretation of messages and motives, thereby harming relationships.[7]

A decade ago the term "community" still meant a physical place. Now it means *network* of users with similar psychographics. Corporate communities also are "ecosystems," using a biological model based on mutual benefit—species that help each other, the way bees help pollinate flora. When technology was in its developmental stages, individual companies competed less with each other for turf and depended more on each other according to the function of their infrastructures. Ecosystems used to change partners according to acquisition or corporate symbiosis. For example, at the end of the twentieth century, newsmaker *Time* relied on entertainer Warner (and vice versa) and merged, attracting the interest of America Online. AOL needed content and relied on Time Warner to supply it in exchange for an electronic delivery platform for online users. The result? *AOL Time Warner*. This mega merger heralded "the dawn of a new media age in which former upstart companies of the Internet could dare to acquire powerful, traditional media companies,"[8] write the authors of *Media Debates: Great Issues for the Digital Age*. Everette E. Dennis and John C. Merrill also document other mergers creating similar ecosystems which, in turn, established the convention of such systems in society. However, in the case of AOL Time Warner, the promise of an Internet platform didn't pan out as anticipated following the collapse of the dot-com boom, and by 2003, the company dropped AOL from its corporate name. This was the saga of a traditional media company bonding with an Internet company at the dawn of the digital age; since then, ecosystems evolve not only for mutual benefit but also to displace geography—yet another indicator of the interpersonal divide—with their own global networks of digital media and content, delivered by branded machine via applications designed for smartphone.

The evolution of ecosystems since the 1990s has followed a distinct interpersonal-divide pattern, an amoeba-like splitting and multiplying following the dictates of technology and accessible services and content.

Traditional media used to join with Internet companies, such as General Electric's NBC division partnering with Microsoft in 1996. Like AOL Time Warner, that partnership essentially ended in 2005, with the exception of the cable news channel MSNBC. By the mid-2000s, Internet companies were acquiring digital platforms, as Google did in 2006, paying $1.65 billion for YouTube. In the first decade of the twenty-first century, media ecosystems metamorphosed by transporting their customers from real to virtual habitat, saturating the landscape so that communication in community was apt to be mediated rather than real. Example: In 2005, Google purchased Android, an operating system for mobile devices. In 2011, it acquired Motorola Mobile, providing smartphones and tablets for the operating system. Corporate leaders used to shun the word "ecosystem" at the dawn of the current century, as its ring sounded monopolistic. Now they make no apologies. In announcing the 2011 purchase of Motorola Mobile, Larry Page, CEO of Google, said in techno-speak, "Motorola Mobility's total commitment to Android has created a natural fit for our two companies. Together, we will create amazing user experiences that supercharge the entire Android ecosystem for the benefit of consumers, partners, and developers. I look forward to welcoming Motorolans to our family of Googlers."[9]

A media ecosystem is many things, but a "family" it is not, at least as the word was once used to describe human relationships. People belonged to a family by birth, blood or marriage. And its extensions included in-laws, grandparents and all manner of first and second cousins, nieces and nephews. Every one of those now is linked to or divided by machine. The term "family" has a distinct corporate ring, as in "our family of products" or "our family of brands," thanks to the prevailing ecosystemic mentality. In the past, one purchased a digital device and then had a choice of accessorizing it from multiple technology companies. Now the choice of a phone or tablet not only involves the hardware but the operating system and associated programs that make up those families of products and brands (including music, games, e-books, TV shows, movies and multimedia), all increasingly dependent on the ecosystem's ability to reach its fair share of the growing global digital audience.[10]

The more the United States relies on a service economy, powered by media and technology, the more consumers are saturated with commercial messages targeting them by the very devices that define their solitary online lives. Since the publication of the first edition of *Interpersonal*

Divide, the United States has become "Consumer Nation," with debt and consumption primary indicators of Wall Street's well-being. Before the Internet age, *investment* defined consumption; now debt does, facilitated by online access that requires credit cards or digital wallets (another ecosystem assessor). The notion that easy credit supercharges production, which in turn fuels the economy, has disenfranchised multiple generations through accumulated student loan debt. In discussing challenges of the modern era, Avery Cardinal Dulles, speaking at Notre Dame University, observed that the communication industry "is almost totally in the hands of advertisers, who use it to market their wares and increase their profits. Their dominant concern is not to relieve poverty or promote justice, but rather to stimulate people's eagerness to buy."[11]

Knowingly or not, too many of us have traded the blessings of liberty founded in the community for the premiums of technology founded in the media ecosystem. As Dennis and Merrill remind us:

> For years media critics like Ben Bagdikian, former dean of journalism at the University of California–Berkeley, had warned about the negative effect of media concentration, especially on newspapers and broadcasting, where independent, family owned papers and broadcast stations fell in to the hands of big chains like Gannett, Thompson, and Newhouse. Although these admonitions seem almost quaint compared to today's really big deals, as one critic called them, they nevertheless reflect deeply held American values that bigness is bad and diversity is good. People often equate freedom of expression and individualism with small-scale social institutions that are close to the people and accessible to all.[12]

Digital communication was supposed to end such monopolies and democratize society, primarily because the equipment facilitated instantaneous, person-to-person interaction. Traditional media, such as newspaper and television chains, were said to have created a consumer society promoting "the idea that the way to be is to buy."[13] According to technology advocate Howard Rheingold in his early work, *The Virtual Community*, "The engines of wealth depend on a fresh stream of tabloids sold at convenience markets and television programs to tell us what we have to buy next in order to justify our existence. What used to be a channel for authentic communication has become a channel for the updating of commercial desire."[14] In hindsight, his assessment of traditional media seems quaint in the current marketing world of Apple,

Google, Microsoft, Amazon, Facebook and Twitter that data-mine our every post, tweet and text and greatly outstrip in scope, breadth and reach any traditional media chain of the 1980s and 1990s.

Still, in the recent past, there have been profiles of interpersonal courage. In the middle of the worst recession since the Great Depression, thousands in the United States and abroad in 2011 began a protest movement, Occupy Wall Street, to express their views about social injustice in real time and place, taking over financial districts in various cities. "Income and wealth inequality in America have been growing for decades with little public outcry,"[15] wrote Bloomberg correspondent Albert R. Hunt. In 2011, he noted, the catalyst for the movement was "the perception that Wall Street and the wealthy were taken care of while average folks suffer. That isn't a fringe view." To be sure, mobile and digital technology helped organize demonstrators in local communities in a manner as predicted by Howard Rheingold in his 2002 book, *Smart Mobs: The Next Social Revolution*, in which he writes that entire populations could be organized (as well as monitored by Orwellian government) thanks to "new tracking capability . . . embedded in the environment."[16] Occupiers of Wall Street were tweeting about their activities onsite from ubiquitous smartphones, demonstrating the power of live-streaming events online. Protestors also used their phones to capture how demonstrators were being treated by police, sharing the video in real time. While this stands as another example of displacing geographic and digital space, as thousands followed the action from Zuccotti Park, protestors may have forgotten momentarily that among the largest monopolies were none other than technology companies such as Google, Microsoft and Apple. According to Hunt:

> There have been few complaints about the wealth that accrued to Microsoft Corp's Bill Gates, Apple Inc's Steve Jobs or Jack Welch of General Electric Co. When taxpayers directly facilitate that success and firms then lavish massive payouts on executives, it would be naïve not to expect public resentment.[17]

The Occupy Wall Street movement triggered that last reaction, helping create what has been labeled the "Anti-Facebook." As CNN reported in 2011, "'Call it Occupy Facebook.' Or, perhaps, 'UnOccupy Facebook,'" a social network startup company capitalizing on "the anti-corporate sentiment bubbling up on Wall Street and beyond," creating a social network called Unthink and aspiring "to be everything that Facebook and rival Google+ are not. . . . "[18] Alas, however, the "Anti-Facebook" movement merely evolved into social media companies with stricter terms of service than Facebook, such as Ello, which promised not to carry advertising or sell users' data.

In the 1990s, when the first edition of *Interpersonal Divide* was being researched, technology and access were supposed to individualize society as mechanical friend. Nicholas Negroponte, the apostle of this view, waxed philosophic about the "post-information age" in his 1995 tome *Being Digital*, noting that technology would know our demographics so thoroughly because of data-mining that there would be no mass audiences. "In being digital I am *me*, not a statistical subset. Me includes information and events that have no demographic or statistic meaning."[19] As an example, Negroponte prophesied that "a machine could call to your attention a sale on a particular Chardonnay or beer that it knows the guests you have coming to dinner tomorrow night liked last time" while also reminding you to buy new tires for a road trip you plan to take to another city in 10 days with clips of restaurant reviews there from culinary experts you read in the past.[20] Negroponte was so steeped in technological consumerism that he failed to foresee the harmful outcomes of the age of big data (discussed in Chapter Three) or acknowledge how machine-driven marketing could erode the knowledge economy, replace it with the consumer economy, and result in automation, unemployment, credit card debt, foreclosure, bankruptcy, redistribution of wealth to the wealthiest, cyber-attacks and Orwellian surveillance by government.

The Search for Acceptance

In dire financial times, we search ever more frantically for acceptance. Without paychecks, let alone steady job or career, we long for a company not listed on the Dow—*the company of others*. However, as the ecosystem economy is empowered rather than immobilized by debt, consumption and fantasy continue to thrive, especially on social networks. In 2009, a Harvard business study analyzed why people spend so much time on social networks and what, exactly, they were viewing.[21] Pictures of people were the biggest draw. Women tended to look at women they know. Men tended to look at women they do *not* know, followed by women they *do* know. From school to work, from romance to estrangement, from the moment we awake to the second we fall asleep,

Internet influences the essential decisions of our lives, including *with whom* we will spend the rest of our lives. Before digital technologies, partners used to meet at work, school and church. Now they often meet by describing themselves on Match.com, eHarmony.com and other social networks—like products in a marketing catalog of potential soul mates, with one out of every six marriages now a result of an online dating service.[22]

According to the Pew Research Center, which first studied online dating habits in 2005, most Americans then "had little exposure to online dating or to the people who use it, and they tended to view it as a subpar way of meeting people. Today, almost half of the public knows someone who uses online dating or who has met a spouse or partner via online dating," with 55 percent of Americans who are in a marriage or committed relationship saying they met their significant other online.[23] As such, partners henceforth and forever are bound by *two* contracts— the standard marriage one and the dating site's Terms of Service. The former is the human contract; the latter, that of the machine.

For millennia, that search for acceptance—in romance, friendship or family—has been intricately linked to the search for community. "Acceptance" is the abstraction—an inner longing for something greater than one's self. "Community" is the external source that provides fulfillment or reaffirmation. Acceptance is associated with the conscience, the notion that right and wrong define our relationships for better or worse; community, with consciousness, the notion that social norms govern actions that impact others with whom we share culture and space. Both are part of the human condition. Past generations found acceptance in community because our interactions there, however challenging or intolerant, taught us essential interpersonal skills. We knew when to look someone in the eyes and "stand ground" and, equally as important, when *not* to do so. We knew how to read body language and tone of voice and adjust for them according to time, place and occasion. We did this because we practiced. As children, we learned that we could stick out our tongues at playmates during recess but not during class. And it mattered at whom we wagged tongues on the school playground. Some would overlook the gesture and others, overreact. We refined our social skills growing up, along with our values—most of which concern treating others as we wish to be treated, the Golden Rule. Schools reinforced that universal lesson. Extended families did, too. And if those families were dysfunctional, we could find mentors in the neighborhood. Now families, schools, neighborhoods and workplaces are wireless, and so are we, feeling displaced in homes and home offices, even though we communicate at ever faster processor speeds.

In attempting to resolve the various digital divides, society in the past two decades unwittingly created an immense interpersonal one. Because technology has so accelerated culture, accompanying us wherever we go, that void warrants more of our attention than ever. A society with weak interpersonal skills cannot influence future innovations in media and technology so that they advance priorities of community, from distribution of wealth to access to education. Machines in the age of big data control our lives because we relegate to them anything we find inconvenient. In turn, they compile data about our every whim or desire and provide answers to our searches without understanding *why* we are searching in the first place. The first edition of *Interpersonal Divide* was about the search for community. In one decade that search was abandoned and the Google search optimized and embraced. As a result, we will continue to spend too much time in virtual rather than real environments—emailing, texting, tweeting, chatting, photographing, browsing, computing and consuming media—increasingly isolated from others, inundated with offers from ecosystems to buy products or services to sate the need to belong. The acquisition of things is a poor substitute for acceptance, just as cyberspace can be a poor substitute for community. Such isolation complicates life, not because life has become complex in reality, but because we have forgotten how to cope with the rigors of the human condition.

The human condition is governed by two conflicting aspects of the psyche. Consciousness tells us that we come into the world alone and we leave it alone. The conscience tells us what is in you is in me. We spend a lifetime between those two polarities, at times being estranged from community, at others seemingly one with it. The goal of ethics, or the ability to lead a stable and productive life, is to harmonize the polarities so that one informs the other. When that occurs, the conscience acts as an inner knowing of right and wrong involving others; consciousness, as an awareness of our place in physical space, hometown to cosmos, shared with others. The conscience demands that we love and are loved by others, that we share meaningful relationships with others, and that we contribute to community. Consciousness requires that we foresee the consequences of our thoughts, words and deeds, enabling us to assess past actions and plan future ones. When the conscience and consciousness harmonize thusly, we realize that how we treat others determines our own well-being and fulfillment. Community, in fact, is founded on that principle, from secular laws to religious morals.

Several theologians have attempted to define conscience, including Dietrich Bonhoeffer—who resisted Hitler and was executed for acting on his beliefs. He writes:

> Conscience comes from a depth which lies beyond a man's own will and his own reason and it makes itself heard as the call of human existence with itself. Conscience comes as an indictment of the loss of this unity and as a warning against the loss of one's self. Primarily it is directed not toward a particular kind of doing but toward a particular mode of being.[24]

Bonhoeffer's 1937 book, *The Cost of Discipleship*, ultimately cost him his life. Imprisoned, however, his conscience blossomed. Bonhoeffer eventually found meaning in "a thorough preparation for a new start and a new task when peace comes,"[25] he wrote shortly before his death in April 1944. He was referring to peace of mind, content that his captivity was a meaningful experience that would safeguard Germany's future. Bonhoeffer, like all great masters of conscience, including Mahatma Gandhi, Mother Teresa and Martin Luther King Jr., realized that peace emanates out of community and is inspired by commitment. One wonders: Would millennials, saturated by media and often oblivious of geographic community, be capable of staging similar social upheavals in real place and time?

In modern times, the word "peace" harkens the media stereotype of a cabin surrounded by evergreens at a tranquil lake. That may be leisure, not peace: *the wherewithal to meet challenges effectively by interacting with others according to a set of firmly held beliefs*. As Bonhoeffer's beliefs indicate, peace usually entails action. That is why activists stage "peace" marches. The *belief* behind a march unites and motivates participants. Peace also involves working with others to contribute to the community or future generations. In a word, peace concerns *others*, not you, an idea so foreign from the economic engines of techno-culture that many of us no longer realize the dullness of our conscience and narrowness of consciousness, forcing us to look for fulfillment in all the wrong cyber places. The question explored here is whether that saturation—70 percent of all waking hours—not only keeps us from the village of humanity but may alter our humane values so that they align with those of the machine.

To understand how humane values are being converted into machine ones, this edition of *Interpersonal Divide* recounts history. From a media history perspective, these debates are not new. Society has faced similar challenges before in times of great technological change. Such change was drastic through the second half of the nineteenth century, when mass media and marketing were conceived, along with the telegraph, telephone and radio. The telegraph has been called the "Victorian Internet." More importantly, perhaps, for a basis of comparison, Western Union owned the telegraph wires upon which the Associated Press relied to communicate the news—an ecosystem prototype. Brand marketing also evolved, along with chain newspapers, whose owners bought out competitors and created magazines out of them, including *Ladies Home Journal* and the *Saturday Evening Post*—not necessarily to serve the public, but to provide a forum for national brand merchandise. From this perspective, readers can fathom the foci of their discontent.

In upcoming chapters, we will document how technological values gradually encroached on humane ones until society no longer could recognize its own morality. Here the case is made, step by step, that universal principles—documented in ethical studies for much of the twentieth century—are increasingly at risk, succumbing to values of the machine. As such readers will evaluate whether "communication technology" is more than a multi-platform delivery system conveying cultural values through sound, sight and touch; they will explore whether such technology, in and of itself, is an independent entity altering those values, precisely because they are rooted in time and place, which technology alters or transcends. The question then becomes whether techno-culture has its own set of values assimilating cultural ones and influencing universal principles because of media globalization.

Chapter Three, "Big Data, Little People," documents how machines overtook human interaction through a series of innovations that undermined the knowledge economy promising new vistas through technical education. The history of this change is documented resulting in economic inequality, institutional bias encoded in machines, social injustice, and a world devoid of critical thinking. Chapters Four through Six document that effect at home, school and work. The typical family has become addicted to digital devices to the extent that the *Diagnostic and Statistical Manual of Mental Disorders* (DSM), published by the American Psychiatric Association, discussed "Internet Addiction Disorder" as a mental condition. Writing in the *American Journal of Psychiatry*, Jerald J. Block, MD, believed such addiction to be so common as to be included in the DSM:

> Conceptually, the diagnosis is a compulsive-impulsive spectrum disorder that involves online and/or offline computer usage and consists of at least three subtypes: excessive gaming, sexual preoccupations, and email/text messaging. All of the variants share the following four components: 1) *excessive use*, often associated with a loss of sense of time or a neglect of basic drives, 2) *withdrawal*, including feelings of anger, tension, and/or depression when the computer is inaccessible, 3) *tolerance*, including the need for better computer equipment, more software, or more hours of use, and 4) *negative repercussions*, including arguments, lying, poor achievement, social isolation, and fatigue.[26]

Increasingly in the home, parents addicted to digital devices are introducing them to their children. In a recent study of 5,000 women, Babycenter.com noted that mothers had acquired smartphones at a rate of 64 percent since 2009, that 51 percent of them are "addicted" to their smartphones, and that 75 percent regularly hand over their phones to children, including toddlers.[27] In that report, some pediatricians believed that giving children iPads is tantamount to allowing them to watch television. We have traveled this path before. The hoopla surrounding media saturation as engagement of youth was covered extensively in the first edition of *Interpersonal Divide*. At the time, many believed that DVDs of images with classical music such as the "Baby Einstein" series founded by Julie Aigner-Clark was creating baby geniuses. We know better now. At the time pediatricians argued successfully that babies shouldn't be watching television at all but interacting interpersonally with their parents. The series, purchased in 2001 by media behemoth Disney, was the subject of much controversy including FTC complaints until the company offered refunds for any DVDs purchased between June 5, 2004, and Sept. 4, 2009.[28] Can we anticipate the same with iPads and smartphones?

Despite technological proliferation, educational scores have plummeted when the opposite was supposed to occur: an informed electorate in touch with global issues. As the *Miami Herald* reported in 2010: "If most of us in the media focused on the issues that really matter—rather than on celebrity tragedies or the political scandals of the day," we might be concerned that the Chinese city of Shanghai topped the world education survey.[29] Apparently, introducing technology into the schools did little then to improve reading comprehension, in which the United States ranked 17th. In math at the time, the United States ranked 31st. In response to PISA scores, then–education secretary Arne Duncan remarked, "The United States has a long way to go before it lives up to the American dream and the promise of education as the great equalizer."[30] According to the digital divide, technology was supposed to be that equalizer.

Case in point: In 2007, the "One Laptop per Child" program by MIT researcher Nicholas Negroponte was making national news. His program was based on the concept of the "digital divide," or the notion that we in America are privileged and so can afford Internet technologies whereas children in certain areas of Africa, say, cannot. The vision assumed as fact a diverse global village in which inclusivity is embraced, celebrated and integrated—literally—into websites, social networks and other applications accessible everywhere. However, Negroponte overlooked that we did not inherit a global village via Internet; we inherited a global mall. Negroponte believed that disenfranchised children deserved access to that mall, but those children did not need Internet; they needed real nets to prevent malaria, as advocated by the "Nothing But Nets" project whose slogan is, "Send a Net. Save a Life." In 2006, Negroponte's laptop project was aided temporarily by the icon of e-commerce, Amazon, which donated one laptop for each consumer one purchased during the holiday season. Its slogan was "Give One. Get One." Compare the two slogans. "Send a Net. Save a Life," versus "Give One. Get One." Nothing more clearly than this depicts the consumerism associated with the United States and Internet ecosystems.[31]

That consumerism did little to halt the Recession of 2008, which propelled unemployment rates to near 10 percent for several years. In the first edition of *Interpersonal Divide*, employees were not being fired because of an economic downturn; nor were they being terminated based on what they wrote in social networks about supervisors. They were being fired for browsing the web when they were supposed to be working. Within a few years, technology, which was supposed to create leisure time (as it enhanced productivity)—yet another unfulfilled promise of the global village—invaded privacy on multiple levels:

Supervisors were screening email; colleges were monitoring Facebook; and employees were being fired via text. "What's the Worst Way to Get Fired: Email, Text, or Tweet?" asks Mark Hachman in *PC Magazine* on the occasion of former Yahoo chief executive Carol Bartz being fired over the telephone rather than in person. What did Bartz do? Via her iPad she sent an email to 13,000 Yahoo employees, noting, "I am very sad to tell you that I've just been fired over the phone by Yahoo's chairman of the board. It has been my pleasure to work with all of you and I wish you only the best going forward."[32] The company deleted her email account. Commenting on the case, workplace consultant Michelle Goodman said a phone call was better than hearing about being fired by accident. "At least it wasn't a text or email but it strikes me as warranting a face-to-face meeting."[33] However, firing four hundred employees via email and text is precisely what Radio Shack did in 2011 as "a quick way to inform employees" that they had a half hour to say their goodbyes to coworkers.[34] How many goodbyes were said interpersonally or electronically was not reported.

Social critic Marshall McLuhan did not foresee this in the 1960s, envisioning a global village. McLuhan is still viewed as an "Internet Nostradamus" who prophesied worldwide civic engagement, thanks to technology. McLuhan never foresaw the web but based his idealism on TV, believing that patterns of low-density lines and dots forced the human brain to interact with the picture tube, to make sense of moving images. His biological model, upon which so much scholarship is based, is flawed scientifically and metaphorically. *Interpersonal Divide* advances a physics paradigm to explain and explore cyberspace, assessing the impact of virtual habitat, which puts a person in two places simultaneously so that consciousness is split and content of messages altered.

McLuhan embraced technology, in part because of the antiestablishment baby boomer generation. In the 1960s activists deplored capitalism and demanded reliable information about the Vietnam War in particular and the government in general. Many of those baby boomers would become dot-com moguls in the 1990s. Now at retirement, they still believe that technology enhances the "information economy." That phrase is used so often that few question its generic meaning. Historian Roszak notes the emptiness of "exuberant talk" about "the information economy" or "the information society."[35] However, he and other social critics failed to assess the gap between baby boomers who used to associate media and technology with *information* and their children and/or grandchildren who continue to associate media and technology with *entertainment*. As technology saturated society, boomers and other adult generations began regressing, associating technology with entertainment too—e-books, games, music, movies, television shows, social networks and the like—because that was what the ecosystem vended and consumers of all ages eventually desired, in homage to the machine. Entertainment is associated now with media and technology available on demand at any hour in any place, compliments of the omnipresent and omnipotent ecosystem. "This is all very good news for the elites controlling enterprises involved in the supply of new ICT products and services, as the message neatly complements the sales and promotional efforts of their own marketing divisions,"[36] writes Paschal Preston in *Reshaping Communications*, which also criticized the prevailing ideas of the so-called "Information Society." One such idea advanced by members of the baby boomer generation (and now abandoned) was that their children would utilize media and technology to access education, thereby achieving social mobility. However, the offspring of baby boomer children—today's college students—are hopelessly in debt. *CNN Money* reported in 2012 that total student loan debt rose by 275 percent since 2003.[37] Rather than the Negropontean digital world of abundance and consumerism, concepts introduced into higher education by baby boomer administrators, they have created a Broke Generation with current student loan debt exceeding $1 trillion.

This is the nature of technology, that is, that of a scorpion. It is what it is. The French-Maltese philosopher Jacques Ellul believed that technology is "a self-determining organism or end in itself whose autonomy transformed centuries-old systems while being scarcely modified in its own features."[38] In simple terms, that means that technology changes everything it touches without changing much itself. Introduce technology into marriage, and love is all about the technology. Introduce technology into the economy, and the economy is all about technology. Introduce it into the home, and home life is about the technology. Introduce it into school systems, and education is about the technology. Introduce it into employment, and you have the same effect. But what is the effect on *you*? Where do you feel it most, at home, school or work? How has it changed you, the real interpersonal you? When did you first allow it and why has it happened? In journal exercises at the end of each chapter, you will encounter questions and experiments to help you derive answers to those questions.

That is why *Interpersonal Divide* is directed at students so that they can see how each digital device that they own—and additional ones that must be purchased to take college courses—are programmed to accept credit cards or digital wallets and thereby generate revenue for their corporate makers. Exposed to arguments that challenge the digital status quo, many students will realize that we *do* have control over ethics and actions.

The last chapter of *Interpersonal Divide* addresses that. To repatriate to the village—to schools, families, workplaces and hometowns—we must analyze the role of technology and media in our lives and then envision which of two futures we desire, one programmed by the machine and the other, by universal values linked to time, culture and place. The final chapter, "Machine versus Moral Code," documents how technology already has become our "third skin," programming society according to two pervasive, insistent values: *connection* and *disclosure*. The machine promotes those values—connecting to others with similar market-based psychographics—and discloses as much as possible in the process in an environment of big data that can predict your range of choices. This insistence is progressing from mobile access to human implants—with social rewards for those who develop according to machine dictates. In exchange for more social choices, the machine demands total loss of privacy.

Interpersonal Divide concludes by giving readers a glimpse of machine society versus communities grounded in time, place and culture whose highest principles are truth-telling, nonviolence and integrity. The second edition prophesies that those who embrace those universal principles might also be able to disengage purposefully from the machine, think critically and sustain interpersonal relationships. According to Lee Rainee, director of Internet, science and technology at the Pew Research Center, "[P]eople who can strategically allocate time and be attentive to its [machine's] nature are going to have an evolutionary advantage over the passive users in as much as it's harder to withdraw into solitude while sustaining a relationship with a piece of media. If you can figure out when to toggle in and off, you will be able to connect the dots and restore yourself. Those people will have it all over others who cannot disengage and discern the silly from the profound."[39]

We not only need to temper use and discern when to use (and *stop* using) media and technology; we also need to use these powerful tools to advance social priorities and contribute to the common good. As philosopher Andrew Feenberg writes in *Questioning Technology*, demands for technology that enhances "humane, democratic, and safe work" can influence the future development of electronic communication.[40] Before that can happen, however, we must reacquaint ourselves with the mediated effects of being digital and take stock of humane values that we may be in danger of abandoning at home, school and work and decide whether this is the future we want for ourselves, our children and our country.

CHAPTER ONE

The Impact of Media and Technology

*Television hangs on the questionable theory that whatever hap-
pens anywhere should be sensed everywhere. If everyone is going
to be able to see everything, in the long run all sights may lose
whatever rarity value they once possessed, and it may well turn
out that people, being able to see and hear practically everything,
will be specially interested in almost nothing.*

—E. B. WHITE,
The New Yorker, 1948

Real and Virtually Real

History is important, the saying goes. Or else we are apt to make the same mistakes. *Media* history is important because communication has the power to change the course of events—in the world and in our lives. Internet, global access, microblogging and social networks have changed the nature of government, economy, education, information and entertainment with near universal access to news, agency reports, distance learning, databases, gaming, stock trading and more, influencing everyday activities. From the 1990s up until the dawn of the twenty-first century, these functions seemed to herald a new era of enlightenment and social evolution, sparking the debate about the "digital divide"—Internet haves and have-nots—that inspired the first edition of *Interpersonal Divide*, which challenged that divide by noting a greater one was developing in how humans interacted with each other and machines. In those early Internet years, the issue of access and the impact on society seemed to resemble what occurred in the 1950s with the introduction of television to the mass audience. The telephone also appeared to have similar influence on social change in the nineteenth century. So did the telegraph before that. Each new medium was a momentous, technological wonder that transformed society and culture. Pro-technology advocates often used media history as an example, claiming that arguments against digital saturation were baseless. We had been through this before, after all.

Or have we? With each new technological invention, from telegraph to telephone to television, the potential for progress seemingly outweighed the prospect for fraud, deceit and disenfranchisement. Fake telegraph messages could be composed. In fact, the 1858 completion of the transatlantic cable—a technological bridge between Europe and America—spawned the first hoax associated with global warming, with newspapers reporting that the cable created magnetic fields pulling the earth ever closer to the sun.[1] The ability of the telegraph "to destroy distance . . . provided unscrupulous individuals with novel opportunities for fraud, theft, and deception,"[2] writes Tom Standage in *The Victorian Internet*. The telephone also destroyed distance, providing more access to more people, especially those involved in banking and commerce. Cases of fraud became widespread as criminals "would assume the identity of another person to call a bank to commit wire transfer fraud," siphoning money out of other people's bank accounts.[3] Concerning television, quiz show scandals of the 1950s showed how producers could dupe the mass audience, providing answers to contestants and thereby fixing outcomes. However, a quarter-century later, in the mid-1970s, satellite dishes combined with cable television to enable televangelist Jim Bakker's *PTL Club* to broadcast live to all his affiliates, requesting donations from the viewing audience. "Instead of waiting days or weeks for videotapes to arrive, local TV stations would be able to pick up PTL's satellite feed and broadcast the program live,"[4] writes Pulitzer Prize–winning journalist Charles E. Shepard in his book *Forgiven*, about the rise and fall of Bakker indicted in 1988 on multiple counts of mail and wire fraud.

Humans talk. We relate. We commune. Talk builds relationships and communities, informing individual and collective awareness, through which we enhance conscience and consciousness. That is why, in our search for acceptance, we must analyze the role that media and technology play in our lives—especially how they shape our identity as individuals who populate communities and as citizens who should contribute to them. The analysis is more vital than ever as never in the history of media and technology has U.S. society (as well as much of the developed world) been exposed to such an onslaught of overt and covert messages as in the twenty-first century. Moreover, the delivery and nature of our interaction with machines has changed dramatically in the past decade, without many people realizing that. In the near future many aspects of our world will be "replaced by computer systems that today are the sole purview of human judgment,"[5] writes Viktor Mayer-Schönberger and Kenneth Cukier in *Big Data: A Revolution That Will Transform How We Live, Work, and Think*. The authors note that the same technologies that entertain us today are being used for a variety of tasks performed by humans in the past, from diagnosing illness and recommending treatments and to identifying criminals before they commit a crime.[6]

Further, these machines are reaping magnificent revenues for the companies that control them, as we shall learn in upcoming chapters. If we opt to ignore the cumulative commercial impact as well as after-effects of saturation—from loss of privacy from data mining to loss of perception from reliance on machines —we not only are apt to commit the same social misjudgments as previous generations, but to do so without realizing what, in fact, has manipulated our choices and values.

In one respect, this is old hat. Media and technology have always manipulated self-image, values and perception. However, the current high-tech era is unique because of the power of the electronic tools, the time that we spend using them, the tasks that we relegate to machines out of convenience, and the influence of the corporations that manufacture them. The net result is a blurring of boundaries. The real and virtually real—including augmented reality, or computer enhanced views of life and locale (as in GPS technology)—have blended to such degree that we cannot always correctly ascertain what is genuine and enduring from what is artificial and fleeting. That type of confusion comes with its own set of interpersonal and societal consequences, complicating our lives and relationships, not because we are necessarily dysfunctional, but because we have forgotten how to respond ethically, emotionally and intellectually to the challenges, desires and opportunities of life at home, school and work.

Our homes, schools and workplaces have been altered by media and technology. *Communication alters habitat.* That is the objective. When you leave a handwritten note under a refrigerator magnet, so your partner knows your whereabouts, you defy time and thus can be in two places at once: in the kitchen and in the car. You don't have to wait until your partner comes home to say you need milk. You leave word and leave. Of course you are really elsewhere, not in the kitchen. But you are there virtually, too, when your partner reads your note. *Communication defies physical laws.* Consider the saying, "If a tree falls in the forest and no one hears it, does that tree actually make a sound?" The answer is decidedly *no.* The tree makes a sound *wave* of certain frequency emanating around the severed trunk. Sound requires ears (human or animal) able to pick up that frequency in the vicinity. There is another scenario, however. A tree that falls without anyone witnessing it also makes a sound if technology has been placed there to record the event. In that case, people listening to the recording can say assuredly that falling timber produces sound, even if no one was at the site to hear it. The effect is the same as that note placed under the refrigerator magnet. A person is at two places at the same time—violating physics. Many social critics influenced by Marshall McLuhan overemphasize biology and overlook physics when assessing the impact of media, believing technology extends and enhances human senses. A microphone placed beside a felled oak may seem to extend the range of the ear, enhancing hearing; it does neither. It creates a secondary set of senses by placing an individual in multiple locations. Advocates of and apologists for media and technology embrace the biological model because it promotes extension and enhancement of senses—which, by *logical* extension, also should enhance identity and humanity. Conversely, the physics model emphasizes a violation of scientific law associated with place. McLuhan never realized that and so, despite his "global village" prophecy—touting television, not Internet—never foresaw cyberspace or the splitting of consciousness that comes with breaches of time and place. When consciousness is split, so is perception. When perception is skewed, so is identity. Symptoms develop from the overuse and consumption of technology and media, which blur and blend the real with the virtually real in ways that McLuhan never imagined.

McLuhan, Revisited

"The medium is the message," wrote media critic and theorist Marshall McLuhan, coining a phrase that seems more prophetic now, in the Internet age, than poetic. McLuhan, though, may be more poet than prophet.

His oft-cited phrase acknowledged the impact of media on messages; however, McLuhan failed to predict the future of mediated communication. Like a line from a poem, his aphorism merely explained pop culture so cogently that his words came to define communication in the television era. McLuhan also coined the phrase "global village," believing that electronic media "re-tribalized" people from various cultures and countries so that they became citizens of the planet, rather than of a place, and hence tended to know more about world events, say, than happenings in their hometowns. "The new electronic interdependence recreates the world in the image of a global village,"[7] McLuhan wrote, noting the impact of media in the Telstar period of the 1960s.

Social critic James Carey credits McLuhan's pioneering spirit to his background in literary studies. "Students of the arts are likely to examine communication with quite a different bias than that advanced by social scientists," he writes, noting McLuhan recognized how machines would produce and recreate in an entirely new aesthetic.[8] That aesthetic would place the human inside the machine. People would humanize machines, a kind of host; it would not automate what people do. People would insert the natural into the mechanical, transforming the world.[9]

Historian Theodore Roszak believes that many of McLuhan's prophesies are based on "zany media metaphysics" predicting generations of cozy technophiles engaged in worldwide civic participation.[10] The idea of telecommunication as human liberator harkens back to this particular McLuhan proclamation. According to Roszak, "McLuhan primarily had television in mind; he insisted that people sitting passively in front of cathode ray tubes, watching a steady display of images from around the world, were somehow becoming more participative citizens."[11] The expression "global village" has become as popular as "the medium is the message." Again the phrase encapsulates truth poetically, bestowing new perspective on an extant aspect of media, rather than predicting new technologies to come.

McLuhan is better known as a media critic than as a professor of English literature, which he was. In addition to *The Medium is the Massage: An Inventory of Effects* (1967) and *Culture is Our Business* (1970), McLuhan also edited *The Selected Poetry of Tennyson* (1954) and *Voices of Literature* (1964). It was only natural for him to tap the universal truths of literature via clever metaphors—a poetic tool—than to measure media's impact on culture, the way a journalism researcher might.

Conversely it was not natural for him to test his theories or gather data to support them. Appropriately, McLuhan's singular talent befitted the times—the literary sound-bite at the beginning of the television era— as powerful as any Shakespearean line. McLuhanisms include such gems as:

- "'Time' has ceased, 'space' has vanished. We now live in a global village."
- "When you are on the phone or on the air, you have no body."
- "All advertising advertises advertising."
- "The future of the book is the blurb."
- "News, far more than art, is artifact."

In many respects, McLuhan's aphorisms are literary artifacts reminiscent of Renaissance masters like Francis Bacon, the great English scholar and poet recognized for these truisms:

- Knowledge itself is power.
- The remedy is worse than the disease.
- Virtue is like a rich stone—best plain set.

McLuhan digested the works of Sir Francis early in his academic career. Indeed, McLuhan's biographer Phillip Marchand acknowledges Bacon's influence on McLuhan in "the art of the aphorism." According to Marchand, "Bacon maintained that the aphorism—the pithy, arresting statement—was useful precisely because it did not explain itself. In its incompleteness and suggestiveness, it invited 'men to enquire further' into a subject. The McLuhan who later became famous for his aphorisms—notably, 'The medium is the message'—was intrigued by this use of language."[12]

McLuhan's interest in Francis Bacon is significant from another aspect, concerning knowledge and technology. Bacon believed that truth and utility were synonymous, directly associated with mechanical invention, meant to ease humankind's fallen state, restoring a sense of transcendence.[13] Policy analyst and author Dinesh D'Souza dubs Bacon "the patron saint of our technological civilization," noting that Bacon believed that "true knowledge is not that which enables us to rise above our wants, it is that which allows us to gratify our wants."[14] Technology embraces such a materialistic philosophy, at least from a marketing standpoint. Poets, however, are known to be positively monkish in their pursuit of knowledge rather than possession. McLuhan, like Bacon, resists that stereotype. The poet in him may have created the aphorism; however, McLuhan the materialist uses it as sound bite in the media.

"I may be wrong," McLuhan once remarked, "but I'm never in doubt." In retrospect, McLuhan was wrong about as often as he was right—standard fare for a typical poet—whose truths are hit-and-miss. But when they hit, they hit *home*, possessing the power of epiphanies. As such, they endure and become clichés until time resurrects them. McLuhan enjoyed such a legacy. Because of the Internet, his stature has grown from media guru to prophet. But the poetic term "global village" refers primarily to broadcast technology, which he deemed superior to books as an educational tool. Television, he believed, stimulated rather than dulled our senses:

> In television there occurs an extension of the sense of active, exploratory touch which involves all the senses simultaneously, rather than that of sight alone. You have to be "with" it. . . . Television demands participation and involvement in depth of the whole being. It will not work as a background. It engages you. Perhaps this is why so many people feel that their identity has been threatened. This charge of the light brigade has heightened our general awareness of the shape and meaning of lives and events to a level of extreme sensitivity.[15]

The late Guido Stempel, distinguished journalism researcher and contemporary of McLuhan, called himself "data oriented," and so he was predisposed to question McLuhan's theories. As Stempel put it in an interview, "I'm guilty of not having completely analyzed the theories of my published research. McLuhan, on the other hand, doesn't bother with data and is guilty of oversimplification,"[16] particularly his idea of "hot" and "cool" media. McLuhan believed that a hot medium is high definition, like a photograph. Conversely a cartoon is a "cool" medium of low definition, requiring viewers to interact imaginatively to receive the message. (One wonders what McLuhan would say about high-definition television, which generates picture quality similar to that of film and sound quality similar to that of high-resolution audio.) In any case, Stempel doubted the validity of McLuhan's theories. "Television is not a 'cool' medium of lines and dots that force the viewer to interact with the screen." According to Stempel, "Television is passive. Except for the remote control. In that sense, television is interactive."

The more one contemplates McLuhan's hot-cold motif, the more unlikely it seems, more reminiscent of oxymoronic poetry than of media. Several theorists have criticized or modified McLuhan's metaphor, including his most famous successor, the late Neil Postman, distinguished author and communications professor, who believed the medium *biases* the message. All media, however sophisticated, are mere tools, according to Postman, and embedded in every tool is an ideological bias, prodding the user to envision reality "as one thing rather than another," causing him or her to value one thing over another and amplifying one or another particular skill or mindset over another.[17] This, wrote Postman, is what Marshall McLuhan meant when he said the medium is the message.

Postman acknowledged that the truth behind the aphorism was not really new but "in short an ancient and persistent piece of wisdom, perhaps most simply expressed in the old adage that, to a man with a hammer, everything looks like a nail. Without being too literal, we may extend the truism: To a man with a pencil, everything looks like a list. To a man with a camera, everything looks like an image. To a man with a computer, everything looks like data."[18]

Similarly, to a man with a metaphor, everything is extended. Part of the problem with McLuhan's metaphor is his core belief that technology extends the human senses. To some extent, this is arguable. But the metaphor is inexact. A hearing aid, for instance, extends the capacity to hear within a physical radius because its purpose is to amplify sound into the ear canal, directly stimulating that sense. A telephone, on the other hand, extends the capacity to hear over tens of thousands of miles. However, it is the distance traveled, rather than the capacity to hear, which is impressive. This eludes McLuhan. Trying to humanize the machine, he is forced to use a biology rather than physics paradigm, as articulated in this book (i.e., "real vs. virtual habitat"), and thus never truly foresees cyberspace—a genuine metaphysical environment with domains and digital divides—that engages as it splits awareness, so we can "visit" new realms, as one does a website, or diverts attention, so we can drive cars and use smartphones. The artist in McLuhan views space creatively, not realistically. Machines can expand or contract space, much like a painter does on canvas, and in doing so, expand or contract time, thereby changing the meaning of places, people and things.[19] This is in keeping with Heidegger's theory of "da sein," German for "to be there," an existential notion that people are present with others while being essentially alone—a perfect metaphor for the illusion of social media and the space in the cloud that technology now occupies. In "Art and Science," Heidegger explains how artists and scientists view space differently, with the artist believing that things do not exist in space but embody or represent it.[20] Scientists view space more realistically, with the view that people, places and things exist in real space and time.

Technology puts a person in two or more places simultaneously and, therefore, influences consciousness and conscience, also as previously discussed. McLuhan acknowledged the impact of electronic media on consciousness and conscience with oracular fervency. He believed that "technological extension of consciousness" metamorphosed humans into mighty beings of expression, enabling us "to reverberate the Divine thunder, by verbal translation."[21] McLuhan prophesied the development of external conscience—in itself, an implausible oxymoron—that would complement and shape individual conscience, instantaneously advancing culture. "No further acceleration is possible this side of the light barrier."[22] In essence, McLuhan theorized that electronic media would evolve human beings biologically into "information systems," extending the reach of physical senses around the globe.

McLuhan's mistake was to focus on humans *as* information systems rather than on humans coping with information *space*. Thus he never foresaw the splitting of consciousness accompanying new technologies. Here is where McLuhan's biological model breaks down. McLuhan emphasized sense instead of space, arguing that the telephone extends the human ear; film, the eye; and television, touch. The notion that television extends the sense of touch has always been problematic, metaphorically and literally. McLuhan's metaphor was based on his unscientific belief that television does not dull but actually supercharges the senses. TV does so, according to McLuhan, because moving images are made up of low-density lines and dots—unlike high-density photography or film—that the TV viewer must learn to decipher in "creative dialogue" with the screen. "By requiring us to constantly fill in the spaces of the mosaic mesh, the iconoscope is tattooing its message directly on our skins," McLuhan asserted in a famous 1969 *Playboy* interview.[23]

Despite mixed metaphors and a penchant for puns (as in "the media is the *massage*")—another incurable Shakespearean trait—McLuhan does deserve respect and attention. He is especially insightful asserting that we must understand how technology changes culture. McLuhan is perhaps singularly responsible for teaching the audience to put less emphasis on content (what a newsmaker says) and more emphasis on the medium (what a newsmaker says on *television*). That kind of insight is needed today. Otherwise, the medium becomes the moral.

America, more than any other society since ancient Rome, embraces entertainment, perhaps to circumvent the human condition. James Howard Kunstler, in particular, makes that observation in his work on community life in the twenty-first century, maintaining that no other society has been so preoccupied with instantaneous make-believe and on-demand fantasy. Americans, he believes, demand fantasy to distract themselves from the hardships and tragedies of life, and because reality is unrelenting, "we must keep the TVs turned on at all waking hours and at very high volume."[24] Kunstler concludes that the emphasis on fantasy in virtual community only deepens our hunger for authenticity in physical community.

The Dawning of Mass Media

With the invention of written language in ancient Mesopotamia some 5,000 years ago,[25] people no longer needed to be face to face to interact; they could express themselves in writing and their messages could be read from afar. The invention of the printing press transformed fifteenth-century society as much as the Internet did twentieth-century society—precisely for this reason. Between 1450 and 1500, the number of books in Europe increased from a few mere thousands to more than 9 million,[26] transforming culture, especially religion. In addition to Bibles, Johannes Gutenberg printed papal coupons called "indulgences," forgiving sins for a fee, and freed up Vatican scribes. They wrote the coupon once, instead of thousands of times, and went to vespers. Granted, couriers still had to hand-deliver indulgences. Several centuries later, the Internet would deliver coupons and other digital messages much more efficiently. Using mobile technology, senders compose a message once and post it on Tumblr or Reddit, clicking a mouse, and then are free to go on to other sites or pursuits, while content is being read at multiple places simultaneously. The Internet also delivers the message without any couriers; so they are free to be elsewhere, too—so free, in fact, that as long as there are electricity and operating systems, communicators no longer need couriers. Virtual habitat has deleted them from the landscape.

Evolution in virtual habitat is similar to that in actual habitat, with a few differences. Occupations, rather than species, disappear from the cyber-landscape. Because there is no "there" there, the fittest survive not by claiming territory but by performing more tasks in less time involving fewer people. The computer software or operating system that accomplishes that goal earns a profit . . . and makes a category of people obsolete. Those folks literally disappear, replaced by others who can multitask, program and analyze more efficiently. In the case of extinct couriers, for instance, cyberspace replaced them with technophiles to make social networks function properly and automatically. The difference, of course, is that couriers made rounds in real habitat and delivered paper messages face to face; technophiles have no faces because they deliver electronic messages in cyberspace, whose salient feature is *invisibility*.

Because of that feature, people de-evolve in virtual environments into symbols (hypertext, pixels and logins) and raw materials (data, hotlinks and code). Cyberspace lacks physical dimensions, including space and time, without which, activities are simulated rather than authentic. Philosopher Andrew Feenberg states that technology incorporates people "into the mechanism" as objects with digital functions rather than true identities.[27] In virtual habitat even governments lose control of citizens and organizations. According to sociologist Manuel Castells in *The Power of Identity*, "State control over space and time is increasingly bypassed by global flows of capital, goods, services, technology, communication, and information."[28] The transformation of society from the real to the virtually real has been occurring since the nineteenth century, affecting how we perceive others and their cultures, communities, priorities, activities and whereabouts, primarily due to universal access to electricity.

Modern media history begins with electricity. The invention of three devices literally transformed society and the American landscape: the telegraph, telephone and radio. These inventions were supposed to bring prosperity to the masses. In fact, nineteenth-century "advocates of electricity claimed it would eliminate the drudgery of manual work and create a world of abundance and peace,"[29] writes Tom Standage in *The Victorian Internet*. Many prophesied the same new world because of Internet and related technologies. In any case, the telegraph, telephone and radio set the stage for twentieth-century inventions, including television and the computer, which influenced our collective view of the world and ourselves before dominating it in the twenty-first century.

With each technological wonder, our perception of community changed and with it, our way of life. The telegraph was invented in 1835 by Samuel Morse, who also devised a code of dots and dashes. Telegraph lines were placed along rail lines to test the device. On May 24, 1844, Morse tapped his famous message—"What hath God wrought?"—from Baltimore to Washington, DC. The phrase is fear-based, suggesting that Morse realized that his telegraph would alter perception, compressing our sense of geography and devaluing the impact of words. The telegraph reduced words to simpler symbols, a kind of code like that used in computing. Before the telegraph, Europe was perceived as a place— a harbor, city, river or mountain range; after the telegraph, "Europe" became a word and much easier to reach. You said "Europe" to a Western Union agent and, viola!, you were virtually there. Fittingly, "telegraph" in Greek means "distance writing."

The telegraph increased the speed of news. Beforehand, reporters had to row out to ships steaming into New York harbor to learn the latest news from abroad. By 1858, news was arriving in America by transoceanic cable.[30] Soon telegraph lines connected the East and West coasts of the United States, enabling the Associated Press to become the world's first mass medium. The AP, to this day, is known as a "wire service." Western Union joined with the AP to create the first media monopoly. Both controlled the content of news until 1875. Finally, over objections of Western Union, the AP was able to lease its own telegraph wire.[31]

As soon as the AP established relative autonomy, using telegraphs to convey news, journalism entered a new age. Researchers have pegged the 1870s as a time when media changed from "the age of communities and place" to "the age of class and groups" (1870–1930) as corporate moguls, including Samuel Morse and Alexander Graham Bell, introduced inventions that altered the perception of physical habitat.[32] The age of class and groups differed notably from the age of communities and place. Priorities changed. Previously newspapers had been emphasizing people and the importance of community—how readers, for instance, might contribute locally to the common good. After the Civil War, however, the focus switched from the character of people to their status in society, defined by wealth or affiliation. Special interest groups, including media companies, were connected not by values, but by wires, roads and railways. Mass communication reached millions of consumers rather than hundreds because media had lost the shackles of place, enabling tycoons to stake claims in the virtual environment and amass fortunes.

Telegraph technology empowered reporters as never before. As the AP realized, Western Union had a vested interest in coverage, attempting to shape the news so that it was in line with corporate priorities. (That conflict of interest still exists to this day.) The telegraph was a powerful communication tool, in itself; but combined with news, the medium rewrote history. Abraham Lincoln relied on the telegraph to learn the latest news from the battlefront. Lincoln was the first U.S. commander-in-chief to command armies from the War Department in Washington. He also relied on news coverage, much like some leaders still rely on CNN. Journalists who telegraphed details of battles influenced military strategy, for better or worse. The AP accepted that responsibility and covered both sides in the Civil War to give coverage a semblance of balance.

Meanwhile, another war was raging in America. Western Union was trying to quash all competitors, including the fledging Bell system, swiftly ascending in virtual habitat. The phone could do more tasks more quickly involving fewer people interacting face to face. The telegraph required agents who knew Morse code. Those agents had to copy and tap messages from customers in Western Union offices and then hand-deliver messages to addressees in physical locations. That inconvenience would make the telegraph obsolete in virtual habitat. In a few decades, long-distance telephone operators working invisibly at mysterious exchanges would replace those agents. Anonymous "Ma Bell" operators would also develop "attitude"—similar to those now at computer support desks—primarily because they lacked face-to-face interaction . . . and could disconnect at will. The focus, then as now, was on the bottom line. As early as the nineteenth century, entrepreneurs realized that those who owned both the medium *and* the new technology (or established partnerships to acquire both) were destined to become powerbrokers. That rule holds true to this day in the evolved media ecosystem. The symbiotic relationship of media and technology—especially their ability to make profit and wield influence—started with the telegraph and would define each invention to come, including the telephone and radio.

Alexander Graham Bell founded his telephone company in 1876. Within a decade, Bell created American Telephone and Telegraph and elevated it to "a parent company," acquiring Western Union along with its influence and power. Telephones altered the nature of news. The media had to retool to deploy the modern technology, just as they had to retool in the twentieth century to use computers. Like computers, telephones impacted coverage by placing reporters increasingly in virtual environments and displacing them from community. The industry transformation happened swiftly. A generation earlier, reporters had to "row for news," meeting ships in harbors to get the latest reports from overseas. Then reporters used telegraphs to gather facts and infor mation but still had to travel to physical locations to interview newsmakers. With the advent of telephones, however, reporters could interview sources without traveling anywhere, relying on quotation—rather than on observation—again without necessarily fact-checking assertions about issues affecting communities.

The characteristics of communication metamorphosed to suit the new medium. Telegraph messages were tapped, not spoken, as email today is tapped and not spoken. But email is tapped on keypads and keyboards (or recited into smartphones, replete with machine misspellings and memes). Telegraphs required agents who knew mysterious codes and preferred brevity, inventing "headline news" a full century before CNN. Symbols like "SOS," the international distress call, replaced phrases. The medium became the message, and users had to adapt. Language changed. The most frequently read word in the telegraph era was *stop*, which replaced periods at the ends of sentences. The telephone did not need code at the user level; it made communication easier and more convenient—the same qualities touted today, concerning computers. The greater the convenience, the greater the impulse to rely on technology to make choices for us. The new device changed the nature of interpersonal communication. People did not have to visit to engage others in dialogue. Neither did they have to pen letters, a nineteenth-century art; they could save time and telephone. Nothing wrong with that, of course, as the sound of a loved one's voice typically generated joy, affirming family ties and renewing relationships. Conversely, the telephone could ease the conscience enough for a person to skip a visit or cancel a trip. Place was dispensable. Because they had options, people began aligning priorities with levels of convenience, deciding when to travel or when to use technology. That impacted relationships. For just as we do not fully appreciate how smartphones affect relationships, Victorian counterparts did not appreciate how new technologies would affect theirs. More importantly, media and technology in that epoch skewed perception about world events that would have enormous social impact. Society still respected the word, as found in the great books, many of which were being written at the time, including works by such masters as Henry David Thoreau, Walt Whitman, Emily Dickinson, Ralph Waldo Emerson and Mark Twain (Samuel Clemens). Media moguls exploited trust in the printed word. Even in the aftermath of our bloodiest war, during which multitudes had perished, preserving the Union and the Constitution, tycoons elevated corporate interests over the common interest.

Several publishers in the 1890s practiced *yellow* or sensational journalism. They obeyed the cardinal rule of virtual habitat—*speed*—the technological touchstone to this day, with computer and cable companies touting processors, gigabytes and networks. The quicker that news is delivered, the more incredible and incorrect it becomes—another rule that still holds true. At the end of the nineteenth century, the media not only could manipulate public opinion; they could create it along with government policy and sell more newspapers in the process. Humanity suffered because of that practice. Two publishing giants in particular, Joseph Pulitzer and William Randolph Hearst, instigated political mayhem in America with overblown news about brutalities in Cuba, ultimately triggering the Spanish-American war.

That was a turning point in journalism. Moguls became more profit-minded and used technology to cut costs. Publishers relied on telegraphs to transmit news, coast to coast. That opened up advertising possibilities. Publishers created new media as vehicles for national brands. One publisher, Cyrus Curtis, owner of the *Tribune and Farmer*, spun off the "woman's page" of his paper—edited by his wife Louise Knapp Curtis—into *Ladies' Home Journal* in 1883. A few years later Curtis purchased the *Saturday Evening Post*, a newspaper dedicated in part to family, morality and literature, for $1,000, and transformed it into a national magazine. Magazines had a geographic advantage over newspapers because they were not bound to local economies and communities. Periodicals, circulated nationally, had longer deadlines than newspapers and so underplayed time elements, preferring "evergreen" features lacking the immediacy of "spot" news (a term emphasizing *place*). Better yet, national media could sell national brands.

Advent of Marketing

"Branding" was invented fifteen years after the telegraph. Its purpose was to distinguish a company's product from that of competitors. William Procter and James Gamble, brothers-in-law, began making candles and soap in 1837 and marked candle boxes with P&G's legendary trademark: the moon-stars icon, which symbolized the brand. In

1886 the company spent $11,000 in a campaign to promote the purity of Ivory Soap. Branding expert Martin Lindstrom notes that within a decade, "P&G became advertising innovators, regularly placing product advertisements in national newspapers and magazines."[33]

Advertising became as indispensable as news. Companies sold brands in nationally distributed magazines. That also homogenized culture. In short order, Coca-Cola became the national drink. Ivory Soap became the cleanser of choice and its maker, Procter & Gamble, the first company to place a color ad in *Cosmopolitan* in 1896. Westclox kept Americans on time. Westclox was the first corporation to advertise its popular alarm clock "Big Ben" in a national campaign, noting in a 1910 advertisement in the *Saturday Evening Post* that this "punctual sleepmeter" would awaken American families with "a deep musical voice . . . on your sleepiest mornings."[34] Overnight, media grew, especially magazines, infiltrating American homes because advertising funded new start-up publications distributed to wider geographic regions, based on those national brands. Soon items on shelves, medicine cabinets, cupboards and rooms began to look alike; eventually, occupants of these homes began to think alike about issues *and* products.

Success came at a cost. Consumers were eager for national brands, and companies like Procter & Gamble wanted to serve that need. In the past, a manufacturer generally made one product and competed with other companies that made a similar product. Competition happened in real habitat—on shelves of local stores. What if one company made two similar products, like soap bars? Would one product cannibalize the other? Procter and Gamble faced that problem with Ivory Soap and Camay, and the company figured out how to sell both without one product winning out over the other: *marketing*. Ivory was billed as a cleanser; Camay, as a beauty bar with moisturizers. This way, both products could compete within the same category but not within the same segment. That approach led P&G to develop a system still being used today: *brand management*. Marketers manage competing products made by the same company, devising strategies for each brand.

Marketing also relied on media and technology. Brand management systems sold products more efficiently, using technology not only to advertise but also to generalize wants and needs. Just as publishers had used technology to shape public opinion and government policy, marketers used technology to shape desire and standard of living. Magazines like *Saturday Evening Post* and *Life* regularly showcased lifestyles at a level above that of their readerships, whetting appetites for consumption during the age of "class and groups." The 1920s has been called the decade of advertising. "The admen went wild," writes Juliet B. Schor in *The Overworked American*, associating consumerism with higher workloads, noting "everything from walnuts to household coal was being individually branded and nationally advertised."[35] That stimulated the U.S. economy, generating jobs for the masses and fortunes for mass media, setting the stage for broadcasting.

In 1898, the Italian-born Guglielmo Marconi had fashioned a crude radio prototype. Two decades later, Westinghouse Radio Station KDKA was broadcasting the results of the 1920 Harding-Cox presidential election. Two years after that, American Telephone & Telegraph Company—another technology behemoth at the time—sponsored the first paid radio advertising commercial, broadcast on AT&T's New York City outlet, WEAF. Almost everyone found the idea of paid advertising over public airwaves repugnant—so much so, writes journalist Ben Bagdikian, that then–secretary of commerce Herbert Hoover warned, "It is inconceivable that we should allow so great a possibility for service, for news, for entertainment, for education and for vital commercial purposes to be drowned in advertising chatter."[36]

A quarter century after its invention, the medium of radio had spawned quandaries impacting us yet:

- The influence of broadcasting on the electorate and commerce.
- The power of corporate ecosystems on people and society.
- The use of technology for commercial gain rather than for social enlightenment.

Radio accelerated America's social clock more than Westclox ever could. The new catchword was "progress." By now the corporate world recognized how technology could make or break fortunes. Western Union proved that in 1877, committing one of the biggest business gaffes of all time. It dubbed the telephone "an electrical toy" and rejected an offer to buy Bell's patents for $100,000.[37] That mistake created a precedent. AT&T eventually gained control of Western Union and marketed both technologies, encouraging customers to use telephones to order telegraphs. The rule of acquisition—buy out, duplicate or integrate new technology—continues to dominate corporate thinking today.

In the first half of the twentieth century, the radio became as popular and as powerful as the telephone. Radio targeted the *individual* listener rather than the entire community. The focus was on the consumer in a house, not on the house in a geographic place. Radio programs like *Captain Midnight* targeted youth and offered boys and girls such premiums as "Flight Patrol" membership cards, "Ringo-Jumpo" bean games, and "Mysto-Magic Weather Forecasting" badges.[38] By 1940, Ovaltine sponsored *Captain Midnight*. Campbell Soup Company was more interested in the New York Drama Company's *The Mercury Theatre on the Air*, founded by entertainers Orson Welles and John Houseman. Welles had proved that mass media could create mass hysteria with his broadcast of *The War of the Worlds* on All Saints' Day, 1938. The infamous hoax about a Martian invasion reportedly struck terror "at the hearts of hundreds of thousands of persons in the length and breadth of the United States."[39] Two years later, when Campbell's Soup acquired the radio show, *Mercury Theatre on the Air* became *The Campbell Playhouse*.

Mass marketing was established. The media of choice were magazines and radio because they could target segments of the audience, identifying potential customers. That practice undermined the media's perception of the importance of community. Until then, newspaper advertising sold to an electric mix of folks living in a geographic area— thereby implying community. Companies sold products and services to families rather than to specific members of families. Radio- and magazine-based marketing took aim at those members by luring them with programming or content suited to their lifestyles and then targeting them with specific name-brand products and premiums, based on social status and purchasing power. Marketing, once a business practice, was now a media tool—just in time for television.

Vision and Values

Television made its public debut at the 1939 World's Fair—an apt forum, as TV would span the globe within a few decades. The essayist E. B. White had prophesied the future of television, maintaining that it would become "the test of the modern world, and in this new opportunity to see beyond the range of our own vision, we shall discover either a new and unbearable disturbance of the general peace or a saving radiance in the sky. We shall stand or fall by television—of that I am sure."[40] White foresaw, perhaps more clearly than any other social critic, how this powerful new medium would homogenize our vision and values.

Television did not gain popularity until after World War II. In 1949 only 2 percent of households had television; within six years, 64 percent of U.S. homes had at least one TV set.[41] By 1959, 90 percent did, a phenomenon that political scientist Robert D. Putnam believes to be "the fastest diffusion of technological innovation ever recorded," including Internet access.[42] (Pippa Norris, author of *Digital Divide*, reports that in 1994 about 3 million people, mostly living in America, had access to the Internet, a figure that increased to 26 million the next year, with worldwide estimates roughly doubling each year after that through 2000.[43]) Television not only spread faster than the Internet; it also transformed home life more thoroughly, especially in light of increased consumerism following World War II. As Bagdikian observes, "Educational, cultural, and political patterns changed as the new electronic box moved into homes. Habits of reading, of doing homework and housework, and of eating family meals were rearranged to place the television set into the daily schedule."[44]

People who did not own televisions in the pre-Sputnik era of the early 1950s lived mostly in remote areas unable to receive a signal. By the end of that decade, however, the number of televisions was fast approaching 85 million, or nearly one set for every two citizens.[45] Americans were also on the move in the 1950s, with families relocating across the country to secure jobs and moving into new suburban neighborhoods whose houses featured garages. People without cars could not fully use their environment, creating two classes of people—those with and without motor vehicles—much like Norris claims about computers, responsible for the digital divide. However, access to automobiles in the 1950s differed significantly from access to computers in the 1990s. The computer industry competes with the auto industry as people decide which large purchase to make in any given year. The auto and television industries complemented each other because television advertising showcased the mobility of cars, featuring them across the expanse of the new U.S. highway system.

Families moved into homogenized homes in ersatz developments with TV antennas, watching television an average four hours per day. Before television, children learned about communities by playing and growing up in and by contributing to them. They engaged in after-school *activities* (rather than passivities). That was soon to change as television-viewing habits increased each decade after the 1950s, with programming wielding more influence on viewers than the neighborhoods in which they lived.

In his book, *The Fifties*, Pulitzer Prize–winning journalist David Halberstam notes that what people saw in real life and on television began to merge, affecting awareness, mainly about community. "[M]any Americans were now living far from families, in brand-new suburbs where they barely knew their neighbors. Sometimes they felt closer to the people they watched on television than they did to their neighbors and distant families."[46] Congress, wary of the impact of the new medium, held hearings in 1952 to determine whether TV was corrupting morals by overemphasizing crime and violence. More hearings occurred two years later because of concern about growing crime rates.[47] The hearings generated some debate, but did not significantly change public attitude. At the time few definitive studies could be cited to make a case for or against television; however, by the 1970s, evidence about TV's influence on children was becoming as indisputable as tobacco's influence on health.

An important study was done in 1973 by Tannis MacBeth Williams of the University of British Columbia. Williams, a psychologist, had studied habits in three Canadian towns: one dubbed "Notel," which had no TV reception but would soon acquire a transmitter; another, "Unitel," which had only one government channel (Canadian Broadcasting Company); and the last, "Multitel," which had the CBC and U.S. network channels. Williams and other researchers analyzed viewer behavior in all three towns before Notel had television and then again, approximately two years later.

The results affirmed the worst suspicions, especially about TV's effect on children. While there was no significant difference in physical and verbal aggression among Unitel and Multitel children, Notel children exhibited nearly twice as much aggression toward each other after television as before. The experiment is explained in detail in Williams's book, *The Impact of Television: A Natural Experiment in Three Communities* (Academic Press, 1986). Williams's study not only showed that television triggered physical and verbal aggression among children; it also affected adult relationships and activities—even sleep. Jane Ledingham, Director of the Child Study Centre at the University of Ottawa, has summarized Williams' study—and television's impact on community—in her paper, "The Effects of Media Violence on Children":

> [Williams' study] found that people spent less time talking, socializing outside the home, doing household tasks, engaging in leisure

activities such as reading, knitting, and writing, and being involved in community activities and sports after television became available. They even slept less. . . . It is clear that television's impact on children arises not only from the kinds of behavior it promotes, but also from the other activities it replaces.[48]

Television viewing impacted community engagement. Some critics argued that TV viewing promoted aggression and some, including Herbert J. Gans, disputed that idea. Gans asserted that his "reading of the existing research suggests that the media encourage violent attitudes and acts only for some people at some times."[49] That may not reassure many in a continuing era of high school shootings; but Gans missed key points about TV-inspired violence. The news media hyped and overplayed violence; communities were typically safer than those depictions. Television viewing not only reduced civic engagement with fewer hours being spent in physical habitat; it altered the perception of that habitat in a continuing cycle of displacement. Robert D. Putnam documented that in his research about the collapse and revival of American communities, noting that "the average American's investment in organizational life (apart from religious groups . . .) fell from 3.7 hours per month in 1965 to 2.9 in 1975 to 2.3 in 1985."[50] Those statistics are the inverse of television statistics in U.S. homes.

As studies still document, television alters reality and with it, consciousness. Marketing exacerbates that effect. In his aptly named book, *The Culture of Marketing, the Marketing of Culture*, social critic and magazine journalist John Seabrook documents the omnipresent, transparent role of marketing. Until recently, marketing analyzed products before promoting them. That ensured accuracy but was not cost-effective. Now campaigns for products are developed while the products themselves are being developed. In fact, campaigns frequently have become indistinguishable from products. "It was said of the movie *Godzilla* that the marketing campaign was better than the movie but in the prerelease hype surrounding *The Phantom Menace*, the marketing and the movie have become the same thing," writes Seabrook. "I go to the supermarket to buy milk, and I see Star Wars has taken over aisle 5, the dairy section. There are figurine mugs of Han Solo and Princess Leia, nine-inch collectibles featuring Emperor Palpatine, an R2-D2 dispenser filled with Phantom Menace Pepsi, and down from that, another big display case filled with Star Wars-themed Frito-Lay potato chips. Pepsi has sunk over $2 billion into promoting the new trilogy. Each of Pepsi's three fast-food franchises—KFC, Taco Bell, and Pizza Hut—has licensed a different planet and festooned their containers with its characters."[51]

Marketing strategies homogenized America as much as subdivisions and chain stores. Our identities no longer were associated with community but with psychographics—statistics categorizing us according to the products that we purchase and the services that we perceive to need. Sociologist Manuel Castells observes that the obliteration of shared identities is equal to the dissolution of society as a meaningful social system. "At first sight," he writes, "we are witnessing the emergence of a world exclusively made of markets, networks, individuals, and strategic organizations, apparently governed by patterns of 'rational expectations' (the new, influential economic theory), except when these rational individuals suddenly shoot their neighbor, rape a little girl, or spread nerve gas in the subway. No need for identities in this new world."[52]

Marketing similarly afflicts the news industry and with it, community journalism, undermining our collective sense of place. Deregulation fostered this effect, with proponents arguing that media "should carry content that appeals to viewers as measured by market behavior," resulting in little need for ownership regulation beyond antitrust enforcement.[53] Hodding Carter III, former chief executive officer of the Knight Foundation, wrote, "Making money is no longer what [corporations] do so you can afford to do journalism. Making money is what you *do*."[54] Carter believed that media conglomerates—ecosystems that view news as content, satellite as delivery, broadcasting as showbiz, digital data as revenue, and so on—concentrate on yearly profits nearing 30 percent, forgetting that that they once were "part of the entire civic enterprise in this country. The public is not an outsider," Carter observed. "The public is the point of the enterprise."[55]

As far as the public is concerned, with respect to journalism, media companies have a time-honored obligation to enlighten people in a republic so that they can make informed decisions in the voting booth. Jefferson, Adams and Madison wrote about the necessity of an informed electorate, with Madison prophesying the future of a republic without access to that information: "A popular government without popular information or the means of acquiring it, is but a prologue to a farce, or a tragedy, or perhaps both."[56] Although there are dozens of historic examples of newspaper editors engaging and informing the public, perhaps Horace Greeley's "The Prayer of the Twenty Millions," published on August 19, 1862, in the *New York Tribune*, ranks as most iconic. Greeley urged Abraham Lincoln to free the slaves, undermining the Confederacy and ensuring liberty to those "loyal to the Union, and willing to shed their blood in her behalf, [who] shall no longer be held, with the Nation's consent, in bondage to persistent, malignant traitors, who for twenty years have been plotting and for sixteen months have been fighting to divide and destroy our country."[57] The open letter prompted a reply by Lincoln stating he would free none, some or all of the slaves to preserve the Union. This was the type of exchange that Madison foresaw for media and citizen engagement, without which democracy lapses into tragedy or farce.

Little is more farcical in the high-tech media age as the machine (aka corporations) enjoying the same rights as a citizen, especially in political campaigns. However, that is precisely what the Supreme Court decided on January 21, 2010, in *Citizens United v. Federal Election Commission* concerning the 2008 release of a film titled *Hillary: The Movie*, a documentary harshly depicting then–senator Hillary Clinton, a candidate for president that year. The case revolved around "video-on-demand," allowing viewers access to the movie at any time, the Court stated. Because the film, replete with political advertising, could be viewed within thirty days of an election, its distribution ran counter to a ban on corporate-funded political expenditures. The Court ruled that some members of "the public might consider *Hillary* to be insightful and instructive; some might find it to be neither high art nor a fair discussion on how to set the Nation's course; still others simply might suspend judgment on these points but decide to think more about issues and candidates. Those choices and assessments, however, are not for the Government to make."[58] The ruling bestowed First Amendment rights on corporations. The media machine subsumed the political one.

Because the First Amendment provides citizens freedom of and from religion, the Court further personalized corporations in *Burwell vs. Hobby Lobby Stores*, stating that corporations controlled by religious families are exempt from paying for contraception coverage for female employees.[59] The ruling was based on the firm's private avowed religious principles, again bestowing personhood on a corporate entity. Some might consider this reminiscent of Madison's prediction of the republic's future as farce, tragedy or both; however, a better case might be made on corporate branding via social media, based on the premise that products are people, too. Marketing consultant Brian Honeyman, writing in Entrepreneur.com, referenced the Hobby Lobby case in noting, "if you're online, you will likely encounter corporations pretending to be people every day as branded profiles and pages on nearly every social media channel."[60] Honeyman asks, "How can brands effectively create personas out of thin air, that are not just convincing, but that win a customer's trust and affection?" In his favor, Honeyman argues for authenticity. Nonetheless, his conclusion blurs the line between people and corporations in the digital world, proclaiming that "great social media accounts are not brands pretending to be people. Rather, they are people pretending to be brands."

The operative word here is "pretend," in which the virtual world (as opposed to the *real* one) excels.

Journal Exercise: *"On Demand Contact"*

Many of us are losing the ability to interact meaningfully with others, face to face, because we opt for on-demand rather than physical contact, relying on technology to mediate our communication. Bombarded with junk mail, email, spam, direct marketing, advertising, texts and premiums, we may ignore the written and spoken word out of distrust or cynicism, because we have become desensitized to language. The visual world also has diminished with a flatness associated with screens. Mostly, technology has altered our perception of time and occasion.

Test the above assertion. During the course of a week, analyze the impact of technology in your electronic exchanges at home or at school/work. Note the following in a detailed journal or even create an online blog to critically evaluate the exercises and assertions of this book:

- How were you contacted: via social network, microblog, blog, email, text?
- Was contact untimely rather than opportune? Be sure to catalogue interruptions at school/work and disruptions at home. Jot down the medium used to make contact, along with the time of and the reason for the contact.
- Determine whether the message:
  o *was timely for the medium, given the reason for contact*
  o *was untimely for the medium, given the reason for contact*
  o *could have been conveyed at a more propitious moment*
  o *probably should have been conveyed face-to-face at a different time*

- Was content capricious rather than cogent? Determine the import of each message, noting whether:
  - *Language was (a) clear, (b) somewhat clear, (c) unclear.*
  - *Content was (a) important, (b) somewhat important, (c) unimportant.*

Conclude your journal entry by:

1. Listing what components of face-to-face dialogue were filtered by the particular medium.
2. Examining whether sight, sound, touch, and so on would have enhanced content read or viewed on a screen.
3. Documenting how the medium may have modified meaning.

CHAPTER TWO

The Age of the Machine

The primal sacredness of life is a protonorm that binds humans into a common oneness.

—CLIFFORD G. CHRISTIANS,
media ethicist

The first tenet of this new culture is that all of reality, including humans, is one big information system.

—JARON LANIER,
computer scientist

....

Rise of Techno-Culture

A significant body of research has been done on the influence of organizational and cultural values on media ethics, especially in the age of globalization—in itself, a technological phenomenon. As counter to that effect, transnational ethical principles—responsibility, fairness, truth—increasingly have been viewed as essential "for guiding the global mass media, with individual decision-making and community-based ethics out of sync with today's worldwide technology."[1] These principles are rooted in culture, time and place—oft overlooked elements of ethics in a mechanized age—prompting the central question of this book: *Does media saturation alter our perception of fundamental principles guiding human behavior for millennia until now?*

To document the rise of techno-culture in society, we must define not only technology but also culture and universality. Definitions are not neutral. Philosopher Don Ihde in *Philosophy of Technology* defines technology broadly as having a concrete component (such as a computer) that humans can utilize, resulting in "a *relation* between the technologies and the humans who use, design, make, or modify the technologies in question."[2] Communication technology certainly falls into this realm. However, other "technologies" including the invention of the wheel in pre-historic eras, often also are included in this broad definition, even though such inventions were never classified as technological in the past. In this chapter we are focusing on communication technology; nevertheless, it behooves us to investigate the term "technology" as a cultural construct.

David E. Nye, a professor of American history at the University of Southern Denmark, reminds us that in the middle nineteenth century, the term "technology" was rarely used with people speaking about "'the mechanical arts' or the 'useful arts' or 'invention' or 'science' in contexts where they would use 'technology' today."[3] Nye also searched prominent American periodicals published between 1860 and 1870 and found "technology" only mentioned 149 times while "invention" was mentioned 24,957 times, adding that the term "technology" began appearing as part of university names.[4]

Traditionally, technology has been associated with knowledge derived from the industrial arts, applied sciences and engineering with each new discovery posing ethical questions about risk.[5] Thus, moral inquiry about technology requires expertise or knowledge in the specific industry, science or mechanism in addition to a grasp of philosophy. Because technology has wide application, many philosophers evaluate risk by assessing technology's impact on civil liberties, personal autonomy or rights such as due process.[6] Invariably, then, the concept of risk associates technology with aspects of scientific and mechanical culture.

The term "culture" likewise is not easily defined but has its roots in anthropology and has expanded over the years to various disciplines that interpreted the concept differently, including use of the term to identify power, inequalities and history.[7] As such, the concept of culture remains elusive. An oft-cited definition emanates from a study of various interpretations of the term by Kroeber and Kluckhohn whose 1952 work described "culture" as follows:

> Culture consists of patterns, explicit and implicit, of and for behavior acquired and transmitted by symbols, constituting the distinctive achievements of human groups, including their embodiments in artifacts; the essential core of culture consists of traditional (i.e., historically derived and selected) ideas and especially their attached values; culture systems may, on the one hand, be considered as products of action, and on the other as conditioning elements of further action.[8]

As such, culture concerns the behavior of communities defined by their history, achievements and actions, as well as the values attached to them. In 1963–64, the University of Birmingham Centre for Contemporary Cultural Studies was instrumental in expanding the definition of culture to include "the interplay of representations and ideologies" of class, gender, race, ethnicity, nationality and media.[9] The Birmingham group also "was among the first to study the effects of newspaper, radio, television, film, and other popular cultural forms on audiences," focusing interpretations on how different audiences responded to media texts.[10] Studies such as these popularized the phrase "media culture" as being distinct from local, regional or national culture, even though newspapers and television stations covered events and issues happening in those locales.

The term "media culture" has since become common in discussing such varied topics as politics, religion and stereotypes associated with class, gender, race, ethnicity and nationality. In fact, it can be argued, digital saturation in the present day has made "media" and "culture" nearly synonymous. However, in terms of journalism ethics, the concept of professionalism in pre-Internet twentieth century led the news industry to claim "cultural authority," or rights to interpret culture because of experience and expertise. Journalism rights as they concern cultural issues typically are associated with licensure. The U.S. State Department Bureau of International Information notes that mandatory licensing of journalists exists in many countries in Asia, Africa and the Middle East.[11] Licensing aside, it has often been argued that just as physicians have the authority to declare medical breakthroughs, or attorneys legal precedents, journalists have unofficial license to analyze, depict and interpret culture through standards of gatekeeping, reporting, editing and ethics.[12]

Licensing and standard newsroom practices increasingly have come under scrutiny as media developed global network capabilities. This led to ethical debates on whether universal principles actually existed, and if so, what were they and how did they affect cultural values. Before addressing the central issue of this chapter—*has techno-culture subsumed national culture, influencing universal principles in the process?*—we must question whether ethics, indeed, can be universal. In a 2006 keynote address at the International Communication Association, sociologist and author Manuel Castells spoke about a new technology boom in the proliferation of blogs worldwide accounting for what he then called an explosion of "I–mass media across cultures." In the question and answer session, Castells was asked: "For centuries in Occidental culture there has been a philosophical debate, entirely conjectural, that universal principles exist or do not exist. We now have some empirical evidence to answer this question. Given the expanse of the blogosphere across cultures, are there any philosophical patterns that qualify now as universal?" Castells replied, "The longing for freedom."[13]

That longing, in and of itself, is not a universal principle but the desire for one. Ethicists have searched for such a principle in the wake of ever-expanding global communication whose history dates back to 1858 when the first trans-Atlantic cable was sent from Queen Victoria of the United Kingdom to President James Buchanan of the United States. As Sandra H. Dickson observes in the *Journal of Mass Media Ethics*, "The pattern of criticisms of the press over the decades underscores the problems caused by the absence of universal ethical standards. Situation ethics . . . are an insufficient moral compass to guide a fast-paced, technologically-driven, bottom-line-oriented industry."[14] In as much as non-journalists are engaging in worldwide communication, that desire for universal standards has heightened in importance in the twenty-first century.

Cultural Values

French media ethicist Claude-Jean Bertrand struggled with the concept of universal principles vs. cultural values. "If a single value exists on which all humans can agree (except a few fanatics), it is the survival of the species, the fate of the planet."[15] However, Bertrand continued, "each culture has specific features . . . female nudity offends in Saudi Arabia and in the U.S., whereas in Europe it has become a normal part of the seaside landscape and of advertising."[16] Survival and nudity, of course, are not ethical precepts but biological ones. How people of varied cultures respond to nudity is associated with a wide array of cultural values lined to social mores, religious convictions and case law. Concerning the latter, the U.S. Supreme Court rejected fines against media outlets for programs featuring cursing and nudity, the *New York Times* reported in 2012, leaving "open the question of whether changes in the media landscape have undermined the rationales" for regulating such content when cable television "and the Internet are not subject to government regulation of ostensibly indecent material."[17] Here again technology and its expansion are at play in an era of global communication.

Nonetheless, ethicist Deni Elliott makes a strong case for universal values beyond social mores or cultural values:

> Viewed from a wide angle, the world's communities and subcommunities appear to be an array of values, a colorful moral kaleidoscope. But these dissimilarities among values, as striking as they are, mask the similarity behind the "colors"—the species-specific "crystals" that create discernible and consistent patterns amid the array of value-colors. The argument for universal values, like moral development theories, builds on the notion of similarities among human behavior that stretch across space, culture, and time.[18]

Elliott bases her argument for moral principles on the benchmarks of space, culture and time.

In a 1997 work titled "Universal Values and Moral Development Theories," she references a 1965 survey from thirteen countries with diverse cultures, citing these similarities of values (compiled by Handley Cantrill):

1. Satisfaction of survival needs
2. Physical and psychological security
3. Sufficient order and certainty to allow for predictability
4. Pleasure: both physical and psychological excitement and enjoyment
5. Freedom to act on ideas and plans for improvement of self and context
6. Freedom to make choices
7. Freedom to act on choices
8. Personal identity and integrity; a sense of dignity
9. Feeling of worthwhileness
10. A system of beliefs to which they can commit themselves
11. Trust in the system on which they depend.[19]

The term "freedom" appears in three of the entries [Nos. 5–7]; the inviolability of life [Nos. 1, 2], justice/fairness [3], pleasure/happiness [4, 9], responsibility/duty [10], integrity/dignity [8], trust [11].

Philosopher Christina Hoff Sommers substitutes the term "moral absolutes" for universal principles in observing that these behaviors are clearly right or wrong and not subject to serious debate in any culture:

1. It is wrong to mistreat a child.
2. It is wrong to humiliate someone.
3. It is wrong to torment an animal.
4. It is wrong to think only of yourself.
5. It is wrong to steal, to lie, to break promises.
6. It is right to be considerate and respectful of others.
7. It is right to be charitable and generous.[20]

These, too, seem to relate to "sanctity of life" [Nos. 1–3], responsibility/duty [No. 4], truth/trust [No. 5], respect [No. 6], and generosity [No. 7].

Clifford G. Christians has written extensively about "protonorm," an overarching universal principle based on human dignity, truth-telling and nonviolence. "The primal sacredness of life is a protonorm that binds humans into a common oneness. And in our systematic reflection on this primordial generality, we recognize that it entails such basic ethical principles as human dignity, truth, and nonviolence."[21]

How do these relate to principles held by journalists across cultures? Are there universal media ethics principles, for example? One such study by Rao and Seow, titled "Globalizing Media Ethics? An Assessment of Universal Ethics Among International Political Journalists," investigated "the possible existence and evolution of universal and global moral imperatives among journalists."[22] The study explored these questions:

- *How do international political journalists who are writing about democracy, nation-state, terrorism, sovereignty and human rights, discuss ethics?*
- *Do they share certain ethical principles?*
- *What are their views about developing a global media ethics code?*

The study, based on both interviews with journalists and analysis of their countries' codes of ethics, identified four principles: "respect[ing] others, tolerance for religious and cultural diversity, tell[ing] the truth with restraint, and freedom and independence."[23]

Another study of journalism ethics codes in Europe identified common principles that emphasized "the truthfulness of information, the prohibition of discrimination on the basis of race, sex, etc., fair means in gathering the information, integrity of the source and the journalist, and freedom of expression and comment."[24] These findings are similar to ones reported in 1980 by the MacBride Commission, which analyzed codes of ethics from sixty countries, identifying these ethical norms: objectivity, impartiality, truthfulness, "responsibility vis-à-vis the public and its rights and interests and in relation to national, racial, and religious communities, the nation, the State, and maintenance of the peace."[25]

The MacBride Commission report was controversial in the United States because it emanated out of UNESCO's International Commission for the Study of Communication Problems. The report called for a new world order concerning information disseminated by mass media, which "precipitated the decision by the U.S. government to withdraw its membership from UNESCO," a move "made on behalf of big mass media and telecommunications industry interests in the United States."[26] Thus, the Reagan administration's emphasis on media marketing over information set the stage for the first modern-day culture war involving global mass media. Indeed, the MacBride report focused in part on universal journalism principles falling prey to U.S. cultural values, noting that those values would be propelled by "a constant flow of messages and stimuli" and noting that even the richest, most ancient cultural identities would fall prey to dominant media's "overpowering influence" and "assimilation."[27]

Media Values

As communication became global via satellite transmission, beginning in the 1960s, the debate about universal principles being influenced by media culture intensified. In *De-Westernizing Media Studies*, editors James Curran and Myung Jin-Park write that the theory of "cultural globalization" took root in 1980 with the premise that "new communications technology, compressing time and space and transcending national frontiers, is bringing into being 'a global village,'" resurrecting the influence of McLuhan.[28] In the 1990s and continuing into the twenty-first century, digital technologies were developed via a market-based paradigm, delivering a global mall rather than a village, as the MacBride Commission prophesied. Presently, the new conventional wisdom concerning universal principles versus cultural values is still being debated, with cultural theorists expressing "infectious enthusiasm about globalization as a process that is increasing international dialogue, empowering minorities, and building progressive solidarity" while political economists "write about globalization as a capitalist victory that is dispossessing democracies, imposing policy homogenization, and weakening progressive movements" rooted in working-class and popular political organizations.[29]

To appreciate the impact of time and space compression, which define techno-cultural values, along with their propensity to transcend and thereby annex national frontiers, a deeper analysis of technology's nature, and its relationship to journalism, is in order. Once again the question arises: *Are media ethics influenced more by technology than by culture?* The latter is defined primarily by place and time, documented geographically by such effects as climate, customs, language and resources and historically by the events, discoveries, politics and economies within national borders. Mass communication technology redefined those markers, gradually transcending them with each new appliance, from the telegraph and telephone of the nineteenth century to the radio and telephone of the twentieth century. Each technological platform increased its geographic reach so that communication in the twenty-first century is defined primarily asynchronous, global and integrated within a digital cloud.

In his 1995 then-futuristic book, *Being Digital*, former MIT technologist Nicholas Negroponte foresaw that progression, defining place, time and cloud:

- *Place Without Space:* "[T]he post-information age will remove the limitations of geography. Digital living will include less and less dependence upon being in a specific place at a specific time, and the transmission of place itself will start to become possible."[30]
- *Being Asynchronous:* "A face-to-face or telephone conversation is real time and synchronous" while email is not. . . . "The advantage is less about voice and more about off-line processing and time shifting."[31]
- *Mediumlessness:* "Thinking about multimedia needs to include ideas about the fluid movement from one medium to the next. . . . [M]ultimedia involves translating one dimension (time) into another dimension (space)."[32]

In 1995, these attributes were futuristic; in 2016, they are commonplace. However, another more pertinent question must be considered with the rise of techno-culture: *Do universal principals metamorphose or remain intact when transported to virtual realms that obliterate or obfuscate space, culture and time?* Even Clifford Christians' well-researched and persuasive argument about the common oneness of humans is based on "reverence for life on earth, for the organic whole, for the *physical realm* [emphasis added] in which human civilization is situated."[33]

Thomas de Zengotita's 2005 book, *Mediated: How the Media Shapes Your World and the Way You Live in It,* posits that loss of time or a sense of time passage in the twenty-first century is embodied in the phrase, *real time.* "Real time: as opposed to what exactly? Well, as opposed to representations that aren't simultaneous with whatever they represent. Instantaneous stock market info—but not just snapshots, the flow across the mediational screen *as* events occur. Hence, 'real time.'"[34] De Zengotita theorizes that two physical phenomena are powerful enough to wrench us from the asynchronicity enveloping us, accident and necessity.[35] This concept will be discussed more in depth in Chapter Six, "Interpersonal Divide at Work," exploring how mobile devices tether employees to their jobs at all hours everywhere every day.

Apart from accident and necessity, most of us live in multiple dimensions, thanks to mobile technology: the real and the virtually real. We have one identity in place and time and another in the digital realm, a phenomenon that author Sherry Turkle analyzed in *Life on the Screen: Identity in the Age of the Internet,* published in 1995, the same year as MIT colleague Negroponte foresaw a social utopia in *Being Digital,* with the word "being" as operative as "digital" when used as a noun, as in digital *being* rather than human being—what Turkle and de Zengotita maintain. "When we step through the screen into virtual communities, we reconstruct our identities on the other side of the looking glass," Turkle writes. "This reconstruction is our cultural work in progress."[36] One of the core observations in her book was the blurring of people and machines, noting that in mass media, in particular, images "of machines have come closer to images of people, as images of people have come ever closer to images of machines."[37] In 1995, that analysis was far less obvious than in 2017 with wired and wireless technology attached to us or within reach at any hour of the day in any "hot spot," another curious phrase associated with place and as ironic as "real time," in that we designate geography now with McLuhanesque terminology, not in hot and cold media as he asserted, but in wireless and non-wireless places. Because of technology's eventual omnipresence, Turkle foresaw that people had two bodies, a physical one and a "technobody," relying increasingly on machine intelligence rather than our own. As such, we began losing our perspective about what is real and virtually real, sometimes with dire consequences, in the wake of accident or necessity.

"Compare a rafting trip down the Colorado River to an adolescent girl using an interactive CD-ROM to explore the same territory. In the physical rafting trip, there is likely to be physical danger and with it, a sense of real consequences."[38] Not so in the virtual world.

Users steeped in virtual environments become immune to the dangers of the real world, as evidenced by statistics associated with distracted driving. Between the years 2010 and 2012, the number of people killed in automobile crashes due to distracted driving averaged about 3,300 per year. In particular, 10 percent of all drivers under the age of twenty who died in crashes were distracted at the time of the crash. The official government site, distraction.gov, also reports that at any given moment in America, some 660,000 drivers "are using cell phones or manipulating electronic devices while driving, a number that has held steady since 2010."[39]

Accidents of all sorts seem to be on the rise perhaps because of the false sense of security provided by the virtual world. Arcade characters simply re-spawn when killed; people do not. There is a general feeling that someone somewhere else is responsible for reporting dangers. In the wake of two deaths involving bear attacks at Yellowstone National Park, a spokesperson interviewed by National Public Radio felt compelled to explain that "Yellowstone is a wild place. This isn't a controlled environment. . . . I fear that some visitors believe that if things were dangerous, we, the National Park Service, would somehow control it."[40]

Accidents occur when virtual and real worlds collide. The mind is engaged in one place while the body exists in another. As author Nancy Baym notes in *Personal Connections in the Digital Age*,

> We may be physically present in one space, yet mentally and emotionally engaged elsewhere. Consider, for instance, the dinner partner who is immersed in his mobile phone conversation. Since he is physically present, yet simultaneously absent, the very nature of self becomes problematic. Where is "he?" The borders of between human and machine . . . are thrown into flux.[41]

Anthropologist Scott Atran takes that conundrum a step further in his essay, "The Fourth Phase of Homo Sapiens," appearing in *Is the Internet Changing the Way You Think?*, noting that people wouldn't need physical libraries or national cultural borders if they could fly like action heroes and surf for relationships, as they do on Internet. Atran observes that cultural values, in particular, had been shaped in the past by politics and religion and were closely aligned with both ethnicity and territory but now "are becoming increasingly detached from their cultures of origin, not so much because of the movement of peoples . . . but because of the worldwide traffic of media-friendly information and ideas."[42]

Indeed, media have been identified for decades as an agent of cultural obliteration, primarily because they introduce into society time, space and language technologies. The term "Internet Revolution," which evolved in the 1980s, concerned the change from mechanical and electrical technology to digital technology. To understand the cultural effect, think of how the invention of the clock—a time technology—changed culture in the Middle Ages. If people had a precise sense of time, everything from church services to shop hours could be scheduled. Cartography became a space technology and had the same effect, revolutionizing warfare and trade. However, media embed language in technologies that also transcend time and place, such as the printing press in the sixteenth century, the telegraph in the nineteenth century, and the television in the twentieth century. In the twenty-first century, the Internet's global reach combined its abilities to embed language while altering and compressing time and place and thus "transformed entire cultural perspectives upon the world."[43]

Commercial Values

The transformation changed economies as well as cultures, moving cultures out of industrialized systems to ones based on information, such as financial services, accounting and software. Law professor Yochai Benkler in his 2006 book, *The Wealth of Networks*, notes that this became possible because of "the move to a communications environment built on cheap processes with high computation capabilities, interconnected in a pervasive network—the phenomenon we associate with the Internet."[44] The economic shift has been accelerated worldwide because of integrated media and digital clouds. Technology writer and author Nicholas Carr notes that as soon as information is digitized, boundaries between media dissolve. "We replace our special-purpose tools with an all-purpose tool. And because the economics of digital production and distribution are almost always superior to what came before—the cost of creating electronic products and transmitting them through the Net is a small fraction of the cost of manufacturing physical goods and shipping them through warehouses and into stores—the shift happens very quickly, following capitalism's inexorable logic."[45] Communication technology has always been a key component of commerce and globalization. However, conventional media, from the telegraph to the television, were controlled and/or regulated by corporate and government entities serving as cultural filters. Until the Internet, there had never been a medium allowing instantaneous global access. Technological diffusion was further accelerated by a host of ever smaller, mobile and more powerful devices programmed for commerce. This cultural effect was the focus of a powerful if prescient analysis aptly titled "Globalization and the Role of the Global Corporation." Allan Bird and Michael J. Stevens identified the creation of an emerging commerce-driven global culture. The authors evaluated the impact of market trends on "the obsolescence of national cultures," concluding that those societies must embrace their core values "if they wish to remain relevant in some viable fashion."[46]

The article cites statistics in its view of globalization, prompted by technological proliferation, leading to these futuristic conclusions:

- *One world, one language:* Probably English with a subset of Mandarin Chinese, Spanish and possibly French.
- *One world, one worldview:* Thanks to global communication media such as CNN, *Wall Street Journal, National Geographic,* etc.
- *One world, one psychographic:* Educated, connected via digital technologies, self-confident, pragmatic, democratic and participatory, individualistic but inclusive, flexible and open and, perhaps most important, unintimidated by national boundaries and culture.

But there is a price for commercial, technology-driven globalization. As Erik Qualman explains in *Socialnomics,* "The winners in a socially driven world are numerous: good companies, good products, employees, consumers, democracy, entrepreneurial talent, and the environment—all creatures great and small. However, it doesn't come without a price: the majority of what we consider to be our personal privacy may be a thing of the past. . . . Andy Warhol's famous statement about fame may very well be flipped on its head and read something like: 'In the future, we'll all have fifteen minutes of privacy.'"[47]

Qualman, however, who touts social media and notes how news finds readers (rather than the other way around), indirectly endorses a deterministic view. He notes that if Facebook were a country, it would be the third largest in the world after China and India, and then adds: "Businesses don't have the choice on whether or not they do social media, the choice is on how well they do it."[48] That is the nature of technology overpowering a wide range of interpersonal choice and replacing it with market-driven options in a specific interface, network or application. And in doing so, in consolidating and consigning interpersonal choice in ever narrower psychographic sectors of globalization—including how we report the news—there seems to be something lacking, as if humans spend most of their day in a representation of the world rather than in the real one.

That last phenomenon is perhaps best articulated again by De Zengotita in *Mediated*:

> [A]n environment of representation yields an aura of surface—as in "surf." *It is a world of effects.* This is another existential consequence of the fact that representations address us by design. We are at the center of all the attention, but there is a thinness to things, a smoothness, a muffled quality—it's all insulational, as if the deities of Dreamworks were laboring invisibly around us, touching up the canvas of reality with digital airbrushes.[49]

This effect has been considered before. From Ellul to McLuhan, technology was viewed as separate from culture but having a profound impact on it. However, digital and mobile technologies have so embedded themselves in almost everything that we do—not only in North American and Europe, but increasingly around the globe—that classic philosophical views of technology no longer apply, indirectly suggesting an alternative deterministic view, namely, a continuous interplay of technology and culture interacting on each other to such extent that we scarcely know the world in which we live, because the real and virtual blend through this interaction.[50]

Turkle has described the impact of this interplay on the self. She once described the computer "as a second self, a mirror of mind. Now the metaphor no longer goes far enough. Our new devices provide space for the emergence of a new state of the self, itself, split between the screen and the physical real, wired into existence through technology."[51] Gradually, because of technology's effect on culture, "we come to see our online life as life itself," no longer the source of complaint but of what we want in an environment that she describes as "gathering clouds of a perfect storm."[52]

The word "cloud" in this usage is not a resurrected cliché, but it could have been, as the digital cloud symbolizes more than weather.

It represents a commercial ecosystem's cluster of infrastructures, platforms, software, storage, security and other data-driven services that we tap into on a regular basis using fixed and mobile technologies. Data are byte-sized raindrops in the digital atmosphere, evaporating from our devices to the cloud, which pours its shared content across the wireless expanse below. Once created, clouds take on distinct structures just as real clouds do. There are public clouds, private clouds, community clouds, etc., forming a vast intercloud ecosystem that alters what we typically we do in homes, workplaces and the digital streets, fulfilling Ellul's prophesy of technology as an inhuman, self-determining organism ("an end in itself") whose autonomy transforms centuries' old systems "while being scarcely modified in its own features."[53]

Determinism as theorized by Ellul is not prominent but subtle primarily because technology gives an individual a sense of control as it establishes itself over society, changing fundamental values. The issue of personal control is explored at length in Baym's *Personal Connections in the Digital Age*. She notes that the separation of the present from communication offers users more control in social networks while simultaneously subjecting them to new forms of control, surveillance and constraint. "We can create new opportunities to converse. We can avoid interactions, talking into a mobile phone (or pretending to) to avoid a co-present acquaintance or letting calls go to voice mail. . . . We can use nonverbally limited media such as text messages or emails to shelter us from anxiety-inducing encounters such as flirting or ending relationships. But just as we can use these media to manage others more strategically, others can also more easily manage us."[54]

In media ethics, control is associated with power or the attempt to control others by assuming power. Power is not a value but the force we exert to express our values. Users and developers of technology are largely oblivious of this philosophical effect "even as it changes who we are, as individuals and as a society."[55] Part of this has to do with users being focused on how to deploy the tool and developers on how to structure, program and disseminate an application for a certain commercial usage. As Carr suggests in *The Shallows: What the Internet is Doing to our Brains*, users as well as societies make choices about technology without considering effects on cultural values, primarily because users lack the power to control the path or pace of technological progress.[56]

Media so dominate our daily lives that nothing is as it was only a decade ago, documenting the meteoric rise of commercially driven techno-culture in society. As Powers writes in *Hamlet's BlackBerry*, "The simple act of going for a walk is completely different today from what it was years ago. Whether you're walking down a big-city street or in the woods outside a country town, if you're carrying a mobile device with you, the global crowd comes along. A walk can still be a very pleasant experience, but it's a qualitatively different experience, simply because it's busier. The air is full of people."[57] That fundamentally changes not only the walk but also the place where we decide to take that walk. Place is redefined by consumer technology. According to Turkle, a place hitherto was defined as "a physical space and the people within it. What is a place if those who are physically present have their attention on the absent?"[58]

Journalism is associated with place. If one takes the standard 5 Ws and H—who, what, where, when, why and how of a conventional news report—and tries to define them in an asynchronous, anonymous, omnipresent digital environment, the "who" may be a person pretending to be someone else; the "what," one or another action by a multitasking person; the "where," somewhere else; the "when," whatever time content is accessed; the "why," the convenience of such access; and the "how," the program that allows access in the first place. This is why some media ethicists often believe that we lack insight into the effects of technology on culture. Those effects are typically found in the design of the user interface and the conventional wisdom that surrounds the creation of that interface. One of the most articulate writers on the topic is computer scientist Jaron Lanier, author of the 2011 book, *You Are Not a Gadget*, who shares insight into how programming decisions are made by technologists. "For instance, it is often claimed by open culture types that if you can't make a perfect copy-protection technology, then copy prohibitions are pointless. And from a technological point of view, it is true that you can't make a perfect copy-protection scheme. If flawless behavior restraints are the only potential influences on behavior in a case such as this, we might as well not ask anyone to ever pay for music or journalism again."[59]

That says much about journalism's current state of affairs in trying to monetize the Internet. The goal of this chapter is not to solve those kinds of practical problems but to make a case that technological values comprise a distinct set of commercial norms apart from cultural and universal values.

Clifford G. Christians has long maintained that technology is not neutral but value-laden, as Ellul suggested. Christians calls Ellul "the most dominating macro thinker on technology," developing the argument that technology refines contemporary culture via "the spirit of machineness."[60] A state of machineness, according to Ellul, has been summarized as artificial, autonomous with respect to values, self-determining, independent of human intervention, proliferative without direction toward an end, and composed of means exhibiting primacy over ends.[61]

According to Lanier, these attributes are the product of "petty designs" that promote freedom, as in "open culture," but is more a freedom for machines resulting in a generation of digital natives "with a reduced expectation of what a person can be, and of who each person might become."[62] Lanier describes programmers thinking about users as parts of the gadget, or machine, and "the vast anonymous crowd" as "an organism with a legitimate point of view."[63] This view is often put forward as a utopian thesis in which one measures social "progress" through techno-science whose innovations "eventually will solve most human problems."[64] Further, the utopian mindset posits that technology not only progresses in that goal but also evolves.

A chief advocate of that view has been Kevin Kelly, co-founder of *WIRED* magazine and author of the 2010 book, *What Technology Wants*. Kelly waxes philosophic on technology's ultimate dominance over culture in a liberating arc that frees us from the dictates of matter and energy. "Look what is coming," he writes: "Technology is stitching together all the minds of the living, wrapping the planet in a vibrating cloak of electronic nerves, entire continents of machines conversing with one another, the whole aggregation watching itself through a million cameras posted daily. How can this not stir that organ in us that is sensitive to something larger than ourselves?"[65] Then he makes a spurious claim about a commercial product—mobile phones—stating that "we can see more of God in a cell phone than in a tree frog. The phone extends the frog's four billion years of learning and adds the open-ended investigations of six billion human minds."[66]

Is a cell phone really more miraculous in design than the biology of a tree frog? The passage above was shared with Distinguished Professor of Evolutionary Biology at Iowa State University, Jonathan Wendel, whose research focuses on molecular and genome evolution, exploring in part how genomes change over evolutionary time. Here is his response:

> There is nothing approaching biological evolution in the technological advances that lead to trinkets such as cell phones, although I can imagine how some might find parallels between technological

advance and a naïve notion that biological evolution also "advances." Evolution consists of constant change, and over the broad sweep of time there may be increased complexity, but this is nothing like technological advance, neither in process nor outcome. Not only that, the tree frog is many orders of magnitude more complex and wondrous than any human-engineered artifact.[67]

Compare Kelly's with Wendell's observations, and one can discern metaphoric versus realistic depictions not only of evolution and tree frogs but also of the culture of techno-science, the new commercial norm in digital society. Objects, people, flora, fauna, past, present and future don't have to be factual; they just have to be representational and subservient to a program engineered for quick, profitable ubiquitous access. In *Hamlet's BlackBerry*, Powers articulates that norm succinctly: "It's good to be connected, and it's bad to be disconnected."[68] He writes that this simple programming idea has enormous implications every waking hour, as well as two corollaries: *The more you connect, the better off you are. The more you disconnect, the worse off you are.* "Together," he writes, "these two propositions prescribe exactly how to manage one's digital existence. You can't be too connected, they say, so we should seek at all times to maximize our time with screens and minimize our time away. And this is just how many of us are living today. We are *digital maximalists.*"[69]

In *Philosophy of Technology*, Ihde remarks that all technologies are embedded in culture. As such, he foresaw the rise of a phenomenon he calls "pluriculture," based on the interaction of techno-culture with national culture which he noted in 1993 was largely a Euro-American phenomenon being adapted successfully into several Pacific Rim Asian cultures.[70] A quarter century later, the embedding and integration of technology in national culture has expanded into every populated continent. According to Lanier, this is cybernetic totalism, a new creed in which nature and culture become "computer peripherals attached to the great computing clouds. The news is no longer about us but about the big new computational object that is greater than us."[71] In this paradigm, humanity and universal principles—including Christians' protonorm about the sacredness of life—succumb to Lanier's digital protonorm: "all of reality, including humans, is one big information system."[72]

That system operates on the bottom line. Another effect of the above technological protonorm is a flattening of visual culture whereby all of reality assumes similar characteristics, from loss of scale to loss of differentiation. "Experience is replaced with facsimile."[73] Facsimile can be manipulated for a wide range of commercial messages. Experience has distinct characteristics that separate it from facsimile, as noted in an anecdote titled "Recalling the Real," as told by de Zengotita in *Mediated*. He asks you to imagine your car breaking down in the middle of Saskatchewan. You have no access to communication whatsoever and realize, finally, that nothing in nature is designed for you. "It isn't arranged so that you can experience it, you didn't plan to experience it, there isn't any screen, there isn't any display, there isn't any entrance, no brochure, nothing special to look at, no dramatic scenery or wildlife, no tour guide, no campsites, no benches, no paths, no viewing platforms. . . . You begin to get a sense of your real place in the great scheme of things. Very small."[74] De Zengotita then discloses the universal principle of the mediated world. The opposite of reality is not phony or illusional or fictional, he writes: It's *optional*.

In a sense, this is what McLuhan was discovering in his famous saying, "the medium is the message." He was warning us about being oblivious to the power of technology and the threat that it posed to culture. As this affects the news, the principle of optional bestows on audience the power to filter highly individualized content, or "The Daily Me," a concept popularized by Nicolas Negroponte in *Being Digital*. In investigating that concept, Harvard law professor Cass Sunstein notes that techno-culture allows people to decide in advance "what they will and will not encounter. They can design something very much like a communications universe of their own choosing. And if they have trouble designing it, it can be designed for them, again with perfect accuracy."[75] Real culture, especially a culture that values free expression and democracy, has two distinct values, according to Sunstein: "*First*, people should be exposed to materials that they would not have chosen in advance. . . . Second, many or most citizens should have a range of common experiences. Without shared experiences, a heterogeneous society will have a much more difficult time in addressing social problems. People may even find it hard to understand one another. Common experiences, emphatically including the common experiences made possible by the media, provide a form of social glue."[76] Of course, in the current day via social media like Facebook, algorithms customize "The Daily Me" to such extent, that people routinely know the products, fads, trends and celebrities of their preferred digital experience. But they may not know the pertinent news, issues, facts and events that shape democracy, state and federal laws, individual health and well-being, and civic and civil rights.

Previously, as media ethics were concerned, the social glue was cemented by cultural values; the human condition, by universal principles. National culture and human condition are being redefined by a commercial techno-culture promulgated by media ecosystems giving users what they want—options—rather than what they need in the aftermath of accident and necessity. In upcoming chapters about big data and the interpersonal divide at home, school and work, we will see how options of the machine are limiting our own, exposing us to values at odds with humane principles that hitherto nurtured our conscience and deepened our awareness for millennia.

Journal Exercise: *"Your Personal Code"*

Before you can assess how, if at all, technology is affecting your personal values and core beliefs, you have to ascertain what those values and beliefs are and how you are coping with or nurturing them in your interpersonal and technological activities. A value system can be expressed in a personal code of ethics. You can keep that code for reference as you view technology more critically and adjust or adapt to your discoveries throughout the reading of this book. A good code also should have a central theme—an overriding principle of service or duty that guides and motivates you when you encounter opportunities or challenges.

In recent years, technological changes across media platforms have dominated discussion, both in academe and the business world. Clifford G. Christians, one of the most distinguished media ethicists, notes that we are living, learning and working in a high-tech world enamored of machines, and one of the effects of that is a worrisome amorality. According to Christians, "In an instrumental age enamored of machines, life becomes amoral, without moral bearings, devoid of moral categories. Moral vocabulary is not understood. Moral distinctions have little meaning. In the process of fabricating expert mechanical systems such as the digital order, the world is sanitized of the moral dimension. In a technological age, the social fashion is to be emancipated from moral standards and to disavow moral responsibility."[77]

Ethics codes remind us about moral vocabularies and categories. Can you create such a code that represents your deeply held beliefs?

Once you have such a code, you can ascertain the impact of technology on your values.

Here's one method to create such a code:

1. **Write a brief statement** about your own values concerning such concepts as responsibility, truth, falsehood, temptation, manipulation, bias and fairness. Length: 25–75 words each.

2. **Check out links for ethics codes** in your chosen career path. For instance, if you plan to enter advertising, journalism or public relations, there are plenty of codes to guide you by major organizations representing those professions. Almost every career path, including blogging and technology, has codes of ethics. Conduct an online search, referencing your career choice and ethics code, as in *"fashion and apparel code* of ethics." You will discover the tenets of the International Textile and Apparel Association. Or you can input *"photojournalism* and code of ethics." You will get a link for the National Press Photographers Association. And so on.

3. **Compare your statements** (in #1 above) with ones in codes that you view online (#2 above). Then revise your codes, if appropriate, clarifying terms or harmonizing content in keeping with high standards of your career path.

4. **Now condense each statement,** articulating your convictions about responsibility, truth, falsehood, temptation, manipulation, bias and fairness, etc. Keep these statements short, about fifty words per item.

6. **Assemble your code in the one document** and revise the wording of each tenet so that all codes are similar in length and read in a consistent and parallel manner. (Common style errors include using the first person, "I," in some codes and not in others and switching verb case or tense.)

7. **Show a draft of your code to a mentor** or role model and/or share yours with peers in a group study or workshop. Ask for a critique and then revise your document again, if necessary.

8. **Insert your code in a blog** and format accordingly, updating or revising your values based on any discovery that stems from upcoming journal exercises in this book.

CHAPTER THREE
....

Big Data, Little People

You might want to create nodes to represent people, organizations or other "cases." When you create a case node, you can record the attributes of the case (for example, a person's age or occupation). Once your case nodes are created, you can code source content relating to a particular case at its node, and then use queries to ask comparative questions based on attributes like age or occupation.

—"Creating Nodes for People, Places, and Other Entities,"
NVivo qualitative data analysis software instructions[1]
....

How People Became Nodes

In Isaac Asimov's famous science fiction story, "Feminine Intuition," published in his 1976 collection *The Bicentennial Man*, researchers created the first robot not pre-programmed to do specific tasks. They labeled the assembly of this model robot "intuition" so as not to leave the impression that the machine was "uncontrolled" or worse, uncontrollable.

Because people might fear irrepressible machines, Asimov begins this story with his fabled "Three Laws of Robotics":

1. *A robot may not injure a human being or, through inaction, allow a human being to come to harm.*
2. *A robot must obey the orders given it by human beings except where such orders would conflict with the First Law.*
3. *A robot must protect its own existence as long as such protection does not conflict with the First or Second Law.*[2]

The title, "Feminine Intuition," affirms a belief that women were better than men at intuition. A female robot "could make correlations far more rapidly and far more precisely than a man could," the protagonist researcher states. "In a day, it could make and discard as many correlations as a man could in ten years. Furthermore, it would work in a truly random fashion, whereas a man would have a strong bias based on preconception and on what is already believed."[3]

The company, United States Robots, builds the machine; but there is a problem. "The trouble is the matter of recognition," the protagonist states. The robot is "correlating magnificently. She can correlate on any subject, but once she's done so, she can't recognize a valuable result from a valueless one. It's not an easy problem, judging how to program a robot to tell a significant correlation when you don't know what correlations she will be making."[4]

Reading this story some forty years later, one can recognize the gender stereotypes but also Asimov's prophetic vision. Big data reduce the global millions of Internet users into *nodes*—interactive redistribution points— or little people, using personal, professional, educational, governmental, psychological, sociological and, most importantly, consumer demographics and psychographics to make seemingly instantaneous correlations of what each user-node likes, dislikes, and is most likely to buy. From an economic standpoint, it really does not matter why the person is buying a product or service; that would be "causation" or, in simpler terms, the reason for the sale. No. All that matters is the sale.

"How is it possible that we live on a world in which so much is free, where so many unprecedented technological advances are available to us without cost?" asks technology blogger Liam McCarty in *Data and Power*. "It is not possible, and those advances are not free: the true cost is data, and the long-term cost could be complete erosion of privacy."[5] McCarty's motive is similar to that of this book. He argues that recognizing the influence of big data in daily lives is the first step in controlling our individual futures rather than yielding that future, for better or worse, to machines. Otherwise, he argues, "those who control the top technology and digital media corporations are disproportionate benefactors of economic inequality."[6]

Economic inequality is only one outcome of a big-data saturated society. Consumer technology, with its social risks and economic rewards, owes its existence to corporate surveillance and government application of that surveillance. In other words, Google uses cookies to track people's consumer behavior, which informs the company what advertisements to put in front of those viewers. The logic here is that such tracking is a win-win situation for viewer and advertiser alike because it literally links buyer and seller. However, the National Security Agency taps into those cookies to potentially spy on anyone using Google's search engine and products. And that's only Google. Smartphone applications utilizing Apple and Google operating systems allow the government to track the location of each device without any warning to owners of Androids and iPhones.[7] Business and government share a commonality when it comes to people in that both do not identify them as such. Each entity is virtually only a node. That viewpoint contributes to economic inequality in big-data policies and practices that result in "little people," or nodes. There are other dangers and risks. In addition to knowing all about each individual from our most popular devices such as iPhones and applications such as Facebook, which surveil and sell simultaneously, the government can compile specific dossiers about our electronic identities which may or may not represent who we truly are. A digital fingerprint differs from a real one. As this book documents, we are more than our cookies say we are. But machines couldn't care less.

This is the reality eroding interpersonal relationships. Consider the ramifications. Security expert Bruce Schneier asks us to imagine the federal government requiring every citizen to carry tracking devices so that the authorities know what we are doing and where we are doing it each second of every day. Moreover, Schneier inquires, what would our reaction be if we had to report to the state police every time we befriended someone? We would rebel if repressive laws were imposed on ourselves, workplaces, families and schools. Those laws would be found unconstitutional. Nonetheless, as Schneier writes, we carry our smartphones everywhere, providing copies of all our digital transactions to email service providers, phone companies, social networking platforms and Internet service providers.[8]

As former government contractor Edward Snowden proved in 2013, the impact of surveillance is more than economic. Snowden copied and distributed classified information compiled by the National Security Agency concerning details of global surveillance. The NSA had assembled data on each person's communication and other electronic transactions, which resulted not only in exposing U.S. top secrets but also our own very human secrets. As CNN reported, certain NSA employees had used the agency's surveillance to spy on their love interests. In one case an employee used the covert system to eavesdrop on a foreign phone number because she suspected her husband was having an affair.[9] In the end, it seemed, nodes (even sleuthing ones) are human beings after all. As the NSA case illustrates, a chief concern is how big data has altered how we live, study, love, work, play and interact with each other interpersonally, collectively and digitally. Computer scientist and author Jaron Lanier believes the Snowden affair revealed the true nature of the Internet myth that users can acquire access to online websites, social media and apps without cost. In sum, Lanier writes in *Who Owns the Future?*, the NSA felt empowered by big data to eavesdrop on everyone. The government simply undermined encryption and privacy software and transformed "free" Internet services into "an Orwellian monster."[10]

Journalist and technology commentator Esther Dyson believes we have come to the end of the Computer Age and are entering another—"perhaps we'll call it the Informatics Age"—in which "humans no longer will be the center of the data solar system, with all of the billions of devices orbiting around us, but will rather become just another player, another node, in an increasingly autonomous data universe."[11] How did this become possible? Dyson identifies three factors that drove us out of the Computer Age and converted people into nodes:

- Nearly universal access to the Internet and World Wide Web.
- Transition from devices like desktops and cell phones, which used to be controlled by people, to intelligent machines controlled by companies and governments.
- Advances in technology regarding tiny, inexpensive sensors embedded in the natural world and working in tandem with processors empowered by Moore's Law, or the doubling of computing capabilities every two years.[12]

As such, the substance of the conversation in the current age has changed from what humans can comprehend to "a ubiquitous decentralized communication, as all these devices begin to talk to one another without our intercession."[13] This is where the really "Big" comes from when we refer to big data, Dyson states.

This is how people in the Computer Age became little in the consumer economy.

From Knowledge to Consumer Economy

The irksome outcome of the big-data revolution, unlike that of the Computer Age, is how it happened without much discussion, debate, input or demurs from people and news organizations. Admittedly, outlets such as the *New York Times, Washington Post* and *Wall Street Journal* have reported on big-data risks to privacy. Many regional papers also have done the same. The problem is declining readerships, down 25 percent between 2012 and 2015, with a mere 16 minutes dedicated to newspapers out of the average 500 minutes Americans spend each day consuming media.[14] At least in the Computer Age, which ended in 2012 with the emergence of big data,[15] there were tangible benefits because of discussion about the "knowledge" economy, a term that came into being in the late 1960s when society increasing began yielding information to machines and later was embraced at the start of the twenty-first century.[16] The knowledge economy would rely on machines that would dispense with national borders as productivity went global, promising upward mobility through formal technical education. There was almost universal acceptance of these promises promoted by news organizations, television networks, educators and legislators. In the decade that followed, only a few social critics recognized the dangers of allowing machines to control social interactions. They included the author of the first edition of *Interpersonal Divide* (2004) along with similar works by Sherry Turkle, such as *Life on the Screen: Identity in the Age of Internet* (1997) and by Jaron Lanier, *You Are Not a Gadget* (2011). Turkle, a clinical psychologist, documented consequences of people interacting more with machines and less with people. Lanier, a computer scientist and philosopher, argued against trust in machines that may cost people their humanity.

Benefits and risks were discussed routinely between 1997 and 2011. For instance, a 2000 report published in *The Future of Children*, a collaboration of the Woodrow Wilson School of Public and International Affairs at Princeton University and the Brookings Institution, discussed many of the potential dangers of increased computer use by children, from obesity to gaming risks, but also foresaw the potential benefits of "computer fluency," or "the ability to use computers to express oneself creatively, to reformulate knowledge, to synthesize information, and to adapt to continuous change."[17] That was supposed to come true in the ensuing years as educational institutions invested heavily in computing equipment to achieve learning goals. After all, the Computer Age promised glowing educational outcomes resulting in widespread investment across school districts to counter any digital divides keeping underrepresented groups from the knowledge economy.

Despite the billions invested in state-of-the-art consumer technology, average educational trends in U.S. fifteen-year-olds from 2000 to

2012 as measured in mathematics, science and reading have neither gained nor lost significantly.[18] Impact of technology was statistically negligible. A more revealing fact about America's so-called technological advantage in relation to digital divides is assessment of global scores against a socioeconomic backdrop. In other words, how effective are school systems in relatively poorer countries like Vietnam, Thailand, Turkey and Indonesia? When viewed in this manner, those entities outshine the hi-tech countries of the United States, Norway and Sweden, which rank near the bottom third of such assessments.[19]

Something else might have been happening in affluent societies whose school children became less fluent in reading, mathematics and science and more fluent in digital distractions. From desktops and laptops to tablets and smartphones, the same technologies meant to inform in school systems were being used to browse, shop, game, chat/Snapchat, eBay, text/sext, Facebook, Instagram, YouTube, tweet and selfie-take. At the college level, students waste about one-fifth of class time using laptops, smartphones and tablets, according to a 2016 study by Bernard R. McCoy, associate professor of journalism at the University of Nebraska-Lincoln. This is more evidence that students place trust in machines providing technological distractions for "free" while compiling data that drives users insistently toward those same aforementioned leisure and social activities. Worse, students are not only using their devices to network socially but they also routinely rely on smartphones to make purchases with credit cards, something even *U.S. News and World Report* cautions against in a 2015 piece titled "Should You Trust Apps That Access Your Credit Card Information?"[20] The answer is no but the practice is yes.

A knowledge economy is based on people and education. A consumer economy is based on nodes and profit. "Nodes in networks represent real-life objects, such as customers, patients, Internet routers, companies, and so forth,"[21] writes management informatics expert and author Bart Baesens in *Analytics in a Big Data World*. Like people, Baesens states, nodes have different relationships—some strong, some weak. Examples: The author of this book might have a stronger relationship with a Facebook friend who collaborated on a paper than with a former neighbor in another city keeping tabs on family affairs. The fact of collaboration alone reveals much about both nodes (authors). If both like to travel, ostensibly to academic conferences, that further affirms and adds another "link." Each link has weight, and the more links between these two authors—from use of a certain software and smart-phone to fondness for Chinese cuisine and Saint Laurent fashion—the firmer the relationship. Big data correlates these links to make predictions on likelihood of future consumer behavior.

Moreover, the terms that big-data analysts use to discuss nodes and relationships speak volumes about what algorithms are measuring and how they are measuring it. Baesens uses the term "ego-nets," representing the "billions of nodes and millions of links" in a network "neighborhood," yet another indication of how objectified "little people" have become in a digital world that focuses on correlation and consumerism. The target, or center of the egonet, is surrounded by like-minded nodes, or "alters" as in "alter-ego," literally a "second self" (or *e-self*) in consumer-psycho-babble. Moreover, the utility of the ego-net is based on the concept of "homophily," which means "love of the same," or the tendency of individuals to associate with others who have like tastes or desires. According to Baesens, "If all of John's friends have a flamboyant personality, what does this say about John? The same reasoning holds in fraud networks: If all of Mary's friends are fraudsters, what kind of behavior do you expect from Mary?"[22] In other words, we don't need to know why John is prone to make ostentatious displays in public or why Mary was driven to break the law; we just need to know that they are, not why they are behaving in such ways. There is no profit in asking why. Consumer economies seek profit, not knowledge.

Technology-based corporations controlling machines reap incredible profits. There was even an app for that (now defunct) on the site of WorldPay Zinc, a PayPal alternative. (Go to https://www.worldpayzinc.com/blog/small-business/19/03/2014/how-much-does-your-business-earn-each-minute.) The app, based on 2013 financial disclosures, is probably conservative in its estimates of revenue and profit of the largest tech companies *by the second*. In one minute on December 18, 2015, when the app still worked and this chapter was being researched, here were profit accumulations: Apple, $70,936; Samsung, $54,731; Microsoft, $41,874; and Google, $23,393. In one minute on that day, Apple's profit was tantamount to or slightly below the average annual salary of typical nuclear power reactor operators, radiation therapists, environmental engineers and administrative law judges.[23] Meanwhile these high-tech businesses along with domestic and global governments were assembling petabytes (one quadrillion bytes) of information on consumers and users that, sadly, are hacked regularly by criminals and

U.S. enemies. Nevertheless, consumers as well as government entities continue to trust digital devices and the machinery that controls them, accepting risks. We do this primarily because we have to rely on "automated, algorithmic systems to accomplish tasks that we cannot or would rather avoid," all being done "without the fluency of computing but out of the recklessness of convenience."[24]

We rely on machines, using them out of convenience, but mostly are oblivious that machines are using us. Trust in algorithmic systems is not based on benefits but on lack of understanding. As previously discussed, the devices we rely on all day every day generate massive amounts of data unrelated to anything in particular until exposed to mathematical formulas culling information through high-speed computer programs. That defines an algorithmic system. All systems in science, industry and society function now through these systems, which assess the level of complexity in a database, create a mathematical structure to consolidate that complexity, and then design software to exploit the information according to a business or government objective. These systems changed the promise of the knowledge economy into the profits of the consumer one.

Consumer economies need to know "where." Location is key in an asynchronous world in which people are tracked 24/7 by mechanized towers communicating with smartphones as we communicate socially through those mobile devices. To be sure, GPS tracking has helped law enforcement solve crimes and pursue criminals. But location is an essential component in something more basic in the big-data world. "Assuming a product is consumed in conjunction with a mobile device, the location of the consumer becomes an important piece of information that may be available to the supplier,"[25] writes Arvind Sathi in *Big Data Analytics*. Machines listen when we engage each other socially. Sathi provides examples such as "I'm at Starbucks in Times Square" or "Looks like we'll be moving to New Orleans sooner than I thought."[26] As we text, Facebook, tweet and crowdsource, data are being compiled as machines measure us according to core consumer statistics. Sathi describes those characteristics in terms of evolutionary stages of consumerism. When a machine detects a person, he or she may begin anonymously and then metamorphose to a named customer based on a device with IP address and social media identity and other factors.[27] With the right interactions, suggested by surveilling machines, the named customer might respond to an advertisement (engagement) and agree to receive information on a product (opted-in). A purchase elevates a person, or identified node, to "buyer," and if a product or service appeals and a review or "like" is gained, the buyer might ascend to "advocate."

It comes down to this: When you turn on your smartphone, you are agreeing to contracts with machines, allowing them to track your whereabouts in exchange for using the carrier's service. Chances are you failed to read the terms of service written in the arcane legal language of the early twentieth century. (That fine print hasn't changed.) That's just the phone. Add to that all the texts, tweets, Snapchats, WhatsApps, Instagrams, photographs, audios, videos, and documents stored in the phone (and later, in the cloud)—all accessible to other machines—and a digital narrative is being written about you, your lifestyle, your state of mind, your health, your wealth, your sex life, your fetishes and more. The bargain is specified in the contract that typical users overlook and also is inherent in how the service functions,[28] writes security specialist Bruce Schneier in *Data and Goliath*. In addition to knowing everything about you—to the point of predicting where you're most likely to be at any given hour in the day—the gossipy device in your pocket also knows whom you interact with and thus has privilege to peep into *their* phones, computers, gaming consoles, Google Glass and other gadgets. There is little you can do to stop the data hemorrhage. Even security savants like Schneier who won't use that snoop of snoops (aka Facebook) cannot dodge data compilation about him because friends, associates and colleagues have sites with "like" buttons on them. Facebook tracks non-users, surveilling Schneier through data linked to those with whom he interacts.[29] "This is a very intimate form of surveillance,"[30] he states.

Indeed. "With every favorite link we bookmark on our browser or search item we enter into the search engine box, we say something about our preferences, values and interests,"[31] writes Elias Aboujaoude, psychiatrist at Stanford University School of Medicine. In this manner, a multitude of machines communicating with each other gradually develop a consumer profile of each user. Aboujaoude adds that our devices, which transmit our location to those machines, offer "unparalleled opportunity to markets and make search engines and sites we subscribe to willing to fight to hold on to every last byte of our private data for as long as possible." Subsequently, argues Aboujaoude, we forfeit an increasingly rare commodity that we coveted a decade ago before the onslaught of machine intelligence began to track our lives: our privacy. People, before they became nodes, used to own personal information about sensitive topics such as health, wealth and sexual preference. Now machines own that data. (Consumers can even purchase select data sets about their life activities, subscribing to services that inform users of their "quantified selves," which involve wearing self-tracking devices that send more intimate information to the ever-inflating cloud.) According to Aboujaoude, owning rather than distributing personal information used to be a source of power. The loss of privacy results in the loss of power when mega-organizations, including government, claim ownership of those data. That fact alone can negate the benefits that omnipresent access affords people in their daily lives.[32] Seldom do we connote the loss of privacy with the loss of power. Gadgets we use each hour of the day have power to change lives, an immense, imperceptible power that we fail to appreciate because we trust our digital distractions. A knowledge economy was supposed to empower people. A consumer economy automates them. Nodes do not require health care. People do.

Computer scientist Jaron Lanier observes that "up until the turn of this century people didn't need to worry about technological advancement devaluing people, because new technologies always created new kinds of jobs even as old ones were destroyed."[33] But the key principle of the big-data economy, which exploits the idea of the "digital commons" of the Computer Age—or sharing knowledge for public good—is to rely on people to create content for free, be it on news sites or entertainment blogs or via social media such as Facebook or Twitter. The irony here is mind-boggling. Users believe that they are accessing digital services for free, when they are not, because the consumer data they provide has value; moreover, users are providing free content, so the corporation doesn't have to. As Harvard Law School professor and author Yochai Benkler argues in *The Wealth of Networks,* the new information systems are not making previous functions and services more efficient or effective; they are fundamentally changing how value is created.[34] Revenue, the sole goal, is multifold. Little people generate big profit as well as data. The more data, the more automated the systems become because people cannot process zettabytes (one sextillion bytes) of information. Only machines can do that. As Lanier observes, this type of economy is survivable as long as limited numbers of people are disenfranchised; he reluctantly cites as dispensable musicians, journalists and photographers. He foresees more than self-driven cars, the robotic assembly lines, the computer-counseled students, and the self-tracked hospital patients. He prophesies the end of working classes.

"What is not survivable is the additional destruction of the middle classes in transportation, manufacturing, energy, office work, education, and health care," which will come if we fail to address the consumer economy.[35]

To do so, we need to know *why* this is vital.

The World Without Why

One of the benefits of big data is the ability to analyze certain situations and make predictions in machine-time, or almost instantaneously, as opposed to days, weeks and months in human-time. And the outcome of those algorithms can benefit humankind. For example, each year the Centers for Disease Control and Prevention are concerned about the rapid spread of influenza. In 2009, Google analyzed American users' 50 million most common search terms and compared that list with CDC data on flu between 2003 and 2008. The experiment was described in *Scientific American*, "Google Flu Trends Found to Be Nearly on Par with CDC Surveillance Data."[36] The idea was to compare what users were searching against a map of locales where the flu virus spread. Machines can do that type of comparison, utilizing 450 million methodologies to identify forty-five search terms that point to where the flu was and when it occurred, doing all this in machine-time rather than in human-time, which would have taken weeks.[37]

Then again, some users do not trust government to compile those epic narratives about their lives for fear about how that information will be used. Keep in mind that machines excel at identifying and compiling data about "who," "what," "where," "when" and "how" but lack human intelligence and so cannot discern "why." Human motivation and decision-making, even in negotiating who drives first at a four-way stop (something self-driving cars cannot achieve), are too complex, random and illogical. However, our criminal justice system is based on the notion that defendants are innocent until proven guilty, requiring juries to discern motives, or *why* a crime may have been committed. "Ubiquitous surveillance means that anyone could be convicted of law-breaking once the police set their minds to it," Bruce Schneier observes, noting the dangers of law enforcement's license to comb through large data sets to undercover nodes of wrongdoing.[38]

The propensity for bias exists as well. If you believe that institutional racism exists, that systems and organizations over time believe falsehoods about under-represented groups, then imagine the long-term consequences if such bias is coded in and programmed into machines. For instance, if machines compile data suggesting that a certain race, gender and age of people living in a given location may have a higher inclination for wrongdoing, and a person with those characteristics happens to wander into a wealthier section of the neighborhood, merchants equipped with apps might be prone to mistake innocent shoppers for potential shoplifters, depriving them of service or worse, accusing them of crimes. "Want to spy on black shoppers and reflexively accuse them of shoplifting? There's an app for that,"[39] writes Jarvis DeBerry, referring to an application called "GroupMe," which links merchants, employees, community leaders and police officers of suspicious-looking people in their midst.[40] There are other apps such as the insensitively named "Ghetto Tracker" designed to warn users when they are wandering into unsafe areas of a city.[41] And if people are unlucky enough to be profiled, targeted and arrested in the "app-net" (a pun on "dragnet"), they will confront penal boards in half of the United States that use data analytics to determine whether to release or keep incarcerated prisoners up for parole.[42]

When it comes to criminal and social justice, people need to know *why*. Knowing why a person has been arrested or crime committed is associated with motive. Knowing why also pertains to laws and policies when certain ethnic, lifestyle and/or social classes are under-represented or disenfranchised. Of the five "W"s and "H" of reputable journalism and educational standards—who, what, where, when, why and how—the "why" is associated with critical thinking so that issues can be addressed publicly in courts and courts of opinion. People, rather than nodes, want to know why, beginning with *"Why are we born?"* and ending with *"Why will we die?"* The best evidence of that comes from Austrian neurologist, psychiatrist and Holocaust survivor Viktor Frankl, who chronicles his survival at the death camp Auschwitz in his masterpiece, *Man's Search for Meaning*, in which he states: "Those who have a 'why' to live, can bear with almost any 'how.'"[43] Perhaps the writer Annie Dillard best captured the importance of why in her 1982 essay, "Total Eclipse": "The mind wants to live forever, or to learn a very good reason why not. The mind wants the world to return its love, or its awareness; the mind wants to know all the world, and all eternity, and God. The mind's sidekick [the body], however, will settle for two eggs over easy."[44] That famous quote might be altered in the big-data age to something along the lines of "The mind wants to live forever, or to learn a very good reason why not. . . . The mind's sidekick, the machine, will settle for two gigabytes over Instagram."

As Mayer-Schönberger and Cukier write in *Big Data: A Revolution that Will Transform How We Live, Work, and Think,* machines now can derive new insights and create new forms of value that will change people's relationships with just about everything and everyone. "Most strikingly, society will need to shed some of its obsession for causality in exchange for simple correlations; not knowing *why* but only *what,*" overturning "centuries of established practices" to challenge "our most basic understanding of how to make decisions and comprehend reality."[45]

When you eliminate the "why" from daily life at home, school and work, you gain immense power over people because you can deal with them as numbers. You are able to compile who did what and how they did it at which location and when. Those facts rarely change and so can be counted. For example, authorities can assemble data on a burglary suspect in possession of a victim's cell phone used in Des Moines, Iowa, to post a selfie to Facebook at 2:03 p.m. on January 2, 2017. We have the "who" (suspect), "what" (cell phone), "how" (posting), "where" (Des Moines), and "when" (2:03 p.m. Jan. 2, 2017). But we don't know "why" he broke into the victim's house to steal the phone (perhaps he bought or borrowed it from the real thief). In a society without "why," the circumstantial evidence alone may be sufficient to charge and convict. Because such data can be assembled in machine-time, authorities can be dispatched to a GPS-identified location to confront the cell-phone-toting suspect who, if he flees for any number of why-based reasons, may be tasered or even shot. Beyond law enforcement, there are other, strange consumer truths that do not require "why" as long as online purchases are made. As Jaron Lanier writes, machines with copious amounts of data may be able to discern odd commercial truths: People with bushy eyebrows who like purple toadstools in spring might hanker for hot sauce on mashed potatoes in autumn. That would enable a hot sauce vendor to place a link in front of bushy-eyebrowed Facebookers posting toadstool photos, increasing the chance of a sale, "and no one need ever know why."[46]

If the Internet of the late twentieth century altered the way we communicate interpersonally, creating a divide as documented in the first edition of this book, then big data will exacerbate that and do one more life- and lifestyle-altering thing: *It will change the way we think.* Big data experts promoting data analytics acknowledge this. The preface of Bill Schmarzo's book, *Big Data: Understanding How Data Powers Big Business*, is dedicated to the theme "think differently." Big data, he writes, forces upon savvy users the empowering new realization of data abundance. Moreover, he observes, the old Internet business models that worked with gigabytes of data are as outdated as the "whip and buggy" in an age of where billions of nodes are processed, requiring business to think like machines so as to embrace the complex logic upon which analytics is based.[47] The complexity is not in the analytics or the correlations they provide that lead to sales. It is in the removal of "why" from our daily discourse. Without the why as an integral component of conversation and analysis, an increasing number of journalists and politicians inevitably will fail to adequately inform citizens. If those citizens get news from social media, they will be prone to believe what is posted there, including fake news and alternative facts that align with their lifestyle choices and political convictions. Teachers will emphasize critical thinking less, and families and employers will cope with decisions without comprehending why those decisions were made. As this book documents here and elsewhere, we will know what and how something occurred as well as where and whom it affects and when. But we will not know why the things that we build and the events that we witness are affecting us because digital distractions are reducing opportunities to ask the "why" questions. Moreover, the cultural transformation has happened gradually so as to be imperceptible to many people. We have lived through gradual transformations before. After all, this is what happened in rural America where only a few decades ago people waved to each other in cars passing in opposite directions. (Now they drive while using cell phones, oblivious to everyone and everything, including on occasion the slow-moving tractors into which they crash.) This is what happened in suburban America when neighbors used to converse with each other on stoops or in urban America when strangers used to interact with each other on the street. One by one, as the first edition of this book prophesied, each aspect of our interpersonal communication and interactions evaporated into the cloud that holds our attention during every waking hour of the day at home, school and work. Even pro big-data enthusiasts like Schmarzo know the new analytic environment will result in organizational change so that business can exploit the nodes at its fingertips. "Old roles will need to be redefined and new roles introduced, creating both opportunities and anxiety for individuals and organizations alike,"[48] he states. "Big data coupled with advanced analytics enables organizations to identify significant material, and actionable insights buried in the data, without having to understand why these insights occur."[49]

The End of Theory

Life without "why" owes its history, in part, to a 2008 commentary— "The End of Theory: The Data Deluge Makes the Scientific Method Obsolete"—by Chris Anderson, then editor for *WIRED* magazine. Anderson knows scientific method as he also was editor for *Nature* and *Science* before editing *WIRED* and later becoming CEO of 3-D Robotics, a consumer and commercial manufacturer of drones. Thus, his insights cannot be easily dismissed. In his commentary, he states that we are living in a world of massive amounts of data which, when coupled with applied mathematics, removes the need for theory. "Out with every theory of human behavior, from linguistics to sociology. Forget taxonomy, ontology, and psychology. Who knows why people do what they do? The point is they do it, and we can track and measure it with unprecedented fidelity. With enough data, the numbers speak for themselves."[50]

The problem with the piece is its genre: *commentary*. In other words, Anderson was sharing an opinion inspired by Peter Norvig, Google's research director, at an O'Reilly Emerging Technology conference in March 2008. Anderson recites what Norvig shared: "All models are wrong, and increasingly you can succeed without them."[51] His influential piece in *WIRED* is not science journalism of the sort one finds in *Nature* or *Science* magazines. It is overenthusiastic hype from Anderson the entrepreneur, not the scientist. Authors Mayer-Schönberger and Cukier address Anderson's overstatement, which suggests big-data analysis has no need for conceptual models in the way that physics or chemistry does. "That is preposterous," they write. "Big data itself is founded on theory. For instance, it employs statistical theories and mathematical ones, and at times uses computer science theory, too."[52]

The absence of critical thinking in the age of big-data consumerism coincides with the media age of opinion. That became the dominant form of content at the turn of the twenty-first century when the Internet eroded the advertising base of news conglomerates that downsized to stay in business. Objective journalism, especially investigative journalism, costs money because it assembles facts that explain the whys of the world. Opinion journalism devoid of fact can be created in pajamas from any location in the world to promote any motive, including the undermining of elections, as we witnessed in the 2016 U.S. presidential campaign. Moreover, Internet news junkies get to comment on the selective and "alternative" facts of commentary, expressing their own opinions often in uncivil ways. Social media segments users via big-data analytics, knowing people with similar lifestyle statistics tend to purchase the same products and services and then write reviews about them, continuing the marketing cycle. The rise of opinion journalism coincides with the demise of objective news reporting," writes Patrick Maines, president of the Media Institute. "Makes one wonder where to turn (outside, perhaps, of the business and financial journals) for investigative and feature news that is not in service to some political party, ideology, or special interest."[53] The Center for Journalism Ethics at the University of Wisconsin notes that the journalism of opinion allows writers and audiences alike to spread the truth as they see or desire it, regardless of the facts upon which objective journalism used to be based.[54]

Algorithms foster such an environment. In *Secrets of the Big Data Revolution*, Jason and Jeremy Kolb note that algorithms do not know what it feels like to read a good book or why some people may prefer one topic over another. "All they know is that people who bought Book A also bought Book B, and people who rated Book B highly also rate Book C highly." A sale is a sale is a sale. Such a mindset brings society closer to a digital version of dystopia according to Simon Head in his aptly titled book, *Mindless: Why Smarter Machines Are Making Dumber Humans*. People become "disembodied objects of speed and efficiency joined to these electronic symbols on the screen—symbols that the 'process assemblers' then move around as they see fit and with the real, corporeal us having to follow orders like members of a digital chain gang, pushed first one way and then another by our virtual overseers."[55]

As a result, communications theory must come into play, addressing a big-data world that believes theory is dead. Before such a world took hold, Wiebe E. Bijker wrote a 1997 book based on past theories of sociotechnical change. His approach is based on the idea, popular in the 1990s, that technology would give humanity more choices because it had previously during such inventions as bicycles, Bakelites and light bulbs. He and others writing in the heyday of Internet diffusion would be wary of books like the one you are reading because it smacks of "determinism," the idea that machines control humans rather than give humans more choices and a greater voice about the direction of their cultures and societies. Determinism is perceived as a pessimistic view of technology because it suggests no intervention can correct problems caused by machines once a machine assumes more power over people than people have over it. However, even theorists like Bijker acknowledge that a machine environment may erode "participatory decision-making" with "the result that technology will really slip out of control."[56]

New York Times journalist John Markoff writes in *Machines of Loving Grace* that optimistic technologists in Silicon Valley believe that innovation and Moore's law— doubling of computing power every two years—are enough to aright problems so that technical progress continues. "Little thought is given as to why one technology wins over others, or why a particular technology arises when it does," he observes. "This view is anathema to what social scientists call the 'social construction of technology'—the understanding that we shape our tools rather than being shaped by them."[57]

That theory happens to be one of the arguments of this book whose goal is to bring the underworld of big data to the attention of those who will be affected the longest by its algorithms. A compilation of views about the benefits and challenges of the current and coming age of analytics can be found in *The Human Face of Big Data*. In one of the sections, "An Ocean of Data," a 1921 dystopian novel titled *We* by Yevgeny Zamyatin is mentioned because it prophesies a future in which every building is made of glass so authorities can spy on citizens around the clock. "Is that the world Big Data will construct?" asks journalist Dan Gardner. "Some pessimists worry that it could. I worry that the pessimists are too optimistic."[58] Gardner mentions Google's interactive Glass as a preview of what is here already or coming soon, with refrigerators that restock themselves and clothing with sensors and Internet connectivity, all compiling data on people. Machines may not know why we do, live and think the way we do; however, they will discern the patterns that drive the behavior until they know us better than we know ourselves. "In that world, not only the buildings would be made of glass; so would our skulls."[59]

The twentieth century technological theorist Jacques Ellul noted that people who rely on technology typically refuse to become aware of the reality they have invited into their lives.[60] In such an environment, people become mere parts of the machine, or nodes, in the case of big data, which Ellul foresaw because of his prescient view of where technology would lead society and why it would disempower people. He foresaw how technology creates problems that require more technology to solve which, in turn, require other technologies to operate until a vast array of machines is assembled that gain power and eventual dominance over human beings.[61] As philosopher and theorist Clifford Christians reminds us, Ellul is often dismissed because critics believe he offers no solutions. Christians asks us to decry such superficiality to see what Ellul offers society—a brutally candid view of reality. "We must smash our modern idols, expose false claims, demythologize today's illusions, and stand squarely before the bloody face of history. We imbue technology, education, and politics with an aura of holy prestige, and it is this sacral transfiguration which enslaves us."[62]

Christians composed that invocation more than thirty-five years ago. Another prophetic scholar, Langdon Winner, wrote more than thirty years ago in *The Whale and the Reactor: A Search for Limits in an Age of High Technology*, that whenever technologists call changes "revolutionary," as so many big-data enthusiasts do, "we tacitly acknowledge that these are matters that require reflection, possibly even strong public action to ensure that the outcomes are desirable. But the occasions for reflection, debate, and public choice are extremely rare indeed. The important decisions are left in private hands inspired by narrowly focused economic motives. . . . Some observers forecast that the 'computer revolution' will eventually be guided by new wonders in artificial intelligence. Its present course is influenced by something much more familiar: the absent mind."[63] Like Asimov and Arendt, Christians and Winner each foresaw the age of machine and a world that correlates without causation and then neglects to assess social impact.

It is with that theoretical thought in mind that we proceed in upcoming chapters to investigate how machines are affecting us at home, school and work.

Journal Exercise: *"Forty-Eight-Hour Social Media Experiment"*

If you are like most readers, you have a Facebook or Twitter account. You might also use other social media such as Instagram, WhatsApp, Snapchat or a different service. Perhaps you order regularly from Amazon or bid on eBay or other sales or auction portal. You are probably accustomed to advertisements appearing regularly on your smartphone, tablet, laptop and computer offering products and services attuned to your age, sex, income, race, hobbies, activities, sports, religion, political affiliation, location, brand preference, lifestyle or other statistic defining who you are and the merchandise and services you use.

For the next forty-eight hours, continue using your digital devices but cease looking at your preferred websites and sales portals. If you are young, visit geriatric sites. If you are male, visit pregnancy sites for women. If you are female, visit erectile dysfunction sites for men. If you are white, visit African-American sites. Heterosexual? Visit gay, lesbian and transgender sites. You get the idea.

To begin, make a list of your lifestyle statistics as identified above (age, sex, income, race, hobbies, etc.) and then choose dramatically different lifestyle statistics and attributes. For instance, think about a hobby you know little about, such as stamp or coin collecting. If you have never invested in gold or silver, visit a site like Apmex.com, which sells bullion. See how long it takes for bullion products to appear on your screen.

Each time a new advertisement appears that bears little resemblance to who you actually are, take note of it in a document.

When your forty-eight-hour experiment concludes, revert to your regular online viewing habits. See how long it takes before those radically different products and services disappear.

Write about the experience in your journal or online blog.

CHAPTER FOUR

Interpersonal Divide at Home

*My kids accuse me and my wife of being fascists and overly con-
cerned about tech, and they say that none of their friends have
the same rules. That's because we have seen the dangers of technology firsthand. I've seen it in myself, I don't want to see that
happen to my kids.*

—CHRIS ANDERSON,
the former editor of *WIRED*, chief executive of 3D Robotics

*First we thought the PC was a calculator. Then we found out
how to turn numbers into letters with ASCII—and we thought
it was a typewriter. Then we discovered graphics, and we
thought it was a television. With the World Wide Web, we've
realized it's a brochure.*

—DOUGLAS ADAMS,
author of *Hitchhiker's Guide to the Galaxy*

··········

Changing Family

The first edition of *Interpersonal Divide* warned that consumer technology was likely to undermine the modern family unless we understood
its nature, which changes everything it touches without it changing
much at all. That effect should be increasingly apparent the more we
understand technology's nature from a programming rather than consumer perspective. Technology changes rapidly. Hardware and applications, especially, rise and fall as fads and trends. But technology's nature
is constant. It is neither moral nor immoral but amoral and pervasive
in its autonomy and anonymity. As early as 2010, technology author
Sherry Turkle noticed a subtle shift in computer use that played a key
role in the changing nature of family and familial relations. Now that
family members were tethered to networks, she wrote, "we really didn't

need to keep computers busy. They keep us busy. It is as though we have become their killer app."[1] Turkle noted that the bonds that bind family now are digital rather than ethical. She called them "the ties that preoccupy. We text each other at family dinners, while we jog, while we drive, as we push our children on swings in the park. . . . When we misplace our mobile devices, we become anxious—impossible really. We have heard teenagers insist that even when their cell phones are not on their person, they can feel them vibrate."[2]

Technology has become a digital appendage. It goes where we do, and we attend to its needs continuously, checking for updates and messages and feeding it text, images, video and emoji. In *The Big Switch: Rewiring the World, from Edison to Google*, Nicholas Carr identifies when and how technology's nature morphed. Seemingly overnight it evolved from stand-alone work stations in the home to necessary utility, affecting families in ways that hitherto were not anticipated. Carr cites a memo dated October 30, 2005, from Microsoft's Bill Gates, warning his company that the family desktop computer was doomed and with it, the selling of software, as vendors increasingly would provide applications like Facebook, transforming Internet into a home utility, such as electricity, heat and water.[3] Moreover, as Gates's prediction became reality, users would create content for such sites because they found the "free" applications enjoyable. This observation was prescient. However, what changed over time, according to Carr, was "the scope, scale, and sophistication of the contributions—and, equally important, the ability of companies to harness the free labor and turn it into valuable products and services."[4]

Creating, consuming and responding to user-generated content came with a price tag, still being levied today: *time*. Family consultants Richard and Linda Eyre note that digital and traditional media are so pervasive and addictive that interpersonal time formerly spent within the home is being stolen. "We are raising a whole generation of kids who communicate better with their thumbs than with their voices."[5] To be sure, teen texting has soared in the past decade with some 88 percent sending messages to friends at least occasionally and 55 percent daily, according to the Pew Research Center.[6] According to a study by Common Sense, American teenagers ages 13 to 18 average about nine hours consuming Internet and media while tweens (ages 8–12) average six hours, excluding time spent at school where more Internet and media typically are used in lesson plans.[7] However, time spent using Internet and media was not confined to tweens and teens. Some 65 percent of adults were using social media regularly in 2015, up from 5 percent a decade earlier.[8] In the past, communication companies produced content that defined family time as "quality time." In essence, those companies divined a concept that allowed excessive web and television use without seeming to violate the conscience, because what time remained for spouses and children would be used wisely in pre-planned activities. Because technological time is asynchronous, or subject to digital signals sent, received, responded to, and so on, family members naturally lose track of linear time (as measured by clock). Also, because content evolved from static websites and downloaded broadcasts to user-generated social media and incessant, insistent application reminders—replete with ringtones—on smartphones, tablets and computers, time and attention were diverted from the family to the devices that went wherever children did. A few scant years ago parents who used cell phones while at Little League games, public parks, Sunday school or dance recitals were chastised; now, they are accepted as digital fixtures. When everyone engages in the same digital behavior, new social norms arise.

In his exegesis of the social media industry, media scholar Alan B. Albarran notes that modern families spend less time watching or listening to content and talking about it as a shared experience and more time creating that content or responding to it with others outside of the family unit. He writes: "In the current media climate of digital content distributed online and viewed at all hours of the day on various media players and devices, the traditional linear communication model has given way to an interactive 'prosumer' process in which consumers of content also act as producers of content in an ongoing feedback loop."[9] That loop cannibalizes time, affecting familial relationships in myriad interpersonal ways. It warps and accelerates time because there are real-life responsibilities that must be executed in the home, from chores to upkeep, compounded not only by our personal use of technology but by the blurring of work and home so that intrusions are the norm and chief cause of familial stress as noted earlier in this chapter and throughout the first edition of *Interpersonal Divide*. But that is not the end of it. Health concerns have arisen because of addictive use of technology.

For years now research has documented that many of us use technology more than we sleep; however, artificial light from televisions, mobile phones, and computer screens "affects melatonin production and throws off circadian rhythms, preventing deep, restorative sleep," according to research at the University of Gothenburg, Sweden.[10] The absence of sleep is a chief source of stress in the typical cyber home, which requires ceaseless parental monitoring to ensure the safety of children who text and use social media at all hours of the day and night. The problem here, of course, is that parents also have similar digital habits and so must confront the temptation to allow children and tweens to take devices to bed. The smartphone, gaming console and tablet are today's bedtime stories that provide a false sense of comfort.

Before technology overtook the modern family at the turn of the century, children engaged in more outdoor activities without parental supervision. They did not require mobile phones and other devices necessitating credit card authorization for access and upgrades. Cris Rowan, a pediatric occupational therapist, also notes that time for chores in the typical home used to instill in children a sense of daily expectation that often is eclipsed now by the myriad hours children spend consuming technology.[11] This has fractured core familial values. There is less time for "hugging, playing, rough housing, and conversing with children," she writes; instead, "parents are increasingly resorting to providing their children with more TV, video games, and the latest iPads and cell phone devices, creating a deep and irreversible chasm between parent and child."[12]

As noted elsewhere in this chapter, technology use has changed the family dynamic, but there are other factors to take into account. The *New York Times* reports that families in the twenty-first century are more diverse ethnically, religiously and attitudinally; U.S. couples marry, divorce and remarry at record rates not seen anywhere else in the world; birth rates are falling dramatically with fewer children in the typical home; and women are now often more educated than their male partners—a reversal from the latter twentieth century.[13] Perhaps more impactful from the traditional family of the last century is a new development: Both partners now work rather than one as breadwinner and one as homemaker.[14] The Pew Research Center has been interested in the changing family, noting two-parent households are in decline in the United States; four in ten babies are born to single women or nonmarried partners; and, thus, fewer children live in two-parent families—a model now no longer believed to be conventional.[15] For the most part, traditional and digital media have covered the transformation of the family, including more variety in race, gender, sexuality and types of families—even to the extent of defining "family" as the home where people feel a sense of belonging.[16] That is a useful term because it connotes place with emotion. We will use that concept to define family here and elsewhere in *Interpersonal Divide*.

Technology, including telephones, became important after World War II in maintaining that sense of belonging. In the first half of the twentieth century, families were extended, with married couples tending to remain in hometowns near grandparents. That changed as relatives dispersed across the country, creating what has become known as the nuclear family (father, mother, children) that populated much of America through the second half of the last century. The farther relatives moved from hometowns, siblings and grandparents, the more they needed communication technology to keep in touch. As technology bridged the physical gaps between relatives, more families changed their attitude about the importance of community—that is, neighborhoods and religious and civic involvement—to the importance of the child, a phenomenon that began in the 1960s and continues to this day. The "child-centered family" was not based on the nuclear one, as the new model was defined primarily by children in the home, no matter how we labeled the lifestyles of their parents or caregivers. Media refocused on the transformation, triggered in part by a cultural shift from real to virtual community. Technology expanded from hometown newspapers and radio stations to multiple platforms, including cable and satellite broadcasting, video and gaming consoles, audio and VHS cassettes and CD-ROMs, and eventually Internet and mobile phones. The needs of the child superseded needs of the community, giving rise to a culture of "self-esteem" that often overlooked the development of civic duty.[17]

Admittedly, previous models like the nuclear family disenfranchised those who failed to fit the mold. It was a positive step to create a new mold that diversified the family and emphasized "belonging" rather than gender roles or race that shaped social mores and sparked community discord in the past. While current families may focus more on children than on communities, they still must deal with civic issues from taxation to safety. However, by resorting to media and technology to bridge familial and social voids, families have allowed new dangers to threaten that sense of belonging, including data-mining by corporations and governments and hacking by cybercriminals and sex offenders. As the *New York Times* reported in a feature aptly titled "Quality Time, Redefined," the living room of the typical modern family no longer is a place to connect interpersonally but serves now as "an entangled intersection of data traffic—everyone huddled in a cyber-cocoon."[18] That cocoon also poses unseen or unforeseen threats upon the family even as one member posts about another on social media, violating privacy or social norms. The living room cocoon also is mined by corporations collecting data and governments amassing profiles of each user. As media scholar Charles Ess writes, "Governments may be (somewhat ironically) the worst culprits. On the one hand, the modern liberal state exists to protect basic rights—including rights to privacy; but, to protect our rights—especially so-called positive or entitlement rights, e.g., to education, health care, disability assistance, family benefits such as child support and salary offsets for maternity and paternity leave, etc.— governments clearly require a great deal of personal information about us."[19] The question for the modern family is two-fold: how are unseen entities using personal information and how are they protecting that information from others intent on harming us?

A larger question is how we may be harming ourselves by failing to monitor and temper use of technology. Elias Aboujaoude, psychiatrist at Stanford University School of Medicine and director of the Obsessive Compulsive Disorder Clinic and the Impulse Control Disorders Clinic, has written about the blurring of familial boundaries because of omnipresent digital access—not only the previously discussed blurring between home and work but a more intimate one—the blurring of our "information-age appendage," or our smartphones. "It is all one big digital life, or afterlife; the Internet just happens to have been our instruction, a 'gateway drug,' of sorts, that has opened the door wide to other addictions."[20] As with all addictions, overuse of Internet not only alters the family dynamic, but also as previously discussed, wastes time. Technology consumption also gives users a false sense of existence, or what Aboujaoude calls, "the sense of being outside of normal rules," so that we engage in ill-advised online activities ranging from start-up investments and illicit cybersex to bankrupt gambling and shopping sprees.[21] While indulging ourselves, family members may forget that real pain results from virtual actions, an epiphany we realize only after paying the financial and emotional bills.

Cause and effect do not happen instantaneously, so we continue addictive habits, especially the case for children who may not have the benefit of real-life experience. The blurring of reality and virtual reality perhaps is most pronounced when teens text and drive, Aboujaoude writes, noting those who do are twenty-three times more apt to crash their vehicles. "How can sending one more smiley face before focusing on the road ever hurt anyone?"[22] To view the heart-breaking accounts of digital tragedies on the road, input the phrase "stories about texting and driving" in your favorite search engine and read about life-changing injuries and death. Hundreds out of 650,000 accounts generated by Google using the aforementioned phrase in 2016 in the preparation of this chapter revealed a subcategory: final texts sent by victims before crashing their vehicles.[23]

Teens in particular do not often realize correlations between texting and accidents because they have an intense relationship with social media. Technology scholar Danah Boyd has focused on the complicated relationships that teens have with Internet and smartphones. "Just because teens can and do manipulate social media to attract attention and increase visibility does not mean that they are equally experienced at doing so or that they automatically have the skills to navigate what unfolds," she writes, "It simply means that teens are generally more comfortable with—and tend to be less skeptical of—social media than adults."[24] Over the years Boyd has been an advocate for technology use and would likely argue against many of the cited observations in this chapter, preferring the view that teens engage in so much social media because they want to be part of a wider world. However, she also has acknowledged some of the commonly overlooked effects on teen use of social media in the home, including the specter of gossip, which seemingly takes on a life of its own when "people choose to share or spread content about others. . . . A rumor shared on Facebook has the potential to spread farther and faster and persist longer than any school rumor could have in the past."[25] Boyd also states that teens inadvertently lapse into the risky belief that "privacy is necessary only for those who have something to hide."[26] That feeling increasingly is being shared by all members of the family, not only tweens and teens.

Changing Relationships

Within a few decades, the modern family has experienced a dramatic and dynamic interpersonal and digital cultural shift. The demographics of the family have changed, as cited earlier in this chapter, having little to do with technology. The nuclear family may be a historical fact, with traditional gender and parental roles altered to suit social mores, ethnic migration and economic realities, among other factors. However, the core values of unconditional love, empathy, trust, responsibility, knowledge and security should remain untouched, without regard to gender and lifestyle roles, under the umbrella of "home" and "belonging." Those ethical principles also should transcend any technical innovation, no? And if not, then we have to reassess the power of the machine to transform our time-honored familial beliefs and ethical principles. Is it not true that the digital family willingly or begrudgingly shares relationships now with machines, coping as best it can with loss of time, privacy and interpersonal engagement? Is it not true that potentially addictive, profit-programmed devices adorn our bodies and living spaces now, insisting on continuous use to the point that our virtual relationships often demand more attention than our interpersonal ones? The effects of that on our interactions were initially documented in the first edition of *Interpersonal Divide*. The question now concerns whether we have reached a tipping point in electronic saturation. It is time to assess how our digital interactions are affecting our value systems and whether those systems are accommodating machine needs rather than human ones.

In his book *Humans Are Underrated*, Geoff Colvin, senior editor at *Fortune*, makes a case for high-achieving people knowing more than advanced machines ever will. One of his first observations is how humans express emotion through words, voice tone and body language, but even more so via facial expression. Machines are not mind-readers; but they are very good at decoding our feelings by analyzing those expressions, especially since people display seven basic emotions—"joy, surprise, sadness, fear, disgust, contempt, anger—and two advanced emotions, frustration and confusion (advanced because they're combinations of other emotions)."[27] Because these expressions are simple and universal, purportedly as human core values and principles are universal, machines are better at reading emotions than people are. Colvin then cites research that affirms how people "connect" with each other, without an external power source as machines do, but by facing each other, interpersonally synchronizing their brains, which actually light up. If one person turns her back, the connection is broken in our brains, as if a charger is yanked from a power-deprived smartphone. If those two people standing back to back use smartphones to interact, the machines may have to sync, but the people will be unable to because the human connection has been lost. All the machine can do is provide a facsimile. "We are designed to empathize" as part of the human condition and cannot experience that emotion through computers, Colvin writes, noting that we have the chance to offer empathic emotion in a world that desperately needs it.[28] In terms of ethical values such as truth-telling, integrity and nonviolence, which have advanced society through the ages, machines only replicate, not duplicate. That is a fundamental lesson of this chapter.

According to an English proverb, the eyes are windows to the soul—a truth that scientists in Sweden tested recently. They successfully associated iris patterns, as unique to individuals as fingerprints, with such character traits as warmth and tenderness versus self-indulgence and impulsiveness.[29] Of course, that's only a correlation; we don't know what causes those iris patterns to develop. What we do know from literature, however, is that the proverb about eyes is true, at least as far as the great love poems are concerned. "Drink to me only with thine eyes / and I will pledge with mine," writes the great English poet and playwright Ben Jonson (1572-1637) to his love Celia. The Romantic poet Lord Byron (1788-1824) references the eyes in one of the most endearing love poems of all time, the first stanza of which reads:

She walks in beauty, like the night
Of cloudless climes and starry skies;
And all that's best of dark and bright
Meet in her aspect and her eyes:
Thus mellow'd to that tender light
Which heaven to gaudy day denies.

Poets have written through the ages about the eyes as windows to the soul. Many of us in less technological times met the love of our lives in a chance encounter when eyes of two strangers locked and unlocked a shiver of recognition and emotion. That encounter was captured in another poem, "First Love," by John Clare (1793-1864):

I ne'er was struck before that hour
With love so sudden and so sweet.
Her face it bloomed like a sweet flower
And stole my heart away complete.
My face turned pale, a deadly pale.
My legs refused to walk away,
And when she looked what could I ail
My life and all seemed turned to clay.

And then my blood rushed to my face
And took my eyesight quite away.
The trees and bushes round the place
Seemed midnight at noonday.

I could not see a single thing,
Words from my eyes did start.
They spoke as chords do from the string,
And blood burnt round my heart.

Are flowers the winter's choice
Is love's bed always snow
She seemed to hear my silent voice
Not love appeals to know.

I never saw so sweet a face
As that I stood before.
My heart has left its dwelling place
And can return no more.

Emotions this intense, when physical surroundings dissolve and in doing so, transform eyesight into sound and then music—an "in-sync" emotion known as synesthesia—cannot be replicated by selfie or Instagram. It can only happen face to face.

Throughout history, technology has helped yoke or dissolve relationships. Case in point: "With each new or expanded application of telephone technology, the relationships among people changed," write Bruce Drushel and Kathleen M. German in *Ethics of Emerging Media*. "So-called 'enhancements' such as voicemail, call-waiting, caller ID, and distinctive caller ringtones dramatically altered the etiquette and civility of conversations.... With other changes, such as call forwarding, people could obscure their locations."[30] In an article titled "This is How Technology Is Affecting Your Relationship," the *Huffington Post* cited statistics revealing the average American spends eleven hours per day on digital media, reason alone to miss eye-locking encounters in physical environs; moreover, new applications offer "unprecedented exposure to the innermost thoughts and actions of others, as well as new avenues to spy on our loved ones, cheat, and cover the tracks."[31] This explains why so many people are divorcing—not because they caught their partner in a bedroom—but because they discovered emotional infidelity on social media. In fact, a prestigious British law firm surveyed couples and found one in seven contemplated divorce due to what partners posted on Facebook, Skype, Twitter, Snapchat and WhatsApp. The firm calls social media "the new marriage minefield."[32] The legal and government website HG.org cites a study that found Facebook to be the leading cause of divorce and notes that four out of five lawyers use social media as evidence in divorce cases.[33]

While studies such as these cite risks of social media and marriage, more unions are being arranged online. Online dating statistics continue to increase in frequency and number. In 2016, some 49,250,000 out of 54,250,000 single people in the United States tried online dating, providing $1.7 billion to the dating industry.[34] The Pew Research Center reports that 41 percent of American adults know someone who uses online dating and 29 percent know someone who has married or entered into a long term partnership via online dating.[35] What isn't being said is how couples meet via dating sites that use algorithms much like Netflix and Amazon do. Companies utilize facial recognition technology—*you liked this face, so perhaps you might like this similar one, too*—to match potential partners.[36] Far from the romantic encounters of yore, with eyes as gateways to souls, machines use algorithms as gateways to profits in a process that is sterile, data-driven and commercial.

In *Vanishing Act: The Erosion of Online Footnotes and Implications for Scholarship in the Digital Age*, co-authored by the author of *Interpersonal Divide*, research showed that convenience was the driving force in new technology. Convenience changed values, customs and cultures. *Vanishing Act* was one of the first to document how Internet was undermining the scientific process because online footnotes routinely disappear within a few years as servers are replaced and folders changed. For instance, a study on medical innovation citing online sources could not be replicated easily because footnotes based on links were untrustworthy. Media historians cannot use URLs effectively because those links are mostly dead after a few years so the entire Internet Revolution cannot be footnoted with primary sources as in the era of the book. True, often some links might still work, but the content may have been altered or refer to entirely different content unrelated to the topic at hand. In documenting that phenomenon, the authors of *Vanishing Act* discovered the role of convenience as one of four factors governing technology use, with the other three being durability and portability of content and space for that content.[37] For instance, words or images on stone could last centuries, scoring high in durability but low on convenience, portability and data storage. Content inscribed in caves was, well, highly inconvenient. You had to travel to the place to cipher the content. Clay tablets were less durable than rock and more portable and convenient, stored in an ancient temple. If the temple was endangered by flood or war, the tablets could be moved to a safer place. More content could be inscribed on them, too. Scrolls provided space for even more content and were lighter, more portable, and hence, more convenient. Handwritten books in monasteries increased space for content and could be stored conveniently on shelves. Printed books increased space for content because of type size and leather bindings and also were durable, portable and convenient.

The more convenient the content, the more people were willing to change customs. Throughout history, convenience was largely beneficial, increasing education of the populace because content could be shared on an ever larger scale. This, too, was the hope for Internet, which changed society as much as the printing press. But Internet differed vastly from rock, clay, scroll and book in one of those four essential technological components: *durability*. Content simply vanished because there was no "there" there. Moreover, with rock, clay, scroll and book, people did not need to purchase additional items to be able to cipher content. They simply went to the cave, temple, monastery or library and held and beheld the content. True, one had to have physical access to the material previously restricted by tribe, religion, government and social class. However, the more people had access to content, the more access increased to a mass scale. Access to online material, however, required a different kind of access—consumer electronics and engineering systems that have little to do with literacy and much to do with profit. To this day, the cost of Internet and devices delivering content is prohibitive for the underclass, affecting educational systems and upward mobility. Those devices and systems, however, promise those who can afford them convenience on a micro and macro scale, from Google glasses to data analytics.

The convenience factor plays a role now in communicating with family members in the same dwelling. We text each other in bedrooms to come to dinner assuming dinner is still served in a family setting like a kitchen or dining room. Often, we just order on our smartphones and wait for the doorbell to ring, speaking to someone else on the device and ignoring the delivery person as we pay for the pizza. That soon will be a thing of the past as those deliveries already are being made by "autonomous pizza delivery vehicles," $22,000 self-driven, 12-mph, four-wheeled bots that use GPS and lasers to navigate with an array of IP cameras to deter thieves.[38] The only inconvenience will be walking to the bot at roadside or driveway as we check Facebook on cell phones.

We consume social networks with a seemingly insatiable appetite. Social media may be a convenient way to establish and maintain relationships but the durability of those relationships may have been undermined in the process. According to *Forbes* magazine, 91 percent of people sleep within arm's reach of a mobile device, making it "safe to say that we are both addicted to our mobile device and dependent on it."[39] The term "arm's reach" in bed used to refer to spouses and romantic partners, dating back centuries in literature, as in the anonymous sixteenth-century poem, "The Lover in Winter": "Christ, that my love were in my arms / And I in my bed again." (Perhaps a modern rendition of that couplet would be: "Christ, that my iPhone were within arm's reach / And I on Facebook again.") Increasingly smartphones in bed are undermining relationships as one study titled "Technoference" found, suggesting that married or partnered women suffered lower levels of relationship satisfaction and higher levels of depressive symptoms because of technology.[40]

Addiction has been linked to depression for decades. Mental health experts warn that Internet addiction affects health, job, finances and relationships and may have "the same troubling effects as substance abuse or gambling addiction."[41] In 2015, CNN reported studies that show excessive technology and Internet use "can create dependence and addiction, neurologically and physically," a condition that afflicts children because their brains should develop primarily through face-to-face relationships.[42] As such, technology overuse quickly becomes compulsive as we seek happiness from others, only to feel unsatisfied after hours of seeking happiness online.

Levels of happiness are especially important in our pursuit of enduring relationships. Sadly, Internet overuse can also affect those levels negatively, especially in young girls, ages 8 to 12, as another study has shown. Researchers theorize that even at a primitive level, "girls need to experience the full pantheon of communication that comes from face-to-face contact, such as learning to read body language, and subtle facial and verbal cues."[43] Internet is two-dimensional, lacking those attributes. To be sure, technology and social media when used judiciously can strengthen existing bonds, as the science-based website Happify reports, with the key factor "between stress and bliss is using our devices mindfully."[44] That lesson is at the core of the first and this edition of *Interpersonal Divide*.

When it concerns happiness, technology can help people pursue that emotion in any number of commercially feasible ways, from winning video games and first dates to more likes and friends on social media. But technology can do little to secure happiness in an enduring manner without interpersonal contact, and even that depends on your genetics. As social psychologist Jonathan Haidt notes in *The Happiness Hypothesis*, research has documented "the strong influence of genes upon a person's average level of happiness" and "that most environmental and demographic factors influence happiness very little."[45] In other words, you can be insanely happy about winning the lottery and changing your living environs from poverty to wealth, but sooner rather than later you will return to a happiness norm largely established by your genes. In the long run, it doesn't much matter what happens to you, writes Haidt: "Good fortune or bad, you will always return to your happiness setpoint—your brain's default level of happiness—which was determined largely by your genes."[46] Certainly, wealth plays an important role in health, longevity and desirable locales that may bring about more occasions for temporary happy conditions; conversely, millions of basically happy people also live in less opulent environs around the globe.

Technology exposes users to judgmental and often hostile content and remarks, especially via social media. One study showed that 19 percent of users decreased face-to-face contact because of something said online and fully 78 percent of users reported rising incivility online, with blocking and defriending commonplace because of arguments.[47] The 2016 presidential election featured an onslaught of hostile tweets by candidates and supporters. One study showed that 65 percent of adjectives used by Republican Donald Trump in tweets were negative, with these words appearing frequently: "phony," "fraudulent," "unethical, "worthless" and, of course, "hostile."[48] According to Haidt, being judgmental is part of the human condition but also can lead to anger, torment and conflict, decreasing happiness; while he doesn't specify the role of technology in exposure to judgmentalism, the sheer hours of average tech use combined with online pejorative content continue to affect us in untold interpersonal ways. Haidt reports that one way to reduce exposure to hostility and to maintain one's level of happiness is meditation, a practice that more people should engage in, but sadly, don't, again because of media and technology consumption, averaging about eleven hours per day during the sixteen to eighteen hours we are awake.[49] There is little time for meditation, let alone the daily chores of existence. Time-consuming electronic media is not invested in the well-being of our family relationships, one of the few components that actually can increase our happiness over time. "Good relationships make people happy, and happy people enjoy more and better relationships than unhappy people,"[50] Haidt writes. The good news is that we can increase our genetic happiness level by actions we choose to take, such as making time for meditation or treating others as we wish to be treated. One surefire way to enhance happiness is by changing our behaviors to become more virtuous in our interactions with others, whether online or in person, showing wisdom, courage, humanity, justice, temperance and transcendence (the belief in something higher than the self).[51] Moreover, virtuous behavior must be choices we make independently. A child raised in a virtuous home doesn't necessarily raise his or her happiness levels by exposure to these values; choices must be made independently and interpersonally to change one's mindset.[52] Luckily, there is always room for improving the human condition based on ethical actions.

Changing Values

The operative word in the human condition is, of course, "human." We need to focus on that in the age of the machine, not only when it comes to ethics but also when it comes to the future, as we shall learn in the last chapter of *Interpersonal Divide*. In his bioethics book, *Shaping Our Lives: On Technology, Flourishing, and a Habit of Thinking*, Erik Parens, senior research scholar at the Hastings Center, a bioethics research institute, points to a critical question for those who hope to lead ethical lives in the machine age. "As soon as we begin asking not only what we have a right to do but also what we ought to do, we find ourselves asking meaningful questions," he writes. "What we think we ought to do depends, in significant measure, on what we think it means to be human."[53] If families want to flourish, each member might ask, what truly makes us happy? "What is the proper relationship between parents and children?" Parens asks. "And, among myriad others, what is our proper stance toward ourselves and the rest of the world?"[54]

Bioethicists like Parens focus on all aspects of the human condition, from our mental states to our physical well-being. Communication ethicists like Sharon Bracci and Clifford G. Christians narrow that broad spectrum to how we communicate and live our ethics in and through language. We express, reflect on and influence the human condition in our relationships with others. The entire purpose of language is to engage others and, through that, establish bonds for better or worse. We are social creatures, Bracci and Christians write; "We live with one another in communities, and it is in our shared, associated lives that we must seek that form of happiness that most fully corresponds to our *human* nature."[55] Bracci and Christians refer to geographical rather than digital communities because our ethical values were shaped in specific locales and cultures, with universal principles like truth-telling, integrity and responsibility evolving across the globe. That historic evolution is important in understanding how we will address the challenges of the machine age.

In *The Question for a Moral Compass: A Global History of Ethics*, science historian Kenan Malik notes that the gods of Judaism, Christianity and Islam, which shaped morals, often were capricious, vain and even vicious, a reflection of how people in ancient times viewed reality. "Not only have human choices to be made against the backdrop of divinely ordered fate, but the gods often force humans to act against their wishes."[56] Centuries later the human condition and morality were shaped more by rational argument than by religious myth or symbolism. Later, in the eighteenth and nineteenth centuries, the rise of the market economy and other aspects of modernism forced philosophers to address who or what would shape moral behavior. "Many suggested a revolutionary answer: humans could," Malik writes. "Human nature, needs, desires, aspirations, and possibilities would act as the warrant for moral good."[57] Now a new question is arising: If we heed machines more than each other in the digital age, will those machines shape our needs, desires and aspirations and, in time, our morality?

There is nothing new in technology's ability to change society, as documented in the first chapter of *Interpersonal Divide*. What *is* new concerns the scope of and objective of change in the twenty-first century, saturated with digital media as we rely increasingly on machines to define human bonds by data programmed for profit rather than the common good. True, society can pass laws to mitigate that effect. This, too, has historic roots. For instance, in the late 1880s, a married woman and her paramour used residential telephones to arrange trysts, leading the deceived husband to devise his own technological deception. He tapped the phone and used those conversations as the basis in a divorce case in Connecticut. That led to the Connecticut Telephone Company asking for a law, which the legislature then passed, that levied fines for wiretapping.[58] The uproar in the 2013 case of Edward Snowden, who exposed U.S. government surveillance of electronic communication—in cahoots with telecommunication companies—is a prime example of technological change in modern times. The average citizen can do little to stop secret government and corporate surveillance that not only targets the home but wherever users roam because of mobile devices. Increasingly new technologies violate our personal space. "Home was the protected place, carefully shielded from the world and its dangerous influences," writes Carolyn Marvin in *When Old Technologies Were New*. "New communications technologies were suspect precisely to the extent that they lessened the family's control over what was admitted within its walls."[59] Suffice to say that the family has lost that control in the age of the machine.

Indeed, society has changed to such extent that we no longer value privacy and the modesty that used to be associated with that virtue. Traditional and social media prod us daily to overshare our most private thoughts, words and deeds. Communication technologies are programmed to tap those data and then instantaneously tempt, taunt and tantalize us to share and consume. "Having sex with anyone and telling your secrets to everyone have a lot in common," writes Wendy Shalit in *A Return to Modesty: Discovering the Lost Virtue*. "Everything is public because there is no longer a private realm. Our dignity is in our secrets. If nothing is secret, nothing is sacred."[60]

That sentence captures the present danger. Western philosophers for centuries understood that people should be autonomous, able to pursue their own goals and sate their own desires. If everyone is doing that independently without a thought about the impact on community and the welfare of others, chaos ensues. Jurisprudence created laws that allow a degree of autonomy while safeguarding communal virtues such as duty, respect, integrity and patriotism.[61] The question we now confront in the age of the machine is whether our devices enjoy more autonomy than humans pursuant to terms of service that allow constant data-mining and intrusion and to which we have agreed, typically without taking time to read the fine digital print. Here are a few clauses to which 1.65 billion Facebook users have agreed:

- You grant us a non-exclusive, transferable, sub-licensable, royalty-free, worldwide license to use any IP content that you post on or in connection with Facebook (IP License). This IP License ends when you delete your IP content or your account (2.1 "Sharing Your Content and Information")
- When you publish content or information using the Public setting, it means that you are allowing everyone, including people off of Facebook, to access and use that information, and to associate it with you (i.e., your name and profile picture) (2.4 "Sharing Your Content and Information")
- You give us permission to use your name, profile picture, content, and information in connection with commercial, sponsored, or related content (such as a brand you like) served or enhanced by us. This means, for example, that you permit a business or other entity to pay us to display your name and/or profile picture with your content or information, without any compensation to you. (4.1 "About Our Advertising and Other Commercial Content Served Or Enhanced by Facebook")
- If anyone brings a claim against us related to your actions, content or information on Facebook, you will indemnify and hold us harmless from and against all damages, losses, and expenses of any kind (including reasonable legal fees and costs) related to such claim. (5.2 "Disputes")
- WE DO NOT GUARANTEE THAT FACEBOOK WILL ALWAYS BE SAFE, SECURE OR ERROR-FREE OR THAT FACEBOOK WILL ALWAYS FUNCTION WITHOUT DISRUPTIONS, DELAYS OR IMPERFECTIONS. FACEBOOK IS NOT RESPONSIBLE FOR THE ACTIONS, CONTENT, INFORMATION, OR DATA OF THIRD PARTIES, AND YOU RELEASE US, OUR DIRECTORS, OFFICERS, EMPLOYEES, AND AGENTS FROM ANY CLAIMS AND DAMAGES, KNOWN AND UNKNOWN, ARISING OUT OF OR IN ANY WAY CONNECTED WITH ANY CLAIM YOU HAVE AGAINST ANY SUCH THIRD PARTIES. (5.3 "Disputes" [Facebook states this in ALL CAPS])

Facebook terms of service, similar to that of other platforms, have dozens more clauses that safeguard its autonomy at the expense of yours.

Alas, applications and machines that deliver content will require more laws safeguarding their autonomy and indemnifying themselves legally at users' expense. Content must stand out, insult, affront, tantalize or violate community standards to engage audiences at ever-outlandish levels merely to remain in business. The biggest corporate communication problem in the early twenty-first century is how to hold family members' multitasking attention. In *The Marketplace of Attention*, communications scholar James G. Webster writes:

> Digital media offer people countless choices. They can spend their time with hundreds of television networks, thousands of expensively produced films and TV shows, and a seemingly endless supply of websites, videos, and tweets. . . . But almost without exception, their creators want attention. With it, they hope to amuse, build social capital, make money, or change the course of human events.[62]

Media corporations not only insist on 24/7 access to family members but also on each one's consent so that they can mine and monitor likes, dislikes, lifestyles and personal data. Ultimately, these analytic practices are designed to appease investors with stock holdings rather than patrons holding devices.

Patrons not only provide data. They generate content, too, raising other legal questions that have yet to be addressed. For instance, if the mega-billion-dollar social media industry is such an important component of the marketplace, and if users provide personal information mined from their devices—in addition to content, including video, audio, photography and text—should we consider those users exploited if they receive no or little compensation for their data and content? "What would it mean to take seriously the notion that access to online communities facilitated by social networking sites comprised a productive resource in the emerging information economy?" asks Mark Andrejevic in "Social Network Exploitation," a chapter in *A Networked Self* about implications of digital media on identity, community and culture. "That is to say, what if we were to describe such sites not just as consumer services or entertaining novelties for the informated class, but as crucial information resources in the networked era?"[63] As such, billions of users worldwide may been seen as exploited workers who spend hours each day allowing their personal information to be mined and sold and who provide content that engages others and generates more data for profit-minded creators and stockholders of Facebook, Twitter, LinkedIn, Instagram and other popular venues.

Consumption is a commodity in itself in the age of machines. According to sociologist George Ritzer in *The Globalization of Nothing*, a book in part about how the Internet feeds the consumer culture—global in scope with the capacity to tap funds for products, real or digital—consumption is not about the purchase of goods to survive. Rather, people see ever-increasing and continuous consumption as an economic necessity. "The collectivity needs Americans to do this not only because it is necessary that what the culture values be reaffirmed regularly, but also because active consumption generates needed jobs and incomes for others."[64] This may be true from an economic standpoint; but it is at odds with family values, especially in the rearing of children who consume entertainment-oriented electronic media at all hours of the day, exposing them to thousands of commercials, offers, sign-ups, downloads, gaming platforms and other digital distractions.[65] This consumption excludes use of digital technology and media for school work and homework, fast becoming a dreaded consideration in the typical U.S. home because children demand time for digital consumption. Moreover, that near continuous consumption has become the chief source of discord in the family, according to *Psychology Today*. Many children who consume electronic media simply cannot turn off the continuous stream of multitasking content. For them, consumption leads to isolation, prompting them to turn to technology for a sense of belonging—the value as previously discussed that symbolizes "home"; as a result, "the more connected they feel to technology, the less connected they feel to the people around them" primarily because technology never shuts off.[66]

Psychologists have warned parents about this effect for most of the past decade. While purveyors of technology sold a bill of digital goods to parents about the importance of Internet and education in the global economy, corporate vendors have been exploiting children's inability to shut off technology, creating what *Psychology Today* calls a "family divide." Programming often depicts parents as incompetent or clueless and offers children independence from parental guidance. Worse, parents increasingly turn to electronic media while in the home, talking on phones, checking email or watching television. Consumption becomes continuous with deleterious effects. "Less connection—the real kind—means that families aren't able to build relationships as strong as they could be," with the result being "children feel less comfort, trust, security and love," writes Jim Taylor in "Is Technology Creating a Family Divide?"[67] Another, potentially more ominous effect may develop in the typical home: Children may look to technology rather than to family for a sense of comfort, trust, security and love. Bonds of affection may turn from parents to machines that develop facsimile feelings on a continuous basis. As Sherry Turkle foresaw in the mid-1990s, "For today's children, the boundary between people and machines is intact. But what they see across that boundary has changed dramatically. Now, children are comfortable with the idea that inanimate objects can both think and have a personality."[68] That effect will be investigated in detail in the last chapter of *Interpersonal Divide*. But first we must assess the impact of technology at school and work.

Journal Exercise: *"Your Digital Inventory"*

Electronic devices are programmed for profit with the intent on driving continuous consumption. Moreover, each device or appliance has the capacity to sell products or services because of omnipresent digital access in the home. Do an inventory on your person (the devices you carry or wear) and room by room (where devices exist or are used). Include smartphones, digital eyewear, televisions, radios, computers, laptops, tablets, gaming consoles, and even kitchen appliances and vehicles with media and Internet access. (Optional: Create and compare two inventories, if possible: one in your dwelling if living independently and another in your former family home.)

After you complete your inventory, noting devices and where you located them (on your person or in a specific room), assess:

1. How much each machine costs (check Internet for original purchase price).
2. How often each machine is on or has access to products and services.
3. How many minutes or hours per day you used a particular device.
4. Cost for Internet access or continuing services from telecommunication vendors such as AT&T or Sprint, satellite or cable television, and downloaded applications such as Netflix or video/computer games.

5. What products and services you remember purchasing through each device in the past month.
6. Electronic media/technology charges on your credit card statement, digital wallet or PayPal statements. (Compare with #5 above.)

After completing your inventory, write a journal entry about the results, focusing on cost and consumption and time spent using devices per day. You may want to conclude your journal entry by (a) evaluating how you used technology in your family home and how you are using it now independently and (b) whether technology created an interpersonal divide between you and other family members (or, conversely, strengthened bonds in some way).

CHAPTER FIVE

Interpersonal Divide at School

Anonymous blog comments, vapid video pranks, and lightweight mashups may seem trivial and harmless, but as a whole, this widespread practice of fragmentary, impersonal communication has demeaned interpersonal interaction. . . . A new generation has come of age with a reduced expectation of what a person can be, and of who each person might become.

—JARON LANIER,
author, programmer, digital media pioneer

....

Educational Distraction

The first edition of *Interpersonal Divide* warned that omnipresent digital access combined with consumer technology would likely transform educational standards and influence ethical values unless communities and school districts emphasized emotional and interpersonal intelligence. "Emotional intelligence," a psychological theory popularized by *New York Times* science writer Daniel Goleman in his insightful book by that title, is defined as a skill set that controls impulses, showcases empathy, and displays competence in interpersonal relationships.[1] "Interpersonal intelligence," coined in the first edition of *Interpersonal Divide*, embraces emotional intelligence but emphasizes social competence in interpersonal relationships as a buffer to the pervasive influence and overuse of consumer technology.

The moral of omnipresent media is distraction, afflicting educators and students alike. Case in point: In 2016 at Palo Alto College, Texas, a community college chancellor sat on stage at commencement, an interpersonal milestone (or, as Facebook would frame it, "life event"). The chancellor knew that ceremonies typically celebrate students and alumni, often by inviting a successful honorary speaker who shares wisdom about the *real* rather than virtual world. Commencement also is a time when administrators distribute degrees in front of parents, relatives and friends as names of graduates are called from rolls. The tradition is steeped in interpersonal engagement. For instance, it includes music, "Pomp and Circumstance No. 1 in D," a military march first performed in 1905 at Yale University in honor of composer Edward Elgar, who received an honorary degree.[2] Other universities adopted the tune to mark milestones of erudition with cap, tassel, gown, hood and alma mater colors—all of which Chancellor Bruce H. Leslie had donned for the occasion. Like many students and parents in the audience, Leslie brought his cell phone to the event. Only he was a dignitary in public view, where a spectator timed his use of the gadget for more than thirty minutes. Later a spokesperson for Leslie stated the chancellor did not provide a reason for his cell phone use but apologized "if people were offended by it."[3] The quote was telling. Leslie not only may have offended people; initially he provided no real reason for fiddling with the device, proffering a television-inspired "non-apology apology," a media phrase, elevated to such status by the online encyclopedia Wikipedia: "a statement that has the form of an apology but does not express the expected contrition."[4]

In retrospect, chancellors are as apt as students to be addicted to smartphones. Half of teens believe they are addicted to their devices, according to a poll conducted for Common Sense Media. The survey found almost 80 percent of teens checked their phones hourly with 72 percent feeling the urge to reply immediately to texts and social network messages.[5] As in the case of the chancellor who twiddled as graduates walked with cell phones in their gowns, 27 percent of parents in the Common Sense survey admitted that they, too, were addicted to their phones, which came as no surprise to their children, 28 percent of whom believed parents were hooked on wireless devices.[6] That also was predictable in as much as a 2015 Pew Research Center study found 89 percent of adult cell phone owners had used their devices during the last social gathering they attended, with as many as 82 percent feeling the phone distracted them from others in their presence.[7] Researcher Sherry Turkle cites this study in a *New York Times* article titled "Stop Googling. Let's Talk," noting that the mere presence of a phone between two people on a table between them is powerful enough to change the nature of a conversation. Turkle also discusses college students with split vision, almost like a split screen on a computer, able to look someone in the eye while typing undetected on their smartphones, dividing attention. "They say it's a skill they mastered in middle school when they wanted to text in class without getting caught. Now they use it when they want to be both with their friends and, as some put it, 'elsewhere.'"[8]

"Elsewhere" is now the norm in the wireless classroom. The proliferation of mobile media and online access has changed the learning climate in high school and college classrooms. To be sure, teachers have successfully used cell phones in class, asking students to fact-check an assertion or provide a link to a video that furthers discussion. Some teachers use applications enabling smartphones to give so-called "clicker quizzes," a response toll that can poll the class on a question or assignment. Also, there are nonprofit Internet start-ups such as Khan Academy that create free content on a range of subjects to enhance traditional schooling. Prestigious universities like Stanford, Harvard and Massachusetts Institute of Technology offer free massive open online courses (MOOCs) in the arts and sciences. But in the everyday classroom in high schools and colleges, the use of mobile technology often only generates distraction. Devices vibrate with new messages or social media posts for student and teacher alike. The more applications on smartphones, the more notifications and temptations to be somewhere else rather than in the classroom. This is why many teachers ban use of smartphones, believing devices are used primarily for socializing and entertainment. That suspicion has been documented, too, with 42 percent of cell phone use in the typical classroom accessing social media and gaming.[9] Other tests and surveys have shown that mobile technology insists on continuous interaction whether by text, email or other ring tone notification. Overwhelmingly such engagement is programmed to entice purchases while surreptitiously gathering data for marketers so as better to target consumers, often with advertising appearing instantly as soon as the user expresses interest on social media. The entire process happens during class. A study by faculty members at West Point found that contrary to conventional wisdom about the utility of classroom technology, students performed markedly better when laptops and tablets were banned in lecture. In classrooms allowing use of the device, students scored 18 percent lower than counterparts in sections where devices were prohibited.[10]

There is no question that social media and Internet often can be instructive, engaging and beneficial to school-age children. Numerous examples abound in the arts and sciences. Here are two recent examples. In 2016, the twelve-year-old singer-songwriter Grace Vanderwaal learned how to play the ukulele by watching YouTube videos and went on to win a million dollars on the competitive talent show "America's Got Talent."[11] Online content also has advanced careers of budding scientists. In 2015, seventeen-year-old Olivia Hallisey helped solve a refrigeration issue in Africa associated with portable diagnostic tests for Ebola by reading online about a silk fiber derivative that keeps proteins stable without requiring cooling temperatures.[12] Whether arts or sciences, Internet inspires innovation. Early on, however, there is one critical component that can cultivate astute use of online resources, and that is parental, peer and teacher guidance on how to access information from reliable sources and avoid dangers from untrustworthy ones.

Online distraction pervades all levels of society. But distraction in children comes with educational consequences: poor comprehension of the written word and, at times, their own emotions at a critical time in their development. Unlike many parents and grandparents, schooled in a literary rather than digital age, lacking incessant distraction, children may never realize the harm being done to their levels of emotional and interpersonal intelligence, precisely because they have no basis of comparison. Reading requires focused attention. That was the hallmark of the literary age. A 2007 research report from the National Endowment for the Arts about reading levels stated that Americans are comprehending less by the written word, warning that the erosion of skills will have "serious civic, social, cultural and economic implications."[13]

Overuse of technology also hinders emotional growth. A University of California study found that children put their ability to recognize *emotions* at risk because of the time they are spending looking at screens instead of each other. According to the study, sixth-graders who did not use technology for a five-day period "were significantly better at reading human emotions than kids who had regular access to phones, televisions, and computers."[14] The irony here concerns school districts promoting emotional intelligence, one of the methods said to address bullying. The Center for Emotional Intelligence at Yale University notes that adolescents who "recognize and understand their own emotional responses to difficult situations" will learn "to act in an intelligent, constructive manner," enhancing peer relations.[15] Bullying is rampant online across age groups and Internet platforms, all of which adolescents routinely access at all hours of the day; thus, the impact of too much screen time, in itself, blunts attempts to teach emotional intelligence because recognition of emotions, in itself, is endangered.

Misuse of social media leads to oversharing, which triggers privacy concerns. Sociologist Carrie James addressed this in a balanced, insightful book titled *Disconnected: Youth, New Media, and the Ethics Gap*, calling for "conscientious connectivity," or making youth aware of the consequences for online engagement. James's work discovered a key aspect of how tweens, teens and young adults think about privacy, a kind of filter, in which "people that you want to see your stuff can see your stuff but not everybody."[16] James explains attitudes about privacy from viewpoints of young users who often lack impulse control (which technology worsens). Engaging with others virtually rather than face-to-face, they may experience the fleeting empowerment that social media bestows. They continue to look to screens to provide that feeling, needing more and more screen time for the same effect, often trusting others who may have ulterior motives. "Regardless of our intentions," James writes, "the online content we post, 'like,' or retweet can be misread, taken out of context, copied, forwarded, and otherwise misused in ways that harm our friends, family members, peers, colleagues, and online connections."[17] Anonymity may accompany online interactions. In worst-case scenarios, fake identities groom school-age children, resulting in cyberstalking and sexting.

Since the 1990s, Internet has been associated with the widespread distribution of child pornography. At the National Strategy Conference on Combating Child Exploitation, former Attorney General Eric Holder Jr. spoke about the explosion of child pornography crimes because of Internet distribution through online communities and networks. Holder noted that the Internet "provides ground for individuals to create, access, and share child sexual abuse images worldwide at the click of a button," with images "readily available through virtually every Internet technology including websites, email, instant messaging/ICQ, Internet Relay Chat (IRC), newsgroups, bulletin boards, peer-to-peer networks, and social networking sites."[18] Increasingly, however, tweens, teens and young adults are contributing to the exploitation by sexting each other, sharing nudity through message, photo, email or social network. As a result, the current online climate not only contains illegal distribution of child pornography but also illicit content sent voluntarily by youth. University of Miami media professors Bruce Drushel and Kathleen M. German observe that unlike criminals who share unlawful images for sexual fulfillment, teenagers distribute "pornographic images of themselves in more targeted manner, often through cellular phones," seemingly "unaware of the potential for humiliation and embarrassment that can occur when these photos and videos are distributed to unintended parties."[19] The authors add that search engines like Google have unprecedented machine ability to capture content, further aggravating privacy concerns because of potentially harmful access and redistribution by others.[20]

The more students learn about technology, the more they will use it responsibly. The more distracted they are, the greater the risk. Advocates often overlook this, believing divided attention is a choice, not a distraction. Clive Thompson, columnist for *WIRED*, has praised the new multitasking awareness in his book, *Smarter Than You Think: How Technology is Changing our Minds for the Better*, noting how annoying it would be for friends to phone you only to report what sandwiches they were eating. Unlike the telephone, online access is part of the "tapestry you can glance at," he says, an optional distraction, inviting your attention "rather than demanding it."[21] However, even Thompson concedes that few young people know how social media and photo-sharing applications function and would have "X-ray vision into the digital world" if they learned a bit of programming.[22] (Happily, some nonprofit start-ups like Code.org, praised in the official blog of the U.S. Department of Education, have been advocating for basic computer code to be introduced in K–12 education.[23])

Choice is vital in the modern age, but a different one than Thompson promotes. Neither is choice optional. It involves reading terms of service and understanding programming to decide whether to click "I agree" and use an application or device.

Otherwise, technology will use you.

Digital Education

At Rio Salado College, you not only learn about technology; it learns about you. It records all your data as you go about your digital day; "when you log on, when you log off, what you view (or don't), how long you're on the site, and so on,"[24] write Jason and Jeremy Kolb in their book about big-data secrets. The authors state that Rio Salado has taken a page out of Amazon's playbook. "These metrics are used to build a data-based profile about you and determine the probability you'll pass your class and graduate."[25] After eight days the college has enough information to focus on students who might underperform as students. That might not be enough. According to the Kolbs, correlations alone do not prove anything; testing does. In other words, the lesson is broader than Rio Salado, whose innovative vision would "reinvent the learning experience to change lives."[26] The point here concerns untested algorithmic profiling, which can be as stereotypical as any kind of profiling if machines are left to their own—and *your*—devices. Schools should not act on correlations alone but should develop healthy skepticism about what machines collect as opposed to what they "know."

No one questions that technology, properly used, can enhance the educational experience, especially involving distance learning. Purdue University makes a strong case for "anytime anywhere education" on its Online Program website, noting that students have access to massive amounts of data in the machine age. In an introduction titled "How Has Technology Changed Education?," Purdue mentions how students collaborate more because of digital connections. In the past, it states, professors were the primary source of information, a situation that has not changed significantly since medieval Europe. "With the worldwide reach of the Internet and the ubiquity of smart devices that can connect to it, a new age of anytime anywhere education is dawning."[27]

The problem with "anytime anywhere education" is the dawning of another era: *truthiness*. The word was coined in 2005 by television entertainer Stephen Colbert and means "the quality of seeming to be true according to one's intuition, opinion, or perception without regard to logic, factual evidence, or the like."[28] At the time truthiness suited the emerging social mediated algorithmic audience segmented into marketing groups with a goal of analyzing consumer behaviors to predict future ones. Students believe what they believe usually because friends in their affinity groups did. Digital natives have been exposed to this norm their entire lives. They came of age as machines began to correlate at ever-faster speeds in an increasingly data-rich environment. Something else occurred, though. Students no longer could easily find primary sources of information, such as historical documents in libraries, or acquaint themselves with groundbreaking discoveries by world-renowned researchers; now there were multitudes of online sources. Hoaxes. Hacks. Stunts. Pranks. Fraud. Counterfeits. Conspiracy theories. Altered photographs. Doctored records. Viral videos. Facts died in the process. "The era of the fact is coming to an end," writes Harvard historian Jill Lepore in the *New Yorker*, creating mayhem, "not least because the collection and weighing of facts require investigation, discernment, and judgment, while the collection and analysis of data are outsourced to machines."[29] Fact no longer was earned by traditional means, including observation, experiment and examination; accessed information was data-mined, crunched, targeted, vended and downloaded. Students look to machines for answers because that is all they have known.

The loss of fact has led to other interpersonal losses.

Childhood friendship is remembered for a lifetime. Before Internet, those friends were defined mostly by those in our neighborhoods or school districts. Now, however, friends come to us digitally via a variety of platforms, from social media to gaming. Once again, it is important to note that these applications can *enhance* existing interpersonal friendships in the same manner that walkie-talkies did in other eras. Social media also can be invaluable when families move, allowing children to maintain friendships years after the relocation. Friends nurture healthy childhood development. Researchers at the University of Florida note that childhood friendship at home and at school plays a key role in emotional growth. Children learn social skills by interacting with friends, and that aids educational performance.[30] However, online friendships are poor substitutes for ones at school and hometowns. While the web offers children more opportunities for friendships, without their ever having to meet in person, it suggests that relationships can be established with a click or a like. As technologists observe, there is a difference between interpersonal and Internet friendship because the others appear only on screens (or hide behind them). That impacts how children negotiate with each other, a basic human skill learned primarily through physical play at school. As the *Huffington Post* reported in "Friendship in the Time of Technology," relationships should be based on honesty—"every stumble, hesitation or stutter in a face-to-face conversation reveals our nature in subtle ways, perhaps even without our volition," making "real-time relationships more trustworthy and hence more permanent."[31]

Internet adds another layer of communication with existing and online friends. Often, however, lines between the two blur and create drama. The Pew Research Center notes that 68 percent of teen social media users have experienced drama with friends in online platforms, with 26 percent of all teens reporting conflict with a friend over something that happened on the web or via text message.[32] Findings in that Pew report also suggest that online interaction can help children during stressful times, lending support; but that also can lead to oversharing with myriad adverse consequences. Worse, the added stress comes during a time when children are growing hormonally as well as socially. Pew reports 40 percent of teen social media users feel pressured to post content that makes them look good to others while 39 percent of teens on social media feel pressure to post so that they will be liked.[33]

High school relationships are difficult to handle interpersonally. Social media and messaging can cause strain during break-ups, which abound in the teen years as boys and girls explore sexuality. Before Internet, those break-ups occurred largely out of the public eye; now they occur on Facebook, Twitter and other mediating venues. Online "friends" often view these dramas as entertainment. In *Breakup 2.0: Disconnecting over New Media*, cyber-anthropologist Ilana Gershon writes that the first sign of trouble are changes to a Facebook relationship status, which she has labeled "a glimpse into other people's disconnections, but a glimpse that tantalizes instead of satisfying."[34] Word about break-ups typically happens at school, home and community *simultaneously* because of oversharing and mobile access, with ex-partners confronting a range of emotional questions, laments and encouragements from friends, parents and relatives (as well as proposals from prospective suitors). The digital aftermath of break-ups can cause emotional problems for weeks on end, affecting schoolwork.

Surveys show hope. Teens overwhelmingly believe that telling someone in person is the most acceptable way of ending a relationship, giving this method an average of 8.4 points on a 1–10 acceptability scale, with 78 percent rating it an 8 or higher, according to the Pew Research Center.[35] In the same report, the Center also states that breaking up by phone is the second most acceptable approach. Breaking up via text received a low rating of 3.4, with a mere 12 percent approving of this break-up method. Here's the bad news: Some 27 percent of teens have broken up with someone via text and 31 percent have been broken up in this manner at one time or another. The disparity here— 78 percent affirming interpersonal break-ups as the social norm and roughly 30 percent experiencing the antithesis—is an apt indicator of stress and pressure many teens experience breaking up digitally.

In bygone eras, we eventually forgot the sorrow of breakups. Not so anymore. Internet surveils and gathers data on users at a dizzying pace with little attention paid to the risk of compulsive use, writes journalist and technology author Andrew Keen.[36] Technology records and remembers every keystroke. The sheer pace of data-gathering outstrips the development of social norms. According to John Palfrey and Urs Gasser of Harvard University's Berkman Klein Center for Internet & Society, "It becomes easier to rationalize harmful behavior in a digital setting" because actions might not seem "real"; moreover, "the digital native doesn't see the reactions of the person he has just harmed" but may do so later in life and "feel regret, depending on the extent of the harm he has caused."[37] Extent can be devastating. Victims of all forms of bullying are more than twice as likely to commit suicide; moreover, according to a report in *JAMA Pediatrics*, cyberbullying—sending messages of a threatening or intimidating nature—is "more strongly related to suicidal ideation compared with traditional bullying," with those victims more than *three* times as likely to harbor suicidal thoughts.[38] In a different study, researchers at the National Center for Telehealth and Technology note that the Internet may introduce new threats to the public and that health campaigns to increase awareness should be a priority in schools and colleges.[39]

As in all social issues, especially ones that threaten the public health, parents and educators should fully assess the impact of technology on educational performance. Thousands of books have touted enhanced learning opportunities in the machine age. *Interpersonal Divide* has taken a different tack by focusing on balancing the online world with the physical one. Researcher Sherry Turkle has foreseen opportunities and risks of mediated worlds. "Like Narcissus and his reflection, people who work with computers can easily fall in love with the worlds they have constructed or with their performances in the worlds created for them by others," she writes, noting that involvement "with simulated worlds affects relationships with the real one."[40]

This is the lesson that educators should take to heart.

Educational Diligence

Reading is fundamental in the machine age, and the news is not all bad. In 2015, the Pew Research Center reported that young adults ages 18 to 29 (spanning the college years) were more likely to have read a book in the past twelve months than older adults.[41] However, there are other interpretations. Cultural critic David Denby, writing in the *New Yorker*, acknowledges that teenagers, "attached to screens of one sort or another, read more *words* than they ever have in the past"; but he notes "they often read scraps, excerpts, articles, parts of articles, messages, pieces of information from everywhere and from nowhere."[42] Denby looks beyond the data. "Lifetime readers know that reading literature can be transformative," he writes, "but they can't prove it. If they tried, they would have to buck the metric prejudice, the American notion that assertions unsupported with statistics are virtually meaningless."[43]

The medium matters when it comes to reading. Technology writer Nicholas Carr believes the experience of reading words on a networked computer, "whether it's a PC, an iPhone, or a Kindle, is very different from the experience of reading a book."[44] According to Carr, books focus our attention by isolating us from digital distractions. Computers do the opposite. As previously noted, digital natives are not sufficiently instructed on how to comb the Internet for verifiable, accurate and/or transformative news and literature. And when it comes to works of art, digital reproduction changes how we "know" material because the experience—seeing a masterpiece in a museum—is replaced with facsimile.[45] Moreover, everyone is an expert in the digital age, including the device displaying facsimiles. As computer scientist Roger Schank notes, throughout human history people furthered education by consulting with the village elder "who might very well have gotten his knowledge by talking to a puff of smoke. Today," he adds, "people make decisions based on evidence they get from the Internet, all right, but that evidence often is no better than the evidence the village elder may have supplied."[46]

To be fair, fact-based education must acknowledge that today's student differs substantially from those of the past. Teaching methods, like just about everything else, including cyber-law and ethics, have not kept pace with machines. Processing speed and storage capabilities have accelerated to the clouds, literally. Education cannot keep pace. "Technological changes are altering the minds of our children, both physically and chemically, which is changing their learning styles and preferences,"[47] write the authors of *Literacy is Not Enough: 21st Century Fluencies for the Digital Age*. They encourage teachers to think globally and abandon ineffective strategies such as lecturing to students or making them memorize facts easily found on the web. However, advocates promoting such methods also should encourage educators to analyze programming, terms of service and educational risks of incessant distraction.[48]

In the end, digital education can supplement traditional learning as long as we mitigate distraction and diligently pursue knowledge. These are themes in *Ethics and Education,* a seminal work published in 1970 by English philosopher R. S. Peters who espoused that pursuit of truth is all that matters in science and education. A proponent of critical analysis, he advanced the idea that education is based on three main criteria, "the first concerning its matter, the second its manner, and the third its cognitive perspective."[49] We extrapolate that in modern terms as data, delivery and deliberation. Throughout *Interpersonal Divide* we have focused on all three, arguing that data define us more now than ever based on delivery systems that surveil and distract us around the clock. Students, in particular, often fail to deliberate the impact of overuse on their psyches as well as the digital consumerism that defines their mores and generation. Mediated communication isolates as much as it collaborates, insulates as it innovates. Without interpersonal engagement, digital natives will lose the authentic connectedness that is the chief attribute of physical community.

Empathy is a byproduct such engagement. The feeling enhances interactions on which "our very bodily experience" depends and "by which we enter deeply into each other's lives,"[50] notes Jeremy Rifkin in *The Empathic Civilization.* Since the Enlightenment, technological products have been touted as rescuing fallen humanity but ultimately have led to an increasingly materialist world. "In the modern era of public schooling," he writes, "the goal set forth by the state educators was to produce batches of 'productive citizens' for the emerging national economies."[51] Technology enables that role. The task, then, is to reintroduce students to their communities and promote interpersonal relationships in a manner that nurtures an empathic rather than disembodied response. "The more deeply we empathize with each other and our fellow creatures," Rifkin writes, "the more intensive and extensive is our level of participation and the richer and more universal are the realms of reality in which we dwell."[52]

If education can instill the empathic response in learners, they will humanize the workplace where technology reigns, often at the expense of interpersonal relationships, as we shall learn in the next chapter.

Journal Exercise: *"Real Time and Place"*

Educational diligence in computer age has three basic requirements:

1. **Know the machine** more like a computer scientist than a consumer, understanding when and how to use it, the cost of such usage (both

in time and funds), and the terms of service that apply to such usage.

2. **Think critically** rather than mechanically (continuously checking social media), primarily through undistracted reading, coming to conclusions based on fact rather than belief.

3. **Feel empathically** by engaging others in real time and place so that inspiration and innovation are derived by authentic rather than facsimile experience.

Test your abilities in these areas by:

- **Analyzing service terms** of favorite applications, such as Facebook or Twitter.
- **Setting aside technology** for the entire time it takes to read a best-selling printed book purely for fun.
- **Leaving mobile technology at home** and spending an entire morning, afternoon, or day interacting with others at a public park or community event.

After doing so, write about the experience, explaining anything new you learned about your use of social media, reading for pleasure, and engaging with others in real time and place.

CHAPTER SIX

....

Interpersonal Divide at Work

*I think we're in the middle of the single greatest technological
inflection point since Gutenberg invented the printing press. I
think the workplace is fundamentally being transformed. . . . I
always used to say, "When I graduate from college, I got to find
a job." When my daughters graduate from college, they have to
invent a job. That's what's new. All right? And then, you may
get lucky and get your first job, but you've got to invent, reinvent.
And nobody wants to trust the people with that truth. Because
it's really scary.*[1]

—TOM FRIEDMAN,
Pulitzer Prize–winning columnist, New York Times

....

Interpersonal Analytics

The first edition of *Interpersonal Divide* was among a handful of technology books to warn that workplaces would change dramatically because of round-the-clock, mediated communication. The effects were
predicted to blur boundaries between home and work, increasing stress
levels due to omnipresent emails, persistent texts and managerial demands. The current, evolving workplace elevates stress to a tipping
point because of machine monitoring and other digital intrusions, to be
explored in this chapter. Combined with accelerated time, our current
digital lives have grown hectic and thorny. We use the same devices or
same applications on different devices at home and at work. They are
always at our fingertips. In a few short decades, the word "touch" has
evolved from "user-friendly" gadgets, as in machines with "a human
touch," to touchscreen smartphones and touchless screens. That says
something about where machines are taking us. The point is simple:
Without relaxation compounded by continuous work demands at any
hour at any place, we risk our health and well-being and cannot fully

experience the joys of community life or fully appreciate family, friends and colleagues.

To be sure, many of the joys of health, well-being and harmony depend on one basic aspect of the workplace: *a paycheck*. Machines may deprive millions of that in the global future. To be sure, mechanization has been an employment issue since the Industrial Revolution. Technology writer Nicolas Carr has written extensively about wealth and automation, trends that existed since the late eighteenth century. The current digital revolution differs from the industrial one when it comes to job creation. According to Carr, the invention of the electric grid funneled massive funds to corporations. For a while, this worked well for the average worker because electricity created tens of thousands of new products, requiring skilled and unskilled laborers. "The arrival of the universal computing grid portends a very different kind of economic alignment," he writes, concentrating wealth in relatively few companies, "eroding the middle class and widening the divide between haves and have-nots."[2] Carr bases his argument on technology that replaces skilled and unskilled workers in what he calls "The YouTube economy," in which everyone plays but relatively few reap rewards.

Even those in the technology sector suffer. In 2016, Foxconn Technology Group, an Apple and Samsung supplier in China, replaced 60,000 workers with robots. If any country should be concerned about automation, China might top that list with its population of 1.35 billion people. In reporting the mass firing—a population larger than Pensacola, Florida—the British Broadcasting Company noted that economists "have issued dire warnings about how automation will affect the job market, with one report, from consultants Deloitte in partnership with Oxford University, suggesting that 35 percent of jobs were at risk over the next twenty years."[3]

Two-thirds of Americans believe that robots will do much of the work currently being done by people, according to the Pew Research Center; however, 80 percent of respondents believe that their own jobs and professions will be largely unaffected.[4] The first edition of *Interpersonal Divide* warned against such counterintuitive reasoning, chronicling the overly optimistic reports about technology transforming society. All aspects of life from living wages to living beings would be improved, if only we could bridge the so-called digital divide and provide Internet access everywhere in the world. *We were promised a global village*, the first edition stated; *we inherited a global mall*. In the process, the gap between "haves" and "have-nots" did not narrow, as was promised; the gap continues to widen each year. A 2015 report titled "Digital America: A Tale of the Haves and Have Mores," by the McKinsey Global Institute, measured the technological economy in all job sectors, lamenting the fact that the United States has achieved only 18 percent of its digital potential. Nevertheless, the executive summary was candid about digitization unleashing widespread economic disenfranchisement: "As digital technologies automate many of the tasks that humans are paid to do, the day-to-day nature of work will change in a majority of occupations. Companies will redefine many roles and business processes, affecting workers of all skill levels. Historical job-displacement rates could accelerate sharply over the next decade."[5] That assessment should sound an alarm for everyone who serves anyone or who assembles anything anywhere: *Robots are in your future, but a steady paycheck might not be.*

This fact may come as a surprise for many millennials, ages 18 to 29. In 2010, the Pew Research Center released a report stating that this generation is confident about the future because they are self-expressive and open to change. Some 24 percent of respondents cited their use of technology as fundamental for future success whereas only 12 percent of Gen Xers believed the same.[6] Millennials, many of whom came of age during the Great Recession (2007–2009), are the first generation to be reared entirely in the age of Internet and rank as the most educated of any generation in American history.[7] Their optimism and confidence have instilled in them a strong work ethic, and their technological prowess has prepared them well for the changing workplace of the future. But their story doesn't end there.

Some millennials have entitlement traits, stating they would not be content to punch a time clock or sit in a cubicle, eking out a living.[8] They aspire to high-paying positions, in part because of their technological prowess. To secure those positions, however, millennials must understand technology from a programming perspective and be imaginative enough to use its power to devise pioneering services as well as create innovative products. Their generation not only will be in competition with peers and rivals in chosen professions. Increasingly their job applications are being analyzed by machines that will monitor performance continuously during their employment. Human resources officers use "talent analytics" to assess productivity, poring over data to determine whether investment in personnel enhances the bottom line or whether some workers are better suited to other tasks rather than ones assigned. Machines may delve into questionable practices, too, potentially invading privacy by measuring absenteeism or health benefits based on age or race of employees or firing and promoting people based on what data predict about likelihood of future performance.[9] In other words, people may be fired by a machine not because they did anything wrong but because of the statistical probability that they will at a later date because of quirks, tendencies or outdated skill sets. While companies may have a legal right to collect and evaluate employees using talent analytics, ethical questions inevitably will come into play concerning how those data are used.

Some business leaders think employee monitoring interferes with productivity. Experts in managerial leadership note that high performance at the workplace has three key components: job satisfaction (appreciating assigned tasks), minimal distraction (focusing on those tasks), and motivation (improving performance).[10] Technology, used appropriately, can enhance job satisfaction by enabling employees to meet deadlines and engage multitudes of people, inviting them to patronize products and services. However, technology often falls short in areas of minimal distraction and motivation. Devices are programmed to distract. Robots simulate encouragement. Typical devices, from smartphones to computers, continually insist that they be used to engage or respond to others—ceaseless notifications of messages, tweets, alerts, calls and more (from home, school and work)—while simultaneously monitoring how tasks are being performed via bottom-line analytics. In the digital workplace, employees respond to two levels of supervision: bosses and machines.

Interpersonal Interference

Machines not only monitor how employees are using devices and applications but also may be programmed to detect moods and behaviors of those employees. Machines monitor employees to an alarming degree in some companies, often under the pretext of improving performance. Stress is measured, too, although usually in a negative light. Examples include tracking a worker's Internet and social media use; tapping their phones, emails and texts; measuring keystroke speed and accuracy; deploying video surveillance; and embedding chips in company badges to evaluate whereabouts, posture and voice tone. Computer scientists even have developed lie detection software that tracks eye movements and blink rates, correctly sensing deceit more than 80 percent of the time.[11] Machines have difficulty detecting virtual lies because falsehood, exaggeration and hoax are conventions on Internet. However, studies have found that employees are more truthful when they know they are being videoed (rather than surveilled)—even more so than in face-to-face interactions—because on some level they know that a machine not only is recording communication but also storing copies of that interaction in files that can be used against them and shared with others.[12]

This effect echoes eighteenth-century philosopher Jeremy Bentham's "panopticon" design for prisons. (That penitentiaries should be associated with Internet surveillance is, in itself, a glimpse into stress that online interactions, especially on social media, generate.) The idea of the panopticon was that no watchman can observe every cell simultaneously. However, a central inspection house encircled by cells allows a watchman to peer into each cell at his choosing with prisoners under the idea that they are being watched all the time, thus enabling one guard to control behavior of the hundreds of prisoners. French philosopher Michel Foucault (1926–1984)—who died before the Internet became conventional—understood the harmful psychological implications of being watched continually. Digital theorist Tim Raynor associates Foucault's take on the panopticon with social media, which he calls "a kind of virtual panopticon" where users "are both guards and prisoners, watching and implicitly judging one another as we share content."[13]

There is growing fear of machines. Simon Head, author of *Mindless: Why Smarter Machines Are Making Dumber Humans*, criticizes employee monitoring at such companies as Walmart and Amazon. Head believes current practices are as inhumane as ones in the industrial late nineteenth and early twentieth centuries.[14] Others have made similar arguments, comparing mass marketing to mass production of earlier centuries, with dehumanizing effects, because people are alienated from each other, measured only by consumption[15]—another digital way to distinguish the "haves" from the "have nots." Head says IT practices devalue human dignity, treating people like machine appendages. "The latest in measurement could put sensors on a name tag to monitor how you move, your tone of voice, whether you are conforming to quantitative norms about doing your job. Chairs have sensors to measure your activity at the desk."[16] Employees so monitored are apt to treat potential customers by the same machine values—those who help the bottom line and those who don't. Media theorist Douglas Rushkoff sees similar effects. "The evolution of the Internet recapitulates the process through which corporatism took hold of our society,"[17] he writes, noting how people tethered to machines no longer engage in interpersonal discourse, even in public spaces. "And this local, day-to-day, mundane pleasure is what makes us human in the first place."[18]

We may know human nature because we live it. What is the nature of machines? Short answer: *connectedness*. At the turn of the century, "connectedness" meant Internet access enabling us to network with people of our choosing, such as friends and family. Social media was put on par with telephones, just another means to communicate, often less expensively than long-distance calls. Now that access is universal, the term "network" no longer defines people but a group or system of interconnected machines. In the process, we have lost control of whom we wish to communicate with, such as we had when using landlines. Machines appropriated that choice. If everyone has access everywhere at any time, and if devices connect us to strangers, acquaintances, families, friends, services and products, do we fully grasp that those entities have access to us? That means if our contacts number in the hundreds or thousands, each one can send us multiple messages and requests on a regular basis. Now add analytics to the mix, with companies data-mining us and then vending that information to clients and other interested parties, and our contact lists (desired and undesirable) continue to multiply exponentially. William Powers, prize-winning journalist and author, noted that a few decades ago we would go for weeks without hearing from a family member or friend. Now we hear from everyone everywhere at home, school and especially work. "The goal is no longer to be 'in touch' but to erase the possibility of ever being out of touch," Powers writes, adding that we "live simultaneously with everyone, sharing every moment, every perception, thought, and action via our screens."[19] Digital natives have never known another life. Their memory is one of continuous interactions suggested and facilitated by machines.

"Memory" is a human and machine term. Technologists view it as petabytes of storage capacity. Humanists view it as life experience. Sophie McBain, Associated Press editor, describes the transformation of human memory since the advent of the Internet. According to McBain, the more we use social media, the more we rely on what servers have stored about our lives, including some of our most intimate or private moments. "With every passing year, we are shackling ourselves more tightly to our digital legacies, and relying more heavily on computer programs to narrate our personal histories for us," she states, adding that it is "becoming ever harder to escape the past, or remake the future."[20] This is especially true when it comes to employment histories, with tweets, texts, emails, photos, videos and blogs that tout our successes or chronicle our failures, often accommodated with the fawning or odious comments of others.

An overriding theme of *Interpersonal Divide* has been to warn against endowing machines with qualities that they do not possess. Their nature is neither human nor inhuman. It is a program. Computers excel at simulating human experience for profit. They are less good at fulfilling human needs, some of which concern satisfaction, recognition and achievement in work. Those career paths are part of the digital record. As Sherry Turkle states in the twentieth anniversary edition of *The Second Self*, the utopian vision of the computer culture of the 1980s was that technology would lead to myriad opportunities for affirmation in every area of our lives. "The reality of simulation culture as it has developed," she writes, "is that those who write the simulations get to set the parameters."[21] In another Turkle book, *Alone Together*, she elaborates on those parameters and our collective response to them. Early on technology wasn't a substitute for interaction with others. It was viewed as a convenience when we were short of time, especially on the job. Soon mediated communication became the platform of choice. "We discovered the network—the world of connectivity—to be uniquely suited to the overworked and overscheduled life it makes possible,"[22] she states.

That life is no longer only our own. Machines also lay claim to it.

Digital communication typically is promoted as the sole means of innovation. Cultural anthropologist Howard A. Doughty has argued that mediated communication often involves "anonymous, invasive, intrusive, ubiquitous, and quite possibly iniquitous technological instruments" that tether us to screens, with most of us "only dimly aware of the extent to which electronic observation and record collection are capturing" data of our lives.[23] Work-related technology is good at capturing data without making sense of it. It correlates without causation, as noted in Chapter Three. Increasingly automation accompanies us up (or down) career ladders. Nonetheless, those who can distinguish between human and machine nature, critically analyzing data, can use technology to serve the common good. They can become servants in the knowledge economy. But what about the millions who lack technical education, especially those in underfunded school districts or who lack training or desire to innovate and reinvent themselves over the long course of a career?

There will always be jobs for people who can do tasks that are too menial for machines. Robots cannot easily do routine service jobs such cleaning a hotel room because machines may lack adequate dexterity, sight and other human traits; so it is cheaper to employ people for these positions. As the *New York Times* reports, "computerization is not reducing the quantity of jobs, but rather degrading the quality of jobs for a significant subset of workers."[24] Society has yet to fully address these concerns, which can have dramatic, civic consequences—including social upheaval—when millions are routinely marginalized by machines. According to finance professor Noah Smith, writing in the *Atlantic*, a society with robotic labor "would be an incredibly prosperous one, but we will need to find some way for the vast majority of human beings to share in that prosperity, or we risk the kinds of dystopian outcomes that now exist only in science fiction."[25]

There is another digital dystopia for those working in the knowledge economy, experiencing ever-higher stress levels affecting mental health. "We're guided by a fatal assumption that the best way to get work done is to work longer and more continuously," write the authors of *The Way We're Working Isn't Working*. "But the more hours we work and the longer we go without renewal, the more we begin to default, reflexively, into behaviors that reduced our own effectiveness—impatience, frustration, distraction, and disengagement," taking "a pernicious toll on others."[26] This insightful book, published in 2010, chronicles many of the concerns in the first edition of *Interpersonal Divide*, including the exhaustion many of us feel when arriving home from work, because we have been living on computer time rather than linear time. Everything seems like an emergency. The cumulative effect of continuous distraction combined with pinging insistence that a device or application must be used, NOW, affects the nervous system. At home, where work continues into the evening hours, we may be too tired to interact meaningfully with family members, lapsing into passive activities like watching television while we reflexively check smartphones because multitasking now is part of human nature.[27] In the end, humans do not function like machines, even as machines increasingly try to function as humans, speaking to us in Siri voices programmed for gender, accent and language.

There is a broad range of digital scenarios that interfere with our lives, especially when work and home blur. Because of mobile devices, our jobs go where we do. Earlier in this book, in deference to the changing demographics of the family—no longer only the "nuclear" father, mother and dependent children—we said that "home" was where one felt a deep sense of belonging. Think about that. If work is everywhere and nowhere simultaneously, as we multitask while navigating such physical impediments as cars and crosswalks, where do we get that grounded feeling of belonging apart from the digital simulations of our lives?

Interpersonal Integrity

In our pursuit of materialism that machines promote, we may lose a fundamental necessity of existence: *integrity*. That word has two definitions, one commonly associated with the condition of something, as in the integrity of data, and the other, with a universal ethical principle. As cited earlier in this book, "integrity" is a core component of what media scholar Clifford G. Christians has labeled the "protonorm," part of human dignity, truth-telling and nonviolence that affirms the sanctity of life, uniting us in a common oneness.[28] On a literal level, integrity means "an undivided or unbroken completeness" as well as "moral soundness."[29] We can claim both meanings to help us overcome the challenges of the workplace.

As noted in the introduction of this book, the dual aspects of the human condition—consciousness and conscience—are keys to restoring interpersonal integrity in any environ, especially the workplace. To recap, we noted the importance of aligning the two seemingly conflicting voices in our head. *Consciousness tells us that we come into the world alone and we leave it alone. The conscience tells us what is in you is in me.* The goal of ethics is to harmonize those polarities so that one informs the other. In other words, they can restore in us *"an undivided and unbroken completeness."* Conscience informs us when our values are affirmed, disregarded or silenced. Conscience acts as an inner knowing of right and wrong involving others. Consciousness, on the other hand, is an awareness of our place in the physical and information space. It helps us foresee how our thoughts, words and deeds affect others so that we can take appropriate action when problems arise. When conscience informs consciousness, and vice versa, we feel grounded, whole, at peace, knowing we have the wherewithal to solve any challenge or address any issue. When we act on our values in this manner, others regard us as a person of integrity. We have attained *"moral soundness."*

In the first edition of *Interpersonal Divide*, the question of work-life balance still seemed possible. Families were advised to shut down Internet access so as to engage with each other interpersonally. Character—the ability to act nimbly with integrity—was emphasized. Since then technology has wielded much more influence on our lives. With the advent of digital appliances and wireless access in every room, technology won out. Work continues to interrupt us wherever we go but especially in the home. The goal of achieving work-life balance has lapsed into myth.[30] Thus, it behooves us to take into account who actually is benefitting from the blurring of home and work, especially when research shows that knowledge workers no longer can distinguish any boundaries whatsoever between home, work and community.[31] What is the effect on our character? On our home life and career? On our self-worth and well-being?

Long-term stress seems to be the primary symptom of the work-life imbalance. In his book *Mediated*, Thomas de Zengotita documents anxiety associated with technology overuse. Everything becomes an emergency, he writes. We begin to perceive "reality" as fretful. Armed with smartphones, we circumnavigate physical space as if we no longer belong in it, because we are "addicted to social and professional busyness" and the false belief of "throbbing connectedness to Something Important."[32] When we are removed from physical environs, because we are preoccupied by devices, what then happens to the "integrity" of place, the unbroken completeness that used to describe nature and the outdoors? What happens to moral soundness, as well as common sense, when managers and employees are in continuous touch with their companies at home, on the road and at work? The more they text, the more they believe that they are on the job, living in machine time and sharing a uniquely digital fear: *Prolonged breaks without contact jeopardize upward mobility.*[33] Is this now human nature? The new norm? Is de Zengotita correct in believing that nothing anymore can awaken us from our technological existence apart from accidents and necessities?

Accidents in physical place jar us back to reality. Increasingly this happens with distracted driving, rates of which have risen to epidemic proportions, with 16 percent of all fatal accidents in the United States attributed to such activities as texting while driving.[34] While the nature of those texts cannot be discerned, presumably a large proportion were work-related. Then there are necessities at home, such as putting down cell phones to warn toddlers about swimming pools. But even this is taking a toll. Emergency physician Robert Glattner, writing in *Forbes* about dangers of texting while parenting, asks, "It is possible that the increasing use of such technology may be partly responsible for the recent uptick in traumatic injuries noted in toddlers and children, which had previously been consistently declining over the past decade."[35] Accident and necessity now "constitute the real," de Zengotita writes, as distinct from virtual simulations of the world: "They are what comes from beyond."[36]

So who wins in the absence of work-life balance? Obviously, it is not the family. Some companies, especially digital ones that heavily surveil employees, are coming to understand that continuous stress may not serve the bottom line. Amazon was criticized nationally for its unreasonable, digital tactics to goad employees into exceeding corporate goals. In 2015, the *New York Times* reported such Amazon tactics as employees belittling each other's ideas, answering emails and texts at all hours, sending secret feedback to supervisors, and generally using technology to demean and advance careers simultaneously.[37] Perhaps the bad publicity from such reports prompted the company to try another approach. In 2016, Amazon piloted a new thirty-hour work week for technical teams, asking employees to work at 75 percent of their salaries from 10 a.m. to 2 p.m. Monday through Thursday with the remaining fourteen hours completed wherever and whenever they wished.[38] This is the flexibility that technology advocates once prophesied for everyone at the workplace, so that we could have more time to enjoy loved ones.

Mostly, the use of technology has had the opposite effect. For instance, children have their own screens so parents can squirrel more time to work while at home. One study of 2,403 respondents found that 58 percent of parents of children ages two to thirteen used technology to babysit their children so that they would not have to, seemingly so they could address work and other issues.[39] Fully 25 percent of couples believe their spouse or partner is distracted by cell phones when they are together.[40] The brave new world of the future must take into account the health and well-being of people, restoring a sense of belonging and balance to their lives and redefining notions of what constitutes success in the knowledge economy.

To do that, we need moral soundness and firmness of purpose. We might begin by accepting how consumer technology has changed our priorities. William J. Byron, SJ, PhD, past president of the Catholic University of America and the University of Scranton, discusses the value of integrity in the business world. Earlier in his career he was a professor of ethical practice in the McDonough School of Business at Georgetown University. One of his several books, *The Power of Principles: Ethics for the New Corporate Culture*, addresses concepts of the pre-Internet era, including such precepts as freedom, individualism, competition, loyalty, autonomy, self-reliance and power. "The structure was vertical; the style was command and control," he writes, noting that the "new horizontal structure" in the current digital era "stresses communication and cooperation."[41] Because of Internet, speed is omnipresent in the global economy and an integral aspect of technology's nature. The more we dwell within the information space, the more we must be able to cope with the electric specter of alacrity in just about every message and partnership. It is difficult to maintain a sense of purpose unless we focus on moral soundness as a requisite goal every day in every exchange and interaction, digital and interpersonal. "In the old days, rank and power shaped the organization," Byron writes. "Today 'mutual understanding and responsibility' are needed."[42] His observations are critical because of the likelihood of an employee changing jobs and professions multiple times in the course of his or her career. "[The] new corporate contract is now explicitly contingent—no job is forever,"[43] Byron states.

As such, we should reconsider what used to be dubbed the "American dream," the success model of the twentieth century. The dream emphasized personal opportunity rather than accountability in a lifelong one-track upwardly mobile career with salary, influence and power as indicators of achievement. Perhaps there is another ethic that future generations can explore, using technology to create greater awareness about environmental concerns and working with scientists and media to restore completeness in physical as well as virtual place. In 2006, Philip J. Vergragt, Visiting Scholar at MIT's Center for Technology, Policy, and Industrial Development, published an insightful paper titled "How Technology Could Contribute to a Sustainable World." In it he spoke about "persisting contradictions between a better life created and supported by technology for the wealthy few, and increasing environmental degradation and persistent poverty for the vast majority" and called for "a deeper exploration and understanding of the nature of technology and its relationship to society."[44] While use of technology for a sustainable future is beyond the scope of this book, the deeper exploration and nature of technology have been the focus of the first and new edition of *Interpersonal Divide.*

The time may have come to embrace a more inclusive dream, writes theorist Jeremy Rifkin in *The Empathic Civilization.* "Although the American dream is still the standard for many," he states, "it has lost some of its hegemony as young people turn their attention to tackling global climate change, restoring the health of the biosphere, protecting the earth's other species, maintaining safe communities, providing universal access to health care, ensuring a high-quality and affordable universal education, living a less materialistic and more experiential lifestyle, and creating communities rich in cultural diversity."[45] This is the new workplace morality, and it entails, in part, the ability to use technology to sustain interpersonal integrity in both the information and living spaces. Otherwise, as we shall see in the next chapter, the rise of robots and artificial intelligence might herald a darker future for humankind.

Journal Exercise: *"Digital Discretion"*

One of the keys to success in the digital workplace is to develop discretion. During tense times:

1. **Accept your gut instinct, but reject your first reaction, especially when using technology.**
   - Learn to feel your ethics as well as irritation. Perception is often distorted when you feel tempted, manipulated or deceived. Relearn physical feelings associated with your values so that when questionable situations arise, you can practice discretion.
   - Accepting your gut instinct is one thing, but acting on it quite another—a maxim that is especially important when using technology. Gut instincts can bring back memories of past experience and thus can cloud the immediate situation.
2. **Don't communicate before thinking.**
   - When you "speak what's on your mind" or "give a piece of your mind," using social media, you also risk betraying yourself, creating more problems and causing bleaker circumstances for yourself and others.
   - Don't telephone, text, email or fax until your emotions subside.
   - If angry, determine if you are reacting because someone is using an uncivil tone of voice or "trigger word" (topics, terms or phrases meant to evoke a reaction).

- ○ Remember to focus on the content, not the word or the tone, to help ease the pressure so you can articulate your viewpoint credibly.
3. **Do not spread rumors or gossip.**
   - Untruths posted online can come back to haunt you, undermining your career. Rumors and gossip destroy teamwork and collaboration and typically worsen, rather than resolve, problems.
4. **Solve problems without creating greater ones.**
   - Use appropriate but penetrating discourse, even when others are inappropriate or uncivil.
   - Do the necessary analysis before judging others' work or person.
   - Embrace a shared set of values that analyzes or honors all viewpoints—even ones with which you disagree—in the interest of diversity and community.

Those are basic tenets of discretion. They are particularly important when others criticize or disapprove of us or our work. Tenets of civility—solving problems without creating greater ones, using insight and information rather than hyperbole and mean-spiritedness—also require us to reflect on levels of offense-taking. What words, terms, topics or phrases may cause an emotional reaction on social media? Are colleagues more civil face to face than online? Does distraction, multitasking and interruption play a role in how employees respond to others using technology?

Evaluate how these questions might pertain to you by following the process below.

Part One: Personal Assessment

In a personal journal contemplate and respond to these questions:

- When I interact with others online, especially on social media, what are my "trigger words"—topics, terms or phrases that evoke a negative response in me and cloud my perception and discernment?
- If I decide to comment, am I taking the time to listen to the argument in question and think critically about the topic so that I represent my views or ideals as powerfully and appropriately as possible? Or do I regret what I have written or expressed? If so, was I distracted or interrupted while formulating my response?
- What are the issues or behaviors, again online or in a class or work environment, that *do not* concern me but nonetheless annoy (slight

irritation), anger (moderate irritation), or outrage me (substantial irritation)?

- What are the issues or behaviors of that *do* concern me and annoy me (slight irritation), anger (moderate irritation), or outrage me (substantial irritation)?
- Am I responding with similar or varying levels of offense-taking at slight, moderate or outrageous issues and behaviors that do not concern me or that do concern me? What does that say about my typical mode of response?

Part Two: Write About It

In your journal or blog, write about your personal assessment, noting any discoveries that might enhance your online character and interpersonal integrity.

CHAPTER SEVEN

Machine versus Moral Code

Look Dave, I can see you're really upset about this. I honestly think you ought to sit down calmly, take a stress pill, and think things over.
— HAL 9000 Computer in 2001: *A Space Odyssey,* after killing the human crew except for Astronaut Dave Bowman

....

Artificial Emotion versus Intelligence

In his Pulitzer Prize–finalist book, *The Shallows*, technology writer Nicholas Carr cites the film *2001: A Space Odyssey* as Dave methodically dismantles HAL's memory because the machine determined that a goal of the mission—ironically, life on another planet—took precedence over the lives of people on board. "Dave, my mind is going. I can feel it. I can feel it. My mind is going. There is no question about it. I can feel it. I can feel it. I can feel it. I'm afraid." Carr's point in his 2011 work was that his brain was being changed by machines. "I can feel it too," he writes. "Over the last few years I've had an uncomfortable sense that someone, or something, has been tinkering with my brain, remapping the neural circuitry, reprogramming the memory. . . . I'm not thinking the way I used to think."[1] He discusses how his concentration wanders when reading a book. He gets fidgety and looks for something else to do. Carr's reaction is ancient history, as far as technology is concerned, as it deals with an Information Age symptom debated since the turn of the century and featured in the first edition of *Interpersonal Divide*. This chapter focuses on something more pressing: machine intelligence and what it is doing not only to our brains but also to our values.

In a 2014 editorial, "Do We Need Asmiov's Laws?," the *MIT Technology Review* recites the fiction writer's three laws that govern the behavior of robots:

- *A robot may not injure a human being or, through inaction, allow a human being to come to harm.*
- *A robot must obey the orders given to it by human beings, except where such orders would conflict with the First Law.*
- *A robot must protect its own existence as long as such protection does not conflict with the First or Second Law.*

The piece points out that Asimov later added a fourth law: "A robot may not harm humanity, or, by inaction, allow humanity to come to harm."[2] Essentially, Asimov not only foresaw the dangers of machine intelligence against people; he foresaw it against all of humanity. The MIT editorial discusses the work of Ulrike Barthelmess and Ulrich Furbach who analyze the history of robots and note that there may be no need for Asimov's laws because the minds and bodies of humans inevitably will be augmented by artificial means and parts. Hence, we will have become cyborgs. The debate no longer will be "human versus machine." We will have merged.

The focus of the MIT editorial concerns machines and bodies rather than machines and morals. Once machines augment the mind, or distract it as Carr noted earlier, as we rely increasingly on devices in our pocket as well as on (and in some cases, *in*) our bodies, what then happens to ethical principles such as truth, fairness, generosity, compassion, responsibility, empathy, and so on? Before discussing that in depth, we need to understand what, exactly, constitutes machine or artificial intelligence and how, if at all, it differs from human intelligence.

A twentieth century mathematician, Alan Turing, devised a simple test. A person would ask questions through a computer terminal to an unseen person or computer and analyze responses. If the person thought responses from a computer came from a person, the machine was deemed intelligent. In the 1980s, another test challenged the Turing model. In her book *Life on the Screen*, technologist Sherry Turkle discusses the Searle test, named after the philosopher who conceived it, John Searle. In his thought experiment, a person who does not understand Chinese positions himself on one side of the wall with stacks of index cards that explain what to do when he receives slips of paper with Chinese questions on them. "The rules tell him such things as when you get the Chinese slip with 'the squiggle-squiggle' sign you should hand out the Chinese card with 'the squoggle-squoggle' sign,"[3] Turkle writes, noting that the person with the index cards becomes skilled in seemingly answering questions in Chinese. But does he understand it, really? Or is he merely acting out a program, like a machine would, that gives the appearance of understanding Chinese but does not understand an ideogram of it?

In *The Mind and the Machine: What It Means to Be Human and Why It Matters*, computer scientist Matthew Dickerson also analyzes the Searle test from the standpoint of a human on one side of the wall and a computer on the other. He acknowledges that the human mind in the experiment doesn't understand Chinese but is just very good at following instructions. The same can be said of the computer. As Dickerson attests, the real minds in such a Searle test are those who designed the computer program—people who really did know Chinese. "But the computer itself is not a mind."[4]

In a later book, *The Second Self*, Turkle addresses the Searle test from the perspective of artificial intelligence advocates. AI scientists purportedly reject the Searle view of a *thinking* entity, or human being, able to answer questions because he or she knows the answers (or really understands Chinese). Rather, those scientists affirm the earlier Turing test because "a perfect simulation of intelligence is intelligence,"[5] Turkle states. However, new research shows AI scientists have a long way to go before achieving that perfection. A 2016 report in the *MIT Technology Review*, titled, "Tougher Turing Test Exposes Chatbots' Stupidity," covered results of an artificial intelligence contest whose results were disclosed at an academic conference. To win a $25,000 prize, teams had to create a virtual assistant who could score at least 90 percent accuracy responding to sentences that had ambiguity, but that most humans would understand, as in "The city councilmen refused the demonstrators a permit because they feared violence." The best two entrants were correct 48 percent of the time compared to 45 percent by random choice.[6]

Alas, English is literally a shape-shifter language because you can change meaning merely by placing words and phrases in different positions in a sentence (assuming people speak only in sentences). Machines have difficulty with illogical concepts such as this. Add to that the various grammar and spelling rules, homophones, tropes, declensions, verb tenses, suffixes, prefixes, and so on—in addition to voice inflections—and you create a rhetorical Turing test that few machines will ever master completely. Look at the various shades of meaning in this example: "Stop drinking this instant! That tea is better for you," which can morph into "Stop that. Drinking this instant tea is better for you," which in turn can morph into "Stop drinking that. This better instant tea is for you." Understanding language, you can see why Apple had to correct its virtual assistant, Siri, when someone asked, "Siri, call me an ambulance," only to hear in response: "Okay, from now on I'll call you 'an ambulance.'"[7]

Humans, unlike current-day robots, also enjoy or suffer from *emotional* intelligence. In *The Glass Cage: Automation and Us*, Carr references the theory that humans have developed two types of knowledge: tacit and explicit. Tacit knowledge happens by experience—at home, school and work—and refers to acts we do without thinking, such as riding a bike. True, someone with that skill typically spends time demonstrating how to ride to another person eager to learn balance and coordination; but then, once mastered, that newer rider just hops on the bike and goes. The skill has become tacit. Take a moment and imagine there is a bike in front of you and you're writing an email to a friend precisely describing, as in an instruction manual, how to move, straddle, push, balance and pedal the contraption. Not so easy. Technical writing is an example of *explicit* knowledge. Do this, then this, and now this. Computers and robots are not very skilled in mastering tacit knowledge. They can feign that knowledge via a computer program, but there are limits. Will they be able to think as humans do and implicitly grasp methods to navigate the real world? According to Carr, "They don't, they haven't, and they won't. Artificial intelligence is not human intelligence. People are mindful; computers are mindless."[8]

Many AI scientists would disagree with that notion, explaining that computers need to learn by experience, just as humans do, to fathom tacit knowledge. After all, to truly learn how to ride a bike, a child has to learn language at home or school—just as the adult had to learn—to comprehend what is being demonstrated or said about balance and coordination. If it takes a village to raise a child, it may take a computer company—or several—to raise a robot so that it masters tacit and explicit knowledge, a stance, frankly, that misses the point about who, precisely, will be programming robots with this knowledge and whether those providers will even understand universal values—truth, fairness, generosity, compassion, responsibility, empathy—rather than proprietary profit. However, beyond that, some question the AI argument about humans requiring a village to learn while robots remain disenfranchised from that optimum. In *Shaping Technology/Building Society*, Wiebe E. Bijker and John Law observe that science and technology differ in that the former evolves "beyond the social world to a reality unfettered by human contingency" whereas the latter relies on that contingency.[9] They also add that technology (and by extension, robots) developed in its own kind of village as "part of a long chain of people, products, tools, machines, money, and so forth."[10] As such, we not only must question the stance of AI scientists who equate artificial with human intelligence, whether or not the machine is *mindful* of that knowledge; we also must probe the nature of *artificial emotion* programmed by microchips rather than neurons. At the core of this argument are mirror neurons in the human brain.

Mirror neurons allow us to feel certain emotions when we do particular things, like embracing a loved one on Valentine's Day. But they do something else as well. They produce the same emotion when we watch *others* embrace affectionately. Those neurons may be why humans feel empathy, comprehend others' intentions and intuit their states of mind.[11] Mirror neurons also are associated with mimicry, learning by observing others. Researchers devised a literal "rule of thumb," observing that people who felt the urge to move their own thumbs by watching others move theirs also were more adept at judging emotions in people. However, there was no correlation in the thumb test when it came to recognizing faces, something machines do by measurement of muscles and bone structure rather than by intuitive or emotional bond.[12]

Robots already have been designed to respond to human emotions. In 2015, Aldebaran Robotics marketed "Pepper," a machine that has been programmed to identify facial expression and then adapt or respond to it, engaging humans in what appears like emotional intelligence. The robotic goal is to interact with humans so they can respond to or accomplish certain tasks or, simply, to help people alleviate stress. The more people responded to Pepper, the stronger the bond between them and the machine. As *Slate* reported, "Robots don't actually feel emotions—yet—but they can appear as though they do. If a robot acts appropriately and convincingly emotional, does it matter that the emotions aren't genuine?"[13] On the upside, robots like Pepper programmed to respond to human emotions might teach autistic children how to improve interpersonal communication; on the downside, they can enable narcissism or addiction. Nevertheless, as Bijker and Law have observed, machines excel at grooming human beings via "social control." From video games that feature robots to the actual robots themselves, social control establishes norms and punishes those who transgress them by creating algorithms that oversee rules of conduct. In the past, that phenomenon was known as human culture. Increasingly, it has become machine culture. The point is, people exposed to machine culture may confuse its artificiality with reality, ironically because our mirror neurons too easily bestow empathy on nonliving entities. This outcome was not anticipated in both the Turing and Searle tests.

In her 2011 book, *Alone Together*, Turkle discusses yet another test devised by Freedom Baird, a graduate of the MIT Media Lab—the "upside-down test." This is the one that matters when we analyze the impact of machines on morals. The upside-down test poses an ethical dilemma. People are asked how they would respond to a biological gerbil being held upside down, causing distress, as well as to a Barbie doll and Furby, an animated toy that uses language to convey feelings (even though the toy has none, of course). The test asks a simple question: "How long can you hold the object upside down before your emotions make you turn it back?"[14] The test shows that almost everyone won't allow the gerbil to be held upside-down, as that would be animal cruelty. But what about Barbie and Furby? Both are inanimate objects, a combination of plastic and paint; shouldn't humans endowed with tacit and explicit knowledge treat both similarly, not caring if either were held upside-down? According to Turkle, "Baird's experiment assumes that a sociable robot makes new ethical demands. . . . Even those who do not think a Furby has a mind—and this, on a conscious level, includes most people—find themselves in a new place with an upside-down Furby that is whining and telling them it is scared. They feel themselves, often despite themselves, in a situation that calls for an ethical response."[15] As the upside-down test demonstrated, personal computing can become too personal because of our mirrored, empathic emotions.

Impersonal versus Personal Computing

To understand such an ethical response, we must examine our technological journey over the past few decades. The large mainframe ominous machines of the 1950s and 1960s were overseen mainly by governments as in a dystopian novel. The objective often was to surveil. As computing branched out into business in the 1970s and 1980s, the objective became to sell products and services, enhancing profits. Government machines still surveilled, but we were oblivious to that fact. We owned personal computers and, as the word "personal" suggests, modified them with software so that they appealed to us. In the decades that followed, computing surveilled as it sold and became mobile and more personal. The devices traveled with us in the form of cell phones, laptops, tablets and then smartphones. No longer were these machines ominously impersonal but ubiquitously "user-friendly," anticipating our desires often before we realized those desires ourselves, as algorithms recoded every moment and measured every move. In an age of big data, information about us—intensely personal information—floated into the computing cloud. The result is far more ominous than in an Orwellian novel because we remain oblivious to corporations and governments compiling or tracking our information generated via social media and countless other applications that analyze us continuously because we used our devices continuously. No longer did we fear computing—far from it; we transferred to our devices affection, even love.

John Markoff's aptly named book, *Machines of Loving Grace*, documents that journey, including what he calls the first electronic person— "Shakey," a six-foot wheeled robot. Shakey was designed to be mobile and autonomous, planning its own actions and performing certain tasks. The team that designed the robot pioneered today's computing technologies embedded in everything from cars to smartphones.[16] The thrust of Maroff's book focuses not on artificial intelligence but on the relationships that may develop between humans and robots. "Machines may eventually look, act, and feel as if they are human, but they are decidedly not,"[17] he writes. Nevertheless, robots that simulate emotions not only through speech but through explicitly learned facial expressions and conventional gestures will be eons more effective than Furby in evoking in us personal feelings. They may become adept at that via programming, intentionally prodding us to transfer to machines human attributes that they lack, establishing psychological bonds associated with ethical values.

Markoff uses the word "grace" in the title of his book. The philosophical concept of grace has been associated with the divine or divine justice, from Augustine of Hippo (AD 354–430) to Emmanuel Kant. Both defined the concept with religious terminology. Augustine wrote that God's grace is limitless and limited only by the perception of humankind; moreover, if people are to enjoy free will, they also inevitably must sin, so that divine grace is a necessary component of human existence and condition.[18] Kant takes that notion a step further, believing that our efforts to aright unethical acts are, in themselves, insufficient, by any repentance or good-deed-doing, thus requiring God's grace, or forgiveness.[19] However, grace can be a secular act, too.

One of the best illustrations of grace in Occidental culture comes from Victor Hugo's fictional masterpiece, *Les Miserables*. The scene is 1815 France. The hero, Jean Valjean, has just been released from a nineteen-year prison sentence for stealing bread for his starving sister and for numerous escape attempts. He is homeless, and no one will give him a night's respite because he is marked as a criminal. Finally he finds a place to stay in the local bishop's residence, where he is treated warmly and whence he leaves at night with the bishop's silver. The next day the police arrive with Valjean and the silver, asking the bishop if this was the thief who made off with the goods. The scene continues:

> "Ah! here you are! "the bishop exclaimed. "I am glad to see you. Well, but how is this? I gave you the candlesticks too, which are of silver like the rest, and for which you can certainly get two hundred francs. Why did you not carry them away with your forks and spoons?"
>
> Jean Valjean opened his eyes wide, and stared at the venerable Bishop with an expression which no human tongue can render any account of.[20]

True, the bishop is associated with religion and does ask Valjean to use the silver to redeem his life of crime; but the act, and the astonishment, are genuine displays of grace and the acknowledgment thereof, as occur in secular society—an experience most of us have only a few times in our lives, if we are fortunate. As for John Markoff's book, *Machines of Loving Grace*, we need only to ponder the irony of the above scene from *Les Miserables* and how it could not have occurred in the digital age when every act and motion are recorded by ubiquitous cameras and satellite positioning of our mobile devices. Moreover, the notion of "robotic grace" is oxymoronic—literally going through the motions without the intended transcendent effects.

Grace is a universal ethical principle, one of the most precious components of the human condition. Descartes cites it as the basis of his own moral code, enabling him to obey the laws and customs of his culture, being clear in his actions and intentions, overcoming immoral desires, and pursuing truth relentlessly.[21] His famous maxim, "I think, therefore I am," speaks to the mind-body dualism of the human condition.[22] That condition is intensely mystifying, typically taking a lifetime to realize because it ultimately addresses the question, "Why do I exist?" That is the question that pre-occupies us. It is part of the human condition, defined by two conflicting aspects of the psyche—consciousness (Descartes' "body"), which tells us that we come into the world alone and we leave it alone, and the conscience (Descartes' "mind"), which tells us what is in you is in me. The goal of ethics is to harmonize the polarities so that one informs the other. This is the basis of Descartes' principle of moral universalism, bestowing respect and equal status to all of humanity.[23] Humanity, in his view, was fallen, necessitating grace, which is not earned by observation nor achieved by good deed. It is bestowed by others in moments when all seems lost, when we erroneously perceive that we have done a great wrong and divulge that to a parent or partner, anticipating condemnation, only to have that person extend his or her arms and embrace us, knowing we merely fell prey to the human condition. Misery doesn't love company; it loves compassion, because of its healing and communal properties reminding us, as Schopenhauer maintained, that we are not separate individuals but unified in a fallen world.[24] The question before us is whether robots can provide that healing and sense of belonging when they assuredly lack conscience and only can simulate consciousness.

The mind-body Descartesian concept was addressed in the 1960s by Harvard philosopher Hilary Putnam. He theorized that the mind is the model for the machine. If humans have souls, he asserted, then it is impossible to discern whether machines have or lack them, an idea that came to be called "functionalism" and which influences AI scientists to this day.[25] Essentially, souls are beyond scientific proof, but the mind isn't; therefore, if a machine thinks like a mind, it too exists, and the comparison ends there. Later in life, Putnam disavowed the mind-machine analogy and rejected functionalism because the mind-body (or conscience-consciousness) paradigm was too complex to philosophically address the question: "What is the nature of mental states?"[26]

An enlightening *New Yorker* article titled "After the Fact: In the History of Truth, a New Chapter Begins," resurrects the Descartesian mind-body theory as fundamental to fact and, thus, truth, noting that the philosopher attempted to prove he does not exist but failed to do so because his mind, or conscience, insisted that he did.[27] The article prophesies what may become of humankind the more we trust machine intelligence and carry it with us in smartphones and later embed it within us as cyborgs, relying on artificial intelligence and simulated emotion to inform us factually about the world at large. In its exegesis on fact, the *New Yorker* article cites a thought experiment by philosopher Michael P. Lynch who describes a society where miniature smartphones are wired into brains. Lynch then depicts an environmental disaster that obliterates the earth's electronic communications grid so that human intelligence crashes, much like failing hard drives of computer networks. "There would be no immediate basis on which to establish the truth of a fact. No one would really know anything anymore, because no one would know how to know. I Google, therefore I am not."[28] That statement is at the core of this chapter. The more we embrace machine intelligence, augmenting the body, the greater the chance we can forfeit our minds (or conscience), along with ethical principles that have existed for millennia.

Utopia versus Dystopia

Intelligence may be fundamental to human evolution but not to the human condition. Because of mind-body interaction, Oxford University philosopher Nick Bostrom notes that human intelligence cannot be separated from consciousness and emotional awareness. He believes that machine intelligence will not develop those nuances but will be fixated on programmed goals, perhaps like HAL in *2001: A Space Odyssey*. A *New Yorker* essay—"The Doomsday Invention: Will Artificial Intelligence Bring Us Utopia or Destruction?"—features Bostrom's work at the Future of Humanity Institute. The article notes the likelihood of intensely goal-oriented artificial intelligence and asks, "How, then, to create a machine that respects the nuances of social cues? That adheres to ethical norms, even at the expense of its goals? No one has a coherent solution. It is hard enough to reliably inculcate such behavior in people."[29]

Another scientist to touch on that topic is David Gelernter, a pioneer in artificial intelligence. Gelernter believes the AI movement is dangerously off-track because a key question has yet to be answered, or even asked: "Does it matter that your brain is part of your body?"[30] Gelernter, like Schopenhauer, believes aesthetics as might be found in the fine arts represent a unifying trait of the human condition. Many models of aesthetic intelligence exist, including Bach and Shakespeare, whose works researchers largely still cannot fathom from a scientific perspective, Gelernter states; thus, AI scientists are blundering forward in ignorance when they speak about replacing that distinctly human aesthetic trait.[31] In a 2016 article in *Time Magazine*, Gelernter calls intelligent machines "zombies." They may resemble and even behave in some manner like human beings but they would lack our chromatic scale of emotions, not knowing fear of heights, heartthrobs of love, or exhaustion of grief. "Perhaps most important, the computer won't feel the existential dread or weird magnetism of death."[32]

In *The Glass Cage: Automation and Us*, Nicholas Carr notes that brain and body are interwoven in an intricate web of thought and intention. "The biological processes that constitute 'thinking' emerge not just from neural computations in the skull but from the actions and sensory perceptions of the entire body."[33] Students of social anthropology know that human bonds are established via empathy, the ability to analyze how our actions impact others and how those actions result in a kaleidoscope of emotions and responses in others. We witness those emotions and responses, feel or intuit them via empathy, and develop a moral compass because of them on the micro level. On the macro level, social mores evolve from these encounters and shape culture. Out of these actions, responses, emotions and mores, laws evolve that attempt to guide human experience—not only in science and logic but in aesthetics from arts to religion. These are the components that constitute culture, and while technology is part of that culture, throughout history it has not been so dominant a force as to rewrite our fundamental moral beliefs.

Through the ages, people had the luxury of time to contemplate the good and bad of their complex interactions with others. Moreover, unlike machines, they had the capability to question actions, emotions, laws and culture and to improve upon them through moral codes. Andrew Keen has documented how this capacity is eroding in the age of big data. "I update, therefore I am,"[34] he writes, tweeting his location and thoughts as they occur while disclosing his location and invading his own privacy. This experience prompted him to re-evaluate philosopher Jeremy Bentham and his utilitarian school about happiness, reduced to a mathematical equation by subtracting pain from pleasure and using that to gauge the quality of existence, much like a machine might, or artificial intelligence. Keen bases some of his argument on the work of Nicholas Carr, previously discussed, in asserting that happiness is not an algorithm of our appetites and desires but must be analyzed morally. To do so, we must embrace "the unquantifiable right to be let alone by society—a right which enables us, as human beings, to remain true to ourselves."[35] Machines, especially ones programmed for profit through incessant interaction with others, are undermining human autonomy, Keen argues. He asks us to take time now to reflect on the consequences of machines dominating and dictating human interactions to a degree that our entire culture is subsumed by artificial intelligence and asks, "[W]hat are the human implications of this great rewriting?"[36]

Philosopher and computer scientist Jaron Lanier has spent much of the past decade addressing that question. He investigates "why" artificial intelligence matters in an age of mindless, corporate big-data correlation that omits causation in algorithms. "When developers of digital technologies design a program that requires you to interact with a computer as if it were a person, they ask you to accept in some corner of your brain that you might also be conceived of as a program."[37] By transforming you from the Descartesian mind-body model to the more Benthamian model of algorithmic happiness, machines can alter culture powerfully because they bestow seemingly legitimate points of view on the wired mob. And when you ask humans to deemphasize "individual humans in the design of society, and when you ask people not to be people,"[38] AI scientists effectively can consider human culture as "one big information system."[39] The repercussions of that exist not only in the present but increasingly in what may be our dystopian future.

No one is arguing that human culture has evolved outside of technological invention. That is the fall-back response of AI scientists who point to social upheavals that shaped culture and communication in past epochs. The advent of the printing press radically shaped culture with printed and later mass-distributed material that challenged the oral culture by insisting on proof, or fact. The telegraph transcended location, as did the telephone, and film, and later broadcasting enhanced mass distribution with sound and sight. Internet did the same by combining all those technologies and distributing them to global audiences, changing culture in such places as the former Soviet Union and in current-day Africa and Asia. But the question in an age of big data and artificial intelligence is whether those dual aspects of technoculture have so saturated society—primarily by shaping how the world is viewed and experienced via human-computer interaction—that our moral code is corrupted by machine code.

This argument has a utopian versus dystopian history, as do most debates about technology's social impact. In her 1988 book, *When Old Technologies Were New*, Carolyn Marvin documents two dominant debates about the topic as it pertains to electricity. One promised unlimited prosperity—"electricity was a gift of God, created for His purposes and conferring obligations on men to further those purposes by using it wisely."[40] Lack of respect for technology and how it alters human discourse could summon the devil, literally. The other argument took a decidedly secular view, questioning whether people "were fundamentally different from electrical machines after all."[41] Out of this argument, embraced to this day by many AI scientists, came the notion that machines one day would be superior to humans, "destined to drive man from his fragile position in the cosmos, rather than to help him establish its security."[42] This alludes to the "technological singularity" by computer scientist Ray Kurzweil who prophesied that machines will meld with our brains, enhancing them by vastly greater capacity and speed for thought and action.[43]

American psychiatrist and author Robert Jay Lifton has been concerned about this phenomenon since the early 1990s. He wrote about human resilience in a fragmented, technological age, making the point that we are social animals who require genuine relationships with others. The more interpersonal those interactions, the more genuine. Human beings thrive, he wrote, when those interactions are "expressed in intimate bonds with other people, in the life cycle, in larger links to history and nature, and in enduring ethical and religious principles."[44] He stated that those bonds have the potential to disintegrate when they are complicated by uncertainty about social roles and rules, "resulting in ad-hoc attitudes and behaviors."[45] That is precisely what Nicholas Carr and Jaron Lanier have been forecasting in their works questioning big data and artificial intelligence.

Langdon Winner, Thomas Phelan Chair of Humanities and Social Sciences in the Department of Science and Technology Studies at Rensselaer Polytechnic Institute, also has been concerned about this phenomenon since the 1980s. In his book, *The Whale and the Reactor: A Search for Limits in an Age of High Technology*, he wrote about society turning to machines to address all manner of pressing human needs and warned against those machines bringing about "debilitating uncertainties or even breakdown unless continually replenished with up-to-the-minute electronic information about their internal states and operating environments."[46] For many, he wrote, the ability of machines to process information in record time, addressing social problems, would appear to be a marriage made in technological heaven. "But is it sensible to transfer this model, as many evidently wish, to all parts of human life? Must activities, experiences, ideas, and ways of knowing that take a longer time to bear fruit adapt to the speedy processes of digitized information processing? Must education, the arts, politics, sports, home life, and all other forms of social practice be transformed to accommodate it?"[47] Winner's book, published in 1986, prophesied the current situation playing itself out in our techno-society. He foresaw machines taking an ever-greater role in shaping culture, creating new institutions and patterns of behavior and, as a consequence, assuming vast powers on agenda-setting, or social priorities establishing mores, or shared beliefs. The more advocates called the innovations "revolutionary," he stated, the more society needed time to reflect upon them with debate about consequences for common life. However, he predicted, few would be prepared to own up to that fact because profit would be programmed into the machines at the expense of moral enrichment, forecasting that the computer revolution "will eventually be guided by new wonders in artificial intelligence" and its present course "influenced by something much more familiar: the absent mind."[48]

According to Yochai Benkler in his 2006 book, aptly titled *The Wealth of Networks*, people who wish to enhance culture are "being systematically curtailed in order to secure the economic returns demanded by the manufacturers of the industrial information economy."[49] However, his call to renegotiate terms of freedom, justice and productivity has been largely ignored because, frankly, doing so was not in the interest of technology entrepreneurs reaping profits in the age of the machine—a global machine programmed for corporations rather than the social good. Now the question before us, he writes, is whether society realizes it has a choice—"a choice about how to be free, equal, productive human beings under a new set of technological and economic conditions."[50]

The pro-technology utopian arguments as used in the past will be affixed to the AI debate. Communication theorist James Carey believed the typical futurist ethos as embraced by "coteries of advertisers and engineers, corporate and foundation executives, and government personnel" identifies "electronics and cybernetics, computers and information with a new birth of community, decentralization, ecological balance, and social harmony."[51] These advocates hold a common set of ideas, conveying that technology is the great benefactor of humankind. This is true especially with what Carey calls the "high-tech glamor firms" in robotics and genetic engineering that promise "a cornucopia of jobs, markets, and products, to rejuvenate ailing economies, to refund declining universities, to reemploy the unemployed" and "even to eliminate, through user friendliness, the last alienation and estrangement between people and their machines."[52] Carey then documents that technological innovation throughout history "has been biased toward the recentralization of power in computer centers and energy grids," including the Pentagon and utility companies.[53]

Technological utopias, as envisioned by AI scientists, rarely happen because of corporate, political and economic interests. Advocates suffer from myopic, or "tunnel," vision. We see what we want to see regardless of what media history tells us, as noted in the research of Carey and others cited in this and previous chapters of *Interpersonal Divide in the Age of the Machine*. Human values may be shaped by technology, but technology is controlled by corporate and government dictates that continuously reconfigure the environment that beneficial technology was supposed to transform.[54] "If there is an overarching theme to modern technology it is that it defies the expectations of its creators, taking on functions and roles that were never intended at creation,"[55] writes technology researcher Evgeny Morozov in *The Net Delusion: The Dark Side of Internet Freedom*. Consequently, media ethicists have advocated for a new technological code that takes Morozov's observations into account, encouraging people to "look beyond the individual benefits to identify the broader social implications of emerging technologies."[56]

Authentic versus Artificial Community

To assess the implications of technology from an ethical perspective, people need to reintroduce themselves into their actual rather than technological communities. This was the focus of the first edition of *Interpersonal Divide* and remains the same in this edition. The word "community" has been appropriated by technologists who speak of the AI community, the Facebook community, the Twitter community, the gaming community, the eBay community, and every narrow subcategory of online dating and consumer communities, from Amazon to Zumba sites. The Institute of Electrical and Electronics Engineers even speaks about "the big-data community," a catchall phrase that not only includes engineers but marketers and minions working collaboratively for global technology profit-centers such as Microsoft, Google and Apple. All of these technological communities are linked, literally, through interconnected server and cloud subsystems across the hemisphere. The problem here, according to researchers J. D. R. and Veronica de Raadt, is that such a system is highly unstable because of proprietary and other technical complications and thus remains unreliable when it comes to moral (rather than multimodal) systems.[57] In this regard the only community that matters includes the place where social interaction occurs "between family, friendship, and common interests, the work of service to the community and the wise management of the resources available to sustain this work."[58] This requires an ethic that shares knowledge of the humanities and frees people from ignorance, reintroducing them into their hometowns and turning knowledge into work, "for life is a task."[59]

In some sense, Nicholas Carr shares belief in that statement when it comes to morals and machines. If we put our faith in machines rather than in our mind-body selves, humanity "may end up eroding one of the foundations of culture itself: our desire to understand the world."[60] In essence, ethics cannot be based on predictive algorithms that excel at correlations but are "indifferent to the underlying causes of traits and phenomena. Yet it's the deciphering of causation—the meticulous untangling of how and why things work the way they do—that extends the reach of human understanding and ultimately gives meaning to our search for knowledge."[61] At some point, Carr argues, artificial intelligence and automation reach a critical mass and begin to alter social norms and morality. "People see themselves and their relations to others in a different light, and they adjust their sense of personal agency and responsibility to account for technology's expanding role. They behave differently too."[62]

In the 1990s, MIT technologist Sherry Turkle was researching that phenomenon in *Life on the Screen*, questioning whether we were living in the computer screen rather than merely observing it. In the decades that followed, we carry, wear and embed our screens. Turkle foresaw this, too:

As human beings become increasingly intertwined with the technology and with each other via the technology, old distinctions between what is specifically human and specifically technological become more complex. . . . Our new technologically enmeshed relationships oblige us to ask to what extent we ourselves have become cyborgs, transgressive mixtures of biology, technology, and code. The traditional distance between people and machines has become harder to maintain.[63]

People since early civilization adhered to one code, the moral one. We developed values often centered on community that helped us survive each other, other species, diseases and natural disasters. The human experience gave rise to ethical principles based on space, culture and time. In 1997, researchers investigated ethical values from thirteen countries with diverse cultures, citing such similarities as freedom, the inviolability of life, justice or fairness, pleasure or happiness, responsibility or duty, integrity or dignity, and trust.[64] Philosopher Christina Hoff Sommers substitutes the term "moral absolutes" for universal principles that warn against mistreatment, humiliation or torment of living beings, including animals, and that promote truth, promise-keeping, respect and generosity.[65] Philosopher Clifford G. Christians condensed the aforementioned principles even further in what he called the protonorm advancing principles of human dignity, truth and nonviolence.[66] No matter which of the so-called universal principles you believe in or embrace, each requires more than correlation; each requires turning knowledge into work, for life is a task; understanding and giving meaning to knowledge; and distinguishing what is uniquely human rather than machine-like.

"What does it mean to be human? More specifically, what does it mean to have a human *mind*? Is the human mind, in all its complexity, just a very complex machine?"[67] asks Dickerson in *The Mind and the Machine*. These are the questions that should engage us in vigorous debate. Until recently, Dickerson observes, most people who asked these questions would have responded that human beings are more than biochemical machines, that throughout history, they were "understood to be *spiritual* as well as *bodily* beings."[68] His use of the word "spiritual" traces back to the Descartesian model of "conscience," an inner knowing of right and wrong in the universal sense according to principles cited earlier and grounded in time, place and culture. However, AI advocates dismiss such dualism because their intent is to reduce human minds to automata so that programs can be written to replace brains with code.[69] That is what scares some futurists because once brains are replaced, why do humans need bodies at all? "Our bodies, after all, are susceptible to disease and aging, with all their many limitations," Dickerson writes. "If our brains are just computers, we might as well carry out our entire existence as part of a computer, where virtual reality could eliminate those limitations."[70]

In *Our Final Invention: Artificial Intelligence and the End of the Human Era*, James Barrat discusses "the plausibility of losing control of our future to machines that won't necessarily hate us, but that will develop unexpected behaviors as they attain high levels of the most unpredictable and powerful force in the universe, levels that we cannot ourselves reach, and behaviors that probably won't be compatible with our survival."[71] Barrat argues that the potential ramifications of artificial intelligence need to be discussed and prepared for because it presents an existential threat to humankind. Anticipating criticism from such a stance, he states as a defense that it is irrational to believe that machines would love people when they are one thousand times more intelligent. "On its own an AI will not feel gratitude for the gift of being created unless gratitude is in its programing," he asserts. "Machines are amoral, and it is dangerous to assume otherwise."[72] Ultimately, Barrat challenges us to decide what is worth preserving about humans that machines cannot replicate. He cites ethical values such as valor and righteousness and aesthetic emotions evoked by the fine arts. Although his outlook about the future impact of AI on society may be bleak, or even extreme, Barrat's goal is the same as this chapter. "The necessity of specifying our values is one of the ways in which the quest for general artificial intelligence compels us to get to know ourselves better."[73]

To glimpse the future of AI, so as to debate it, we must consider four possibilities (paraphrased below) as proposed in the 1990s by Sir Roger Penrose, an English mathematical physicist known for his contributions to general relativity:

- **Option A, strong artificial intelligence (or functionalism).** If scientists program the right computations, awareness will result.
- **Option B, computational simulation.** Machines will be able to simulate awareness but will lack it, along the lines of the Searle test referenced earlier.

- **Option C, physical consciousness (preferred by Penrose).** Humans possess awareness located in the brain that cannot be replicated by computation.
- **Option D, inexplicable consciousness.** Human awareness cannot be explained in scientific terms.[74]

In the end, the debate about AI concerns ethics and the human condition. One of the foremost authorities on that topic is political theorist Hannah Arendt in her book, *The Human Condition.* "The task and potential greatness of mortals lie in their ability to produce things— works and deeds and words—which would deserve to be and, at least to a degree, are at home in everlastingness, so that through them mortals could find their place in a cosmos where everything is immortal except themselves,"[75] Arendt writes. She believed that the debate about technology has led humanity astray because of promises by its creators about the great benefits that will ensue with its adoption, easing rigors of life on this planet. "The question therefore is not so much whether we are the masters or slaves of our machines, but whether machines still serve the world and its things, or if, on the contrary, they and the automatic motion of their processes have begun to rule and even destroy world and things."[76]

Social theorist Jeremy Rifkin notes that technology since the Enlightenment advanced "the radical idea of human progress, a wholly new vision of earthly immortality for Western civilization to rally around."[77] Belief in progress eventually overtook belief in religious redemption and eternal life. "To believe in progress is to believe in a future that is always improving, enlarging, and above all, enduring. There is no end to progress. It is unstoppable, relentless." As such, Rifkin argues, technology has become a secular messiah in a material world that increasingly lacks ethical principles that define the human condition, chiefly empathy, or the ability to feel what others do even though an event or emotion is happening to others and not us. The issue before us concerning artificial intelligence is whether we will empathize with machines that do not return the favor and implications of that transference on humanity itself. That topic, alas, is beyond the scope of this edition of *Interpersonal Divide*. A future one will measure how long-standing ethical values and moral principles—shaped in linear time, geographic place and social culture—are faring as big data and intelligent machines claim ever-expanding roles in the human experience.

Journal Exercise: *"Artificial versus Human Acumen"*

Sir Roger Penrose, an English mathematical physicist known for his contributions to general relativity, proposed four possible outcomes for the future of artificial intelligence:

- **Option A, strong artificial intelligence (or functionalism).** If scientists program the right computations, awareness will result.
- **Option B, computational simulation.** Machines will be able to simulate awareness but will lack it, along the lines of the Searle test referenced earlier.
- **Option C, physical consciousness (preferred by Penrose).** Humans possess awareness located in the brain that cannot be replicated by computation.
- **Option D, inexplicable consciousness.** Human awareness cannot be explained in scientific terms.

Review your journal exercises from each of the preceding chapters. After doing so, compose a journal entry for this chapter, asking yourself questions posed by computer scientist Matthew Dickerson:

- *What does it mean to be human?*
- *What does it mean to have a human mind?*
- *Is the human mind, in all its complexity, just a very complex machine?*

Upon concluding your journal entry, review the four options above by Penrose and write a paper or blog post advocating for one of those views.

NOTES
....

Preface

1 Pippa Norris, *Digital Divide: Civic Engagement, Information Poverty, and the Internet Worldwide* (Cambridge, UK: Cambridge University Press, 2001), 4.
2 Stephen Ohlemacher, "Consumption of Media Rising for Americans," Associated Press, Dec. 15, 2006; http://future-of-journalism.blogspot.com/2006/12/research-americans-spend-more-time on.html.
3 "Americans Spend More Time on Media Than Anything Else," Media Giraffe Project, Dec. 15, 2006; http://future-of-journalism.blogspot.com/2006/12/research-americans-spend-more-time-on.html.
4 "Mobile Technology Continues to Steal Share of US Adults' Daily Time Spent With Media," *eMarketer*, April 22, 2014; http://www.emarketer.com/Article/Mobile-Continues-Steal-Share-of-US-Adults-Daily-Time-Spent-with-Media/1010782.
5 Jeffrey M. Jones, "In US, 40% Get Less Than Recommended Sleep," Gallup, Dec. 19, 2013; http://www.gallup.com/poll/166553/less-recommended-amount-sleep.aspx.
6 C. George Benello. "Technology and Power: Technique as a Mode of Understanding Modernity" in *Jacques Ellul: Interpretive Essays*, ed. Clifford G. Christians and Jay M. Van Hook (Urbana, IL: University of Illinois Press, 1981), 92.
7 Jaron Lanier, *Who Owns the Future?* (New York: Simon and Schuster, 2013), 19.
8 Giles Slade, "Alone Together: Interviewing Sherry Turkle and Michael Bugeja," *Huffington Post*, Jan. 20, 2011; http://www.huffingtonpost.com/giles-slade/alone-together-reviewing-_b_803256.html.
9 Manuel Castells, *The Power of Identity* (Oxford, UK: Blackwell, 1997), 2.
10 James Howard Kunstler, *Home from Nowhere: Remaking Our Everyday World for the 21st Century* (New York: Simon & Schuster, 1996), 299–300.

[11] Roger Silverstone, *Media and Morality: On the Rise of the Mediapolis* (Malden, MA: Polity, 2007), 5.

[12] David E. Nye, *Technology Matters* (Boston: MIT Press, 2007), 7.

[13] Nye, *Technology Matters*, 9.

[14] Robert D. Putnam, *Bowling Alone: The Collapse and Revival of American Community* (New York: Simon & Schuster, 2000), 26.

[15] Ben H. Bagdikian, *The Information Machines* (New York: Harper & Row, 1971), 1.

[16] Marie Winn, *The Plug-in Drug: Television, Computers, and Family Life* (New York: Penguin, 2002), x.

[17] Lelia Green, *Communication, Technology and Society* (Thousand Oaks, CA: Sage, 2002), 150.

[18] See Michael Bugeja and Daniela Dimitrova, *Vanishing Act: The Erosion of Online Footnotes and Implications for Scholarship in the Digital Age* (Litwin Books, 2010), for in-depth information about this phenomenon.

[19] Fair use involves the purpose and character of the use (commercial vs. educational), the nature of the copyrighted work (published vs. unpublished), the amount and substantiality of the portion used in relation to the copyrighted work as a whole (qualitative vs. quantitative), and the effect of the use on the potential market or value of the copyrighted work (adverse vs. no effect). See *The First Amendment Handbook*, 6th edition, (Arlington, VA: The Reporters Committee for Freedom of the Press, 2003), 91.

[20] Laura J. Gurak, *Cyberliteracy: Navigating the Internet with Awareness* (New Haven, CT: Yale University Press, 2001), 162.

[21] Gurak, *Cyberliteracy*, 162.

Introduction

[1] Parker J. Palmer, *The Company of Strangers* (New York: Crossroad, 1981), 39.

[2] Palmer, *Company of Strangers*, 48.

[3] Kate Losse, "The Return of the Selfie," *New Yorker*, May 31, 2013; http://www.newyorker.com/tech/elements/the-return-of-the-selfie.

[4] See "Polish Tourist Tries to Snap 'Selfie,' Falls Off Bridge and Dies," *Daily News*, Nov. 5, 2014; http://www.nydailynews.com/news/world/polish-tourist-dies-snapping-selfie-article-1.2000250; Trevor Mogg, "Man Shoots Himself in the Head Taking Gun Selfie," *Digital Trends*, Aug. 5, 2014; http://www.digitaltrends.com/mobile/man-shoots-himself-in-head-while-posing-for-gun-selfie/; Kyle Wiggers, "Forest Service Says No More Bear Selfies—Unless It's with Smokey," *Digital Trends*, Oct. 29, 2014; http://www.digitaltrends.com/photography/forest-service-says-no-more-bear-selfies/.

[5] Palmer, *Company of Strangers*, 21.

[6] According to Robert D. Putnam, author of *Bowling Alone: The Collapse and Revival of American Community* (New York: Simon & Schuster, 2000), civic virtue is closely related to "social capital," whose vitality requires a dense

to sell products and services, enhancing profits. Government machines still surveilled, but we were oblivious to that fact. We owned personal computers and, as the word "personal" suggests, modified them with software so that they appealed to us. In the decades that followed, computing surveilled as it sold and became mobile and more personal. The devices traveled with us in the form of cell phones, laptops, tablets and then smartphones. No longer were these machines ominously impersonal but ubiquitously "user-friendly," anticipating our desires often before we realized those desires ourselves, as algorithms recoded every moment and measured every move. In an age of big data, information about us—intensely personal information—floated into the computing cloud. The result is far more ominous than in an Orwellian novel because we remain oblivious to corporations and governments compiling or tracking our information generated via social media and countless other applications that analyze us continuously because we used our devices continuously. No longer did we fear computing—far from it; we transferred to our devices affection, even love.

John Markoff's aptly named book, *Machines of Loving Grace*, documents that journey, including what he calls the first electronic person— "Shakey," a six-foot wheeled robot. Shakey was designed to be mobile and autonomous, planning its own actions and performing certain tasks. The team that designed the robot pioneered today's computing technologies embedded in everything from cars to smartphones.[16] The thrust of Maroff's book focuses not on artificial intelligence but on the relationships that may develop between humans and robots. "Machines may eventually look, act, and feel as if they are human, but they are decidedly not,"[17] he writes. Nevertheless, robots that simulate emotions not only through speech but through explicitly learned facial expressions and conventional gestures will be eons more effective than Furby in evoking in us personal feelings. They may become adept at that via programming, intentionally prodding us to transfer to machines human attributes that they lack, establishing psychological bonds associated with ethical values.

Markoff uses the word "grace" in the title of his book. The philosophical concept of grace has been associated with the divine or divine justice, from Augustine of Hippo (AD 354–430) to Emmanuel Kant. Both defined the concept with religious terminology. Augustine wrote that God's grace is limitless and limited only by the perception of humankind; moreover, if people are to enjoy free will, they also inevitably must sin, so that divine grace is a necessary component of human existence and condition.[18] Kant takes that notion a step further, believing that our efforts to aright unethical acts are, in themselves, insufficient, by any repentance or good-deed-doing, thus requiring God's grace, or forgiveness.[19] However, grace can be a secular act, too.

One of the best illustrations of grace in Occidental culture comes from Victor Hugo's fictional masterpiece, *Les Miserables*. The scene is 1815 France. The hero, Jean Valjean, has just been released from a nineteen-year prison sentence for stealing bread for his starving sister and for numerous escape attempts. He is homeless, and no one will give him a night's respite because he is marked as a criminal. Finally he finds a place to stay in the local bishop's residence, where he is treated warmly and whence he leaves at night with the bishop's silver. The next day the police arrive with Valjean and the silver, asking the bishop if this was the thief who made off with the goods. The scene continues:

> "Ah! here you are! "the bishop exclaimed. "I am glad to see you. Well, but how is this? I gave you the candlesticks too, which are of silver like the rest, and for which you can certainly get two hundred francs. Why did you not carry them away with your forks and spoons?"
>
> Jean Valjean opened his eyes wide, and stared at the venerable Bishop with an expression which no human tongue can render any account of.[20]

True, the bishop is associated with religion and does ask Valjean to use the silver to redeem his life of crime; but the act, and the astonishment, are genuine displays of grace and the acknowledgment thereof, as occur in secular society—an experience most of us have only a few times in our lives, if we are fortunate. As for John Markoff's book, *Machines of Loving Grace*, we need only to ponder the irony of the above scene from *Les Miserables* and how it could not have occurred in the digital age when every act and motion are recorded by ubiquitous cameras and satellite positioning of our mobile devices. Moreover, the notion of "robotic grace" is oxymoronic—literally going through the motions without the intended transcendent effects.

Grace is a universal ethical principle, one of the most precious components of the human condition. Descartes cites it as the basis of his own moral code, enabling him to obey the laws and customs of his culture, being clear in his actions and intentions, overcoming immoral desires, and pursuing truth relentlessly.[21] His famous maxim, "I think,

network of reciprocal social relations: "A society of many virtuous but isolated
individuals is not necessarily rich in social capital," 19.

[7] Putnam, *Bowling Alone*, 19.

[8] Everette E. Dennis and John C. Merrill, *Media Debates: Great Issues for the Digital Age* (Belmont, CA: Wadsworth, 2002), 34.

[9] Mike Isaac, "Google to Acquire Motorola Mobility," *WIRED*, Aug. 15, 2011; https://www.wired.com/2011/08/google-motorola-acquisition/.

[10] Graham Spencer, "Mapping The Entertainment Ecosystems of Apple, Microsoft, Google & Amazon," *MacStories*, Oct. 16, 2012; http://www.macstories.nct/stories/mapping-the-entertainment-ecosystems-of-apple-microsoft-google-amazon/.

[11] Avery Cardinal Dulles, "Challenges to Moral and Cultural Renewal," Notre Dame Center for Ethics and Culture; http://web.archive.org/web/20060426104810/http://ethicscenter.nd.edu/events/5yrdulles.shtml

[12] Dennis and Merrill, *Media Debates*, 34.

[13] Howard Rheingold, *The Virtual Community* (Cambridge, MA: MIT, 2000), 305.

[14] Rheingold, *Virtual Community*, 305.

[15] Albert R. Hunt, "Real Grievances Fuel Occupy Wall Street Protests," *Bloomberg News*, Oct. 24, 2011; https://www.bloomberg.com/view/articles/2011-10-23/real-grievances-fuel-occupy-wall-street-protests-albert-r-hunt.

[16] Howard Rheingold, *Smart Mobs: The Next Social Revolution* (New York: Perseus, 2002), xxi.

[17] Hunt, "Real Grievances."

[18] Doug Gross, "Upstart Unthink Wants to Become the New Anti-Facebook," CNN, Oct. 26, 2011; http://www.cnn.com/2011/10/26/tech/social-media/unthink-social-network/index.html?hpt=hp_c2.

[19] Nicholas Negroponte, *Being Digital* (New York: Knopf, 1995), 164.

[20] Negroponte, *Being Digital*, 165.

[21] Sean Silverthorne, "Understanding Users of Social Networks," *Harvard Business School Newsletter*, Sept. 14, 2009; http://hbswk.hbs.edu/item/6156.html.

[22] See *Dating Sites Reviews*, "Current Online Dating and Dating Services Facts & Statistics," http://www.datingsitesreviews.com/staticpages/index.php?page=online-dating-industry-facts-statistics.

[23] Aaron Smith and Monica Anderson, "5 Facts About Online Dating," Pew Research Center, Feb. 13, 2014; http://www.pewresearch.org/fact-tank/2014/02/13/5-facts-about-online-dating/

[24] Dietrich Bonhoeffer, *Writings Selected*, ed. by Robert Coles (Maryknoll, NY: Orbis, 1998), 100.

[25] Bonhoeffer, *Writings*, 118.

[26] Jerald J. Block, M.D., "Issues for DSM-V: Internet Addiction," *American Journal of Psychiatry*, March 2008; http://ajp.psychiatryonline.org/cgi/content/full/165/3/306.

[27] "Parent Debate: Do iPads and Smartphones Really Teach Toddlers to Read?," *Good Morning America*, Oct. 25, 2011; http://abcnews.go.com/Technology/parent-debate-ipads-smartphones-teach-toddlers-read/story?id=13626381.

[28] Timothy Noah, "Baby Einstein's Quasi-Recall," *Slate*, Oct. 25, 2009; http://www.slate.com/articles/news_and_politics/chatterbox/2009/10/baby_einsteins_quasirecall.html.

[29] Andres Oppenheimer, "Here's What Really Happened in 2010," *Miami Herald*, Dec. 26, 2010; http://www2.ljworld.com/news/2010/dec/29/key-news-americans-may-have-missed/.

[30] US Department of Education, "Secretary Arne Duncan's Remarks at OECD's Release of the Program for International Student Assessment (PISA) 2009 Results," Dec. 7, 2010; https://www.ed.gov/news/speeches/secretary-arne-duncans-remarks-oecds-release-program-international-student-assessment-

[31] Michael Bugeja, "Global Village Idiots," *The Ecologist*, Nov. 1, 2006; http://www.theecologist.org/blogs_and_comments/commentators/other_comments/269530/global_village_idiots.html.

[32] Mark Hachman, "What's the Worst Way to Get Fired: Email, Text, or Tweet?" *PC Magazine*, Sept. 8, 2011; http://www.pcmag.com/slideshow/story/287430/what-s-the-worst-way-to-get-fired-email-text-or-tweet#fbid=bN4AoL6_Ixx.

[33] Susanne Kim, "Hello, You're Fired: Yahoo CEO and Breakup Etiquette," ABC News, Sept. 7, 2011; http://abcnews.go.com/blogs/business/2011/09/hello-youre-fired-yahoo-ceo-and-breakup-etiquette/.

[34] Associated Press, "You've Got Mail, About Your Layoff," Aug. 31, 2006; http://www.chron.com/business/article/You-ve-got-mail-about-your-layoff-1902185.php.

[35] Theodore Roszak, *The Cult of Information* (Berkeley, Calif.: University of California Press, 1994), pp.xiii–xiv.

[36] Paschal Preston, *Reshaping Communications*, (Thousand Oaks, CA: Sage, 2001), 243.

[37] Tami Luhby, "Fed: Student Loans Soar 275% Over Past Decade," *CNN Money*, May 31, 2012; http://money.cnn.com/2012/05/31/news/economy/fed-student-loans/index.htm?iid=EL

[38] Jacques Ellul, "The Autonomy of the Technological Phenomenon," in *Philosophy of Technology: The Technological Condition*, ed. Robert C. Scharff and V. Dusek (Oxford, MA: Blackwell, 2003), 346.

[39] Interview with Lee Rainie, the director of Internet, science, and technology research at the Pew Research Center, conducted 8:05 a.m. in Ames, Iowa, Dec. 12, 2014.

[40] Andrew Feenberg, *Questioning Technology* (London: Routledge, 1999) 220.

Chapter One

[1] "The Global Warming Hoax of 1874," the Museum of Hoaxes; http://hoaxes.org/archive/permalink/the_global_warming_hoax_of_1874

[2] Tom Standage, *The Victorian Internet* (New York: Berkeley, 1999) 106.

3 "The History of Wire Fraud," Laws.com; http://fraud.laws.com/wire-fraud/wire-fraud.

4 Charles E. Shepard, *Forgiven* (New York: Atlantic Monthly Press, 1989), 68.

5 Viktor Mayer-Schönberger and Kenneth Cukier, *Big Data: A Revolution That Will Transform How We Live, Work, and Think* (New York: First Mariner, 2014), 12.

6 Mayer-Schönberger and Cukier, 12.

7 Marshall McLuhan and Quentin Fiore, *The Medium is the Massage: An Inventory of Effects* (San Francisco: HardWired, 1996 reprint), 67.

8 James Carey, "The Roots of Modern Media Analysis," in *James Carey: A Critical Reader*, ed. Eve Stryker Munson and Catherine A. Warren (Minneapolis: University of Minnesota Press, 1997), 39.

9 Carey, "The Roots of Modern Media Analysis," 51.

10 Theodore Roszak, *The Cult of Information* (Berkeley, CA: University of California Press, 1994), 149.

11 Roszak, *The Cult of Information*, 161.

12 Phillip Marchand, *Marshall McLuhan: The Medium and the Messenger* (New York: Ticknor & Fields, 1989), 57.

13 David F. Noble, *The Religion of Technology: The Divinity of Man and the Spirit of Invention* (New York: Penguin, 1997), 49.

14 Dinesh D'Souza, *The Virtue of Prosperity: Finding Values in an Age of Techno-Affluence* (New York: Free Press, 2000), 178.

15 D'Souza, *The Virtue of Prosperity*, 125.

16 Personal interview conducted May 3, 2000.

17 Neil Postman, *Technopoly: The Surrender of Culture to Technology* (New York: Vintage, 1993), 14–15.

18 Postman, *Technopoly*, 15

19 Carey, "The Roots of Modern Media Analysis," 41.

20 Martin Heidegger, "Art and Space" in *The Heidegger Reader*, ed. Guenter Figal, (Bloomington, IN: Indiana University Press, 2007), 308.

21 Marshall McLuhan, *Understanding Media: The Extensions of Man* (Cambridge, MA: MIT Press, 2002), 57.

22 McLuhan, *Understanding Media*, 61.

23 "The Playboy Interview: Marshall McLuhan," *Playboy Magazine*, March 1969, 61.

24 James Howard Kunstler, *Home from Nowhere: Remaking Our Everyday World for the 21st Century* (New York: Simon & Schuster, 1996), 23.

25 James W. Chesebro and Dale A. Bertelsen note that the first oral language was formulated some 7,000 years ago and the first principles of phonetic alphabetic some 4,000 years ago in the Sinai and Canaan in 2000 B.C. See *Analyzing Media: Communication Technologies as Symbolic and Cognitive Systems* (New York: Guilford Press, 1996), 14.

26 Chesebro and Bertelsen, *Analyzing Media*, 17.

27 Andrew Feenberg, *Questioning Technology* (London: Routledge, 1999), 183–84.

28 Manuel Castells, *The Power of Identity* (Oxford, UK: Blackwell, 1997), 243.

29 Standage, *The Victorian Internet*, 211.

[30] *The Associated Press—The First 50 Years*; http://www.ap.org/anniversary/nhistory/first.html.

[31] *The Associated Press—The First 50 Years.*

[32] Donald Shaw, Bradley J. Hamm, and Diana L. Knott, "Technological Change, Agenda Challenge, and Social Melding: Mass Media Studies and the Four Ages of Place, Class, Mass and Space," *Journalism Studies* 1, no. 1 (2000), 57.

[33] Martin Lindstrom, *Clicks, Bricks & Brands* (London: Kogan Page, 2001), 5.

[34] "Westclox History"; http://clockhistory.com/westclox/company/ads/benseries/bigintro.htm.

[35] Juliet B. Schor, *The Overworked American: The Unexpected Decline of Leisure* (New York: Basic Books, 1992), 119.

[36] Ben H. Bagdikian, *The Information Machines* (New York: Harper & Row, 1971), 161

[37] David Mercer, *The Telephone: The Life Story of a Technology* (Westport, Conn.: Greenwood Press, 2006), p. 41.

[38] "Captain Midnight: The Premiums," Old Time Radio; http://www.otr.com/cm_premiums.html.

[39] *The Philadelphia Inquirer*, Nov. 1, 1938, as cited in *Popular Writing in America*, Donald McQuade and Robert Atwan (New York: Oxford University Press), 127.

[40] E. L. Boyer, *Ready To Learn: A Mandate For The Nation* (Princeton, NJ: Carnegie Foundation for the Advancement of Teaching), 79.

[41] "Children and Television Violence," by John Murray, *Kansas Journal of Law & Public Policy* 4, no. 3 (1995): 7; http://www.nisbett.com/child-ent/children_and_television_violence.htm.

[42] Robert D. Putnam, *Bowling Alone: The Collapse and Revival of American Community* (New York: Simon & Schuster, 2000), 221.

[43] Pippa Norris, *Digital Divide: Civic Engagement, Information Poverty, and the Internet Worldwide* (Cambridge, UK: Cambridge University Press, 2001), 28

[44] Bagdikian, *The Information Machines*, 229.

[45] "Highlights of 1960," The Boomer Initiative; http://www.babyboomers.com/years/1960.htm.

[46] David Halberstam, *The Fifties* (New York: Villard Books, 1993), 195.

[47] For a retrospective of Congressional hearings on the impact of television, see "The Forgotten Battles: Congressional Hearings on Television Violence in the 1950s," by Keisha L. Hoerrner, *Web Journal of Mass Communication Research* 2, no. 3 (June 1999); http://www.scripps.ohiou.edu/wjmcr/vol02/2-3a-B.htm.

[48] "The Effects of Media Violence on Children," Jane Ledingham, C. Anne Ledingham, and John E. Richardson, http://www.indiana.edu/~cspc/media.htm.

[49] Herbert J. Gans, *Popular Culture & High Culture: An Analysis and Evaluation of Taste* (New York: Basic Books, 1999), 49.

[50] Putnam, *Bowling Alone*, 62.

[51] John Seabrook, *Nobrow: The Culture of Marketing, the Marketing of Culture* (New York: Vintage, 2001), 152–53.

52 Castells, *The Power of Identity*, 356.

53 Adam Candeub, "Media Ownership Regulation, the First Amendment, and Democracy's Future," *UC Davis Law Review* (April 2007): 1552.

54 Hodding Carter III, Ohio University speech, May 3, 2002.

55 Ibid.

56 James Madison to W. T. Barry, Aug. 4, 1822; http://press-pubs.uchicago.edu/founders/documents/v1ch18s35.html.

57 Horace Greeley, "The Prayer of the Twenty Millions," *New York Tribune*, Aug. 19, 1862; http://www.civilwarhome.com/lincolngreeley.html.

58 *Citizens United v. Federal Election Commission* (2010); https://supreme.justia.com/cases/federal/us/558/08-205/opinion.html.

59 *Burwell v. Hobby Lobby Stores, Inc.* (2014); http://www.supremecourt.gov/opinions/13pdf/13-354_olp1.pdf.

60 Brian Honeyman, "How Being More Self-Aware Can Help Your Brand Succeed on Social Media," Nov. 18, 2014, Entreprenuer.com; http://www.entreprencur.com/article/239816

Chapter Two

1 Clifford G. Christians, "Universalism versus Communitarianism in Media Ethics," in *The Handbook of Global Communication and Media Ethics*, ed. Robert S. Fortner and Mark Fackler (Malden, MA: Wiley-Blackwell, 2011), 393.

2 Don Ihde, *Philosophy of Technology* (New York: Paragon, 1993), 47.

3 David E. Nye, *Technology Matters* (Cambridge, MA: MIT Press, 2007), 12.

4 Nye, *Technology Matters*, 12.

5 Kristin Shrader-Frechette, "Technology," in *Encyclopedia of Ethics*, ed. by Lawrence C. Becker and Charlotte B. Becker (New York: Routledge, 2001), 1687–90.

6 Shrader-Frechette, "Technology." pp. 1687–1690.

7 See Renato I. Rosaldo, "Defining Culture" in *Redefining Culture: Perspectives Across the Disciplines*, ed. John R. Baldwin (Mahwah, NJ: Lawrence Erlbaum, 2008), ix–xiv.

8 A. L. Kroeber and C. Kluckhohn, *Culture: A Critical Review of Concepts and Definitions* (Cambridge, MA: Peabody Museum, 1952) 81.

9 Douglass Kellner, "Cultural Studies," in *Encyclopedia of Ethics*, ed. Lawrence C. Becker and Charlotte B. Becker (New York: Routledge, 2001), 365.

10 Kellner, "Cultural Studies," 365.

11 See "Free Press: Government Licensing of Journalists and Organizations," International Information Program, U.S. State Department, Dec. 3, 2010; http://iipdigital.usembassy.gov/st/english/publication/2010/11/20101123145400nayr0.7504171.html#axzz24BnPe9jJ.

12 Sandra L. Borden and Peggy Bowers, "Ethical Tensions in News Making: What Journalism Has in Common with Other Professions," in *The Handbook of Mass Media Ethics*, ed. Lee Wilkins and Clifford G. Christians (New York: Routledge, 2009), 354.

13 The author of this book asked the question on June 19, 2006, as a member of the audience attending the event.

14 Sandra H. Dickson, "The 'Golden Mean' in Journalism," *Journal of Mass Media Ethics* (1988): 33.

15 Claude-Jean Bertrand, *Media Ethics & Accountability Systems* (New Brunswick, NJ: Transaction Publishers, 2000), 29.

16 Bertrand, *Media Ethics*, 29.

17 Adam Liptak, "Supreme Court Rejects F.C.C. Fines for Indecency," *New York Times*, June 21, 2012; http://www.nytimes.com/2012/06/22/business/media/justices-reject-indecency-fines-on-narrow-grounds.html

18 Deni Elliott, "Universal Values and Moral Development Theories," in *Communication Ethics and Universal Values*, ed. Clifford G. Christians and Michael Traber (Thousand Oaks, CA: Sage, 1997), 68.

19 Elliott, "Universal Values," 71.

20 Christina Hoff Sommers, "Teaching the Virtues," *Chicago Tribune*, Sept. 12, 1993, 16.

21 Clifford Christians, "The Ethics of Being in a Communications Context," in *Communication Ethics and Universal Values*, ed. Christians & Michael Traber (Thousand Oaks, CA: Sage Publications, 1997), 12–13.

22 Shakuntala Roa and Ting Lee Seow, "Globalizing Media Ethics? An Assessment of Universal Ethics Among International Political Journalists," *Journal of Mass Media Ethics: Exploring Questions of Media Morality* (2001): 101.

23 Roa and Seow, "Globalizing Media Ethics?," 118.

24 Tina Laitila, "Journalistic Codes of Ethics in Europe," *European Journal of Communication* (December 1995): 527.

25 The McBride Commission Report, "Many Voices, One World, 1980," 241; http://unesdoc.unesco.org/images/0004/000400/040066eb.pdf

26 See Andrew Calabrese, "The MacBride Report." Global Policy Forum; http://www.globalpolicy.org/component/content/article/157/27023.html.

27 The McBride Commission Report, 30–31.

28 James Curran and Myung Jin-Park, "Introduction," in *De-Westernizing Media Studies*, ed. Curran and Jin-Park (New York: Routledge, 2005), 5.

29 Curran and Park, "Introduction," 8.

30 Nicholas Negroponte, *Being Digital* (New York: Knopf, 1995), 165.

31 Negroponte, *Being Digital*, 167.

32 Negroponte, *Being Digital*, 72–73.

33 Christians, "The Ethics of Being in a Communications Context," 7.

34 Thomas de Zengotita, *Mediated: How the Media Shapes Your World and the Way You Live in It* (New York: Bloomsbury, 2005), 195.

35 De Zengotita, *Mediated*, 213.

36 Sherry Turkle, *Life on the Screen: Identity in the Age of the Internet* (New York: Simon and Schuster, 1995), 178.

37 Turkle, *Life on the Screen*, 178.

38 Turkle, *Life on the Screen*, 236.

[39] See updated statistics at "What is Distracted Driving," distraction.gov; https://www.distraction.gov/stats-research-laws/facts-and-statistics.html

[40] Linda Wertheimer, "Yellowstone Tourists Warned to Watch for Bears," *National Public Radio*, June 18, 2012; http://www.npr.org/2012/06/18/155263982/yellowstone-tourists-warned-to-watch-for-bears.

[41] Nancy K. Baym, *Personal Connections in the Digital Age* (Cambridge, UK: Polity Press, 2011), 3.

[42] Scott Atran, "The Fourth Phase of *Homo sapiens*" in *Is the Internet Changing the Way You Think?*, ed. John Brockman (New York, Harper Perennial, 2011), 159.

[43] Ihde, *Philosophy of Technology*, 58.

[44] Yochai Benkler, *The Wealth of Networks: How Social Production Transforms Markets and Freedom* (New Haven, CT: Yale University Press, 2006), 3.

[45] Nicholas Carr, *The Shallows: What the Internet Is Doing to Our Brains* (New York: W.W. Norton & Company, 2011), 88–89.

[46] Allan Bird and Michael J. Stevens, "Globalization and the Role of the Global Corporation," *Journal of International Management* 22, no. 4 (2016): 395; http://www.sciencedirect.com/science/article/pii/S1075425303000577.

[47] Erik Qualman, *Socialnomics* (New York: Wiley, 2011), xv.

[48] Qualman, *Socialnomics*, xxii.

[49] De Zengotita, *Mediated*, 15.

[50] See Jozef Keulartz, Maartje Schermer, Michiel Korthals, and Tsjalling Swierstra, "Ethics in Technological Culture: A Programmatic Proposal for a Pragmatist Approach," *Science Technology Human Values* (January 2004): 3–29.

[51] Sherry Turkle, *Alone Together: Why We Expect More from Technology and Less from Each Other* (New York: Basic Books, 2011), 16.

[52] Turkle, *Alone Together*, 17.

[53] Jacques Ellul, "Autonomy of the Technological Phenomenon," in *Philosophy of Technology: The Technological Condition*, ed. Robert Scharff and V. Dusek (Malden, MA: Blackwell, 2003), 386.

[54] Baym, *Personal Connections*, 4.

[55] Carr, *The Shallows*, 3.

[56] Carr, *The Shallows*, 47.

[57] William Powers, *Hamlet's BlackBerry: A Practical Philosophy for Building a Good Life in the Digital Age* (New York: Harper, 2010), 18.

[58] Turkle, *Alone Together*, 155–56.

[59] Jaron Lanier, *You Are Not a Gadget: A Manifesto* (New York: Vintage, 2011), 107.

[60] Clifford G. Christians, "Media Ethics in Education," Report, US Media Summit II, Middle Tennessee State University, Dec. 1, 2007, 41.

[61] Ihde, *Philosophy of Technology*, 33.

[62] Lanier, *You Are Not a Gadget*, 3–4.

[63] Lanier, *You Are Not a Gadget*, 4.

[64] Ihde, *Philosophy of Technology*, 60.

65 Kevin Kelly, *What Technology Wants: Technology Is a Living Force That Can Expand Our Individual Potential—If We Listen to What It Wants* (New York: Penguin, 2010), 358.

66 Kelly, *What Technology Wants*, 358.

67 Email interview with author, June 20, 2012.

68 Powers, *Hamlet's BlackBerry*, 35.

69 Powers, *Hamlet's BlackBerry*, 35.

70 Ihde, *Philosophy of Technology*, 128.

71 Lanier, *You Are Not a Gadget*, 45.

72 Lanier, *You Are Not a Gadget*, 27.

73 Eric Fischl and April Gornik, "Replacing Experience with Facsimile," in *Is the Internet Changing the Way You Think?* ed. John Brockman (New York: Harper Perennial, 2011), 145.

74 De Zengotita, *Mediated*, 13–14.

75 Cass R. Sunstein, *Republic.com 2.0* (Princeton, NJ: Princeton University Press, 2007), 3.

76 Sunstein, *Republic.com 2.0*, 5–6.

77 Clifford G. Christians, "Philosophical Issues in Media Convergence," *Communications and Convergence Review* 1, no. 1 (2009): 4.

Chapter Three

1 "Creating Nodes for People, Places and Other Entities," NVivo9 Help; http://help-nv9-en.qsrinternational.com/nv9_help.htm#concepts/about_nodes.htm.

2 Isaac Asimov, "Feminine Intuition," in *The Bicentennial Man* (New York: Ballantine Books, 1976), 12–13.

3 Asimov, "Feminine Intuition," 18.

4 Asimov, "Feminine Intuition," 19–20.

5 Liam McCarty, *Data and Power* (Palo Alto, CA: Five Star Publishing, 2015), 47.

6 McCarty, *Data and Power*, 81.

7 Ashkan Soltani, Andrea Peterson, and Barton Gellman, "NSA Uses Google Cookies to Pinpoint Targets for Hacking," *Washington Post*, Dec. 10, 2013; https://www.washingtonpost.com/news/the-switch/wp/2013/12/10/nsa-uses-google-cookies-to-pinpoint-targets-for-hacking/

8 Bruce Schneier, *Data and Goliath* (New York: Norton, 2015), 47.

9 Evan Perez, "NSA: Some Used Spying Power to Snoop On Lovers," CNN, Sept. 27, 2013; http://www.cnn.com/2013/09/27/politics/nsa-snooping/

10 Jaron Lanier, *Who Owns the Future?* (New York: Simon and Schuster, 2013), xxiii.

11 Esther Dyson, "The Pulse of the Planet," in *The Human Face of Big Data*, ed. Rick Smolan and Jennifer Erwitt (Sausalito, CA: Against All Odds Productions, 2012), 102.

12 Dyson, "The Pulse of the Planet," 102.

13 Dyson, "The Pulse of the Planet," 102.

[14] Mathew Ingram, "Print Readership Is Still Plummeting, and Paywalls Aren't Really Helping," *Fortune*, June 1, 2015; http://fortune.com/2015/06/01/print-readership-paywalls/

[15] Steve Lohr, "The Age of Big Data," *New York Times*, February 11, 2012; http://www.nytimes.com/2012/02/12/sunday-review/big-datas-impact-in-the world.html?_r=0.

[16] Peter Drucker, "The Next Society," *Economist*, Nov. 1, 2001; http://www.economist.com/node/770819.

[17] Margie K. Shields and Richard E. Behrman, "Children and Computer Technology: Analysis and Recommendations," *The Future of Children* 10, no. 2 (Fall/Winter 2000); https://www.princeton.edu/futureofchildren/publications/journals/article/index.xml?journalid=45&articleid=200&sectionid=1303.

[18] See National Center for Education Statistics' scores from the Program for International Student Assessment, 2000–2012; https://nces.ed.gov/surveys/pisa/pisa2012/pisa2012highlights_6.asp.

[19] Daniel Caro and Jenny Lenkeit, "Which Countries Punch Above Their Weight in Educational Rankings?" *The Conversation*, Nov. 23, 2015; https://theconversation.com/which-countries-punch-above-their-weight-in-education rankings-49698.

[20] Susan Johnson Taylor, "Should You Trust Apps That Access Your Credit Card Information?" *US News and World Report*, Sept. 1, 2015; http://money.usnews.com/money/personal-finance/articles/2015/09/01/should-you-trust-apps-that-access-your-credit-card information.

[21] Bart Baesens, *Analytics in a Big Data World* (New York: Wiley, 2014), 130.

[22] Baesens, *Analytics*, 129

[23] Rachel Zupek, "15 Jobs That Pay $70,000 Per Year," CNN, Aug. 27, 2008; http://www.cnn.com/2008/LIVING/worklife/08/27/cb.jobs.that.pay.70k/index.html?iref=hpmostpop.

[24] McCarty, *Data and Power*, 195.

[25] Arvind Sathi, *Big Data Analytics* (Boise, ID: MC Press, 2012), 13.

[26] Sathi, *Big Data Analytics*, 41.

[27] Sathi, *Big Data Analytics*, 49.

[28] Schneier, *Data and Goliath*, 2.

[29] Schneier, *Data and Goliath*, 31.

[30] Schneier, *Data and Goliath*, 2.

[31] Elias Aboujaoude, *Virtually You: The Dangerous Powers of the E-Personality* (New York: W. W. Norton, 2011), 245.

[32] Aboujaoude, *Virtually You*, 250–51.

[33] Lanier, *Who Owns the Future?*, 15.

[34] See Yochai Benkler, *The Wealth of Networks: How Social Production Transforms Markets and Freedom* (New Haven, Yale University Press, 2006) pp. 27–28.

[35] Lanier, *Who Owns the Future?*, 16.

36 Katie Moisse, "Google Flu Trends Found to Be Nearly on Par with CDC Surveillance Data," *Scientific American*, March 17, 2010; http://www .scientificamerican.com/article/google-flu-trends-on-par-with-cdc-data/.

37 See Viktor Mayer-Schoenberger and Kenneth Cukier, *Big Data: a Revolution That Will Transform How We Live, Work, and Think* (New York: First Mariner, 2014), 2.

38 Schneier, *Data and Goliath*, 92.

39 Jarvis DeBerry, "Anti-Shoplifting App Is Excuse to Surveil Black People," nolo .com, Oct. 14, 2015; http://www.nola.com/opinions/index.ssf/2015/10/anti -shoplifting_app.html.

40 No author, "Stores Using App to Detect Shoplifters Accused of Racial Profiling," *CBS News*, Oct. 15, 2015; http://www.cbsnews.com/news/mobile-app -groupme-used-to-counter-shoplifting-in-georgetown-accused-of-racial -profiling/.

41 Lydia O'Connor, "Ghetto Tracker" App That Helps Rich Avoid Poor Is as Bad as It Sounds," *Huffington Post*, Sept. 4, 2013; http://www.huffingtonpost .com/2013/09/04/ghetto-tracker_n_3869051.html.

42 Mayer-Schönberger and Cukier, *Big Data*, 158.

43 Viktor Frankl, *Man's Search For Meaning* (Boston: Beacon Press, 2006), 56. Frankl's philosophical reference here emanates from the philosophy of Friedrich Nietzsche.

44 Annie Dillard, "Total Eclipse," in *Teaching a Stone to Talk* (New York: Harper Perennial, 2013), 24.

45 Mayer-Schönberger and Cukier, *Big Data*, 6–7.

46 Lanier, *Who Owns the Future?*, 115.

47 Bill Schmarzo, *Big Data: Understanding How Data Powers Big Business* (New York: Wiley, 2013), ix.

48 Schmarzo, *Big Data*, 37.

49 Schmarzo, *Big Data*, 55.

50 Chris Anderson, "The End of Theory: The Data Deluge Makes the Scientific Method Obsolete," *WIRED*, June 23, 2008; http://www.wired.com/2008/06/ pb-theory/.

51 Anderson, "The End of Theory."

52 Mayer-Schönberger and Cukier, *Big Data*, 71.

53 Patrick Maines, "Opinion Journalism vs. Objective News Reporting," The Media Institute, Aug. 15, 2013; http://www.mediacompolicy.org/2013/08/articles/ media-criticism/opinion-journalism-vs-objective-news-reporting/.

54 Stephen J. A. Ward, "In Your Face: The Ethics of Opinion Journalism," Center for Journalism Ethics, Feb. 8, 2011; https://ethics.journalism.wisc.edu/2011/02/08/ in-your-face-the-ethics-of-opinion-journalism-2/.

55 Simon Head, *Mindless: Why Smarter Machines Are Making Dumber Humans* (New York: Basic Books, 2014), 21.

56 Wiebe E. Bijker, *Of Bicycles, Bakelites, and Bulbs: Toward a Theory of Sociotechnical Change* (Cambridge, MA: MIT Press, 1997), 80–81.

[57] John Markoff, *Machines of Loving Grace* (New York: HarperCollins, 2015), xvii.

[58] Dan Gardner, "An Ocean of Data," in *The Human Face of Big Data*, ed. Rick Smolan and Jennifer Erwitt (Sausalito, CA: Against All Odds Productions 2012), 14.

[59] Gardner, "An Ocean of Data," 16.

[60] David C. Menninger, "Marx in the Social Thought of Jacques Ellul," in *Jacques Ellul: Interpretive Essays* ed. Clifford G. Christians and Jay M. Van Hook (Urbana, IL: University of Illinois Press, 1981), 25–26.

[61] C. George Benello, "Technology and Power: Technique as a Mode of Understanding Modernity" in *Jacques Ellul: Interpretive Essays* ed. by Clifford G. Christians and Jay M. Van Hook (Urbana, IL: University of Illinois Press, 1981), 93.

[62] Clifford G. Christians, "Ellul on Solution: An Alternative but No Prophecy," in Christians, *Jacques Ellul*, 148–49.

[63] Langdon Winner, *The Whale and the Reactor: A Search for Limits in an Age of High Technology* (Chicago: University of Chicago Press, 1986), 117.

Chapter Four

[1] Sherry Turkle, *Alone Together: Why We Expect More from Technology and Less from Each Other* (New York: Basic Books, 2011), 279

[2] Turkle, *Alone Together*, 280.

[3] Nicholas Carr, *The Big Switch: Rewiring the World, from Edison to Google* (New York: W. W. Norton, 2013), 69.

[4] Carr, *The Big Switch*, 139–40.

[5] Richard M. and Linda Eyre, *The Turning: Why the State of the Family Matters, and What the World Can Do About It* (Sangar, CA: Familius LCC, 2014), 102.

[6] Amanda Lenhart, "Teens, Technology, and Friendships," Pew Research Center report, Aug. 6, 2005; http://www.pewinternet.org/2015/08/06/teens-technology-and-friendships/.

[7] Vicky Rideout, "Common Sense Census: Media Use by Tweens and Teens," San Francisco: Common Sense, 2015), 15; https://www.commonsensemedia.org/research/the-common-sense-census-media-use-by-tweens-and-teens.

[8] Andrew Perrin, "Social Media Usage: 2005–2015," Pew Research Center report, Oct. 8, 2015; http://www.pewinternet.org/2015/10/08/social-networking-usage-2005-2015/.

[9] Alan B. Albarran, ed., *The Social Media Industries* (New York: Routledge, 2013), 106.

[10] David Volpi, "Heavy Technology Use Linked to Fatigue, Stress, and Depression in Young Adults," *Huffington Post*, Aug. 2, 2012; http://www.huffingtonpost.com/david-volpi-md-pc-facs/technology-depression_b_1723625.html.

[11] Cris Rowan, "The Impact of Technology on the Developing Child," *Huffington Post*, July 29, 2013; http://www.huffingtonpost.com/cris-rowan/technology-children-negative-impact_b_3343245.html.

[12] Rowan, "The Impact of Technology."

[13] Natalie Angier, "The Changing American Family," *New York Times*, Nov. 25, 2013; http://www.nytimes.com/2013/11/26/health/families.html?.

[14] Belinda Luscombe, "How the American Family Has Changed Dramatically," *Time*, Dec. 9, 2014; http://time.com/3624827/how-the-american-family -has-changed-dramatically/.

[15] Pew Research Center, "The American Family Today," Social Demographic Trends Project, Dec. 17, 2015; http://www.pewsocialtrends.org/2015/12/17/ 1-the-american-family-today/.

[16] Megan Burton, "One, Big, Happy TV Family," *Odyssey*, Oct. 26, 2015; https:// www.theodysseyonline.com/how-american-tv-families-change-over-years.

[17] John K. Rosemond, *A Family of Value* (Kansas City, MO: Andrews and McMeel, 1995), 55, 67.

[18] Alex Williams, "Quality Time, Redefined," *New York Times*, April 30, 2011; http://www.nytimes.com/2011/05/01/fashion/01FAMILY.html.

[19] Charles Ess, *Digital Media Ethics*, 2nd edition (Malden, MA: Polity, 2014), 54.

[20] Elias Aboujaoude, *Virtually You: The Dangerous Powers of the E-Personality* (New York: W. W. Norton, 2011), 11.

[21] Aboujaoude, *Virtually You*, 57.

[22] Aboujaoude, *Virtually You*, 155.

[23] Jim Goad, "10 Grimly Ironic Texting-While-Driving Car Crashes," thoughtcatalog.com, June 10, 2014; http://thoughtcatalog.com/ jim-goad/2014/06/10-grimly-ironic-texting-while-driving-car-crashes/.

[24] Danah Boyd, *It's Complicated: The Social Lives of Networked Teens* (Yale University Press, New Haven: 2014), 13.

[25] Boyd, *It's Complicated*, 145.

[26] Boyd, *It's Complicated*, 63.

[27] Geoff Colvin, *Humans Are Underrated: What High Achievers Know That Brilliant Machines Never Will* (New York: Penguin, 2015), 26.

[28] Colvin, *Humans Are Underrated*, 83.

[29] Matts Larsson, Nancy L. Pederson, and Hakon Stattin, "Associations Between Iris Characteristics and Personality in Adulthood," *Biological Psychology* 75, no. 2 (2007), Department of Behavioral, Social and Legal Sciences, Center for Developmental Research, Örebro University, 701 82 Örebro, Sweden; http:// www.ncbi.nlm.nih.gov/pubmed/17343974.

[30] Bruce Drushel and Kathleen M. German, *The Ethics of Emerging Media: Information, Social Norms, and New Media Technology* (New York: Continuum, 2011), 3.

[31] Jessica Leader, "This Is How Technology Is Affecting Your Relationship," *Huffington Post*, Oct. 17, 2014; http://www.huffingtonpost.com/2014/10/17/ technology-changing-relationships_n_5884042.html.

[32] Slater and Gordon law firm, "The New Marriage Minefield," April 30, 2015; http://www.slatergordon.co.uk/media-centre/press-releases/2015/04/ social-media-is-the-new-marriage-minefield/.

[33] HG Legal Resources, "Facebook Has Become a Leading Cause in Divorce Cases," HG.org; https://www.hg.org/article.asp?id=27803.

[34] Latest statistics can be found at Statisticbrain.com: http://www.statisticbrain .com/online-dating-statistics/.

[35] Aaron Smith, "15% of American Adults Have Used Online Dating Sites or Mobile Dating Apps," Pew Research Center, Feb. 11, 2016; http://www .pewinternet.org/2016/02/11/15-percent-of-american-adults-have-used -online-dating-sites-or-mobile-dating-apps/.

[36] Samantha Murphy Kelly, "How Online Dating Sites Use Data to Find 'The One,'" Mashable.com, Oct. 14, 2013; http://mashable.com/2013/09/14/ online-dating-data/.

[37] Michael Bugeja and Daniela Dimitrova, *Vanishing Act: The Erosion of Online Footnotes and Implications for Scholarship in the Digital Age* (Duluth, Minn.: Litwin Books, 2010) pp. 11–18.

[38] Trevor Moog, "Dominos Has Built a Self-Driving Robot for Pizza Deliveries," digitaltrends.com, March 18, 2016; http://www.digitaltrends.com/cool-tech/ dominos-pizza-delivery-robot/.

[39] Daniela Newman, "4 Technology Trends Disrupting How We Communicate," *Forbes*, May 13, 2014; http://www.forbes.com/sites/ danielnewman/2014/05/13/4-technology-trends-disrupting-how-we -communicate/.

[40] Brandon T. McDaniel and Sarah M. Coyne, "'Technoference': The Interference of Technology in Couple Relationships and Implications for Women's Personal and Relational Well-Being," *Psychology of Popular Media Culture* 5, no. 1 (January 2016), 85–98.

[41] Rosalyn Carson-DeWitt, MD, "What is Internet Addiction?," *Everyday Health*, Oct. 10, 2015; http://www.everydayhealth.com/internet-addiction/guide/.

[42] Catherine Steiner-Adair, "Are You Addicted to the Internet?," CNN, July 17, 2015; http://www.cnn.com/2015/07/17/opinions/ steiner-adair-internet-addiction/.

[43] Matt Richtel, "Does Technology Affect Happiness?" *New York Times* blog, Jan. 25, 2012; http://bits.blogs.nytimes.com/2012/01/25/ does-technology-affect-happiness/?_r=0.

[44] Lindsay Holmes, "All the Ways Technology Can Influence Our Happiness," *Huffington Post*, April 17, 2015; http://www.huffingtonpost.com/2015/04/17/ happiness-and-technology_n_7081254.html.

[45] Jonathan Haidt, *The Happiness Hypothesis* (New York: Basic Books, 2006), 87.

[46] Haidt, *The Happiness Hypothesis*, 86.

[47] David Cohen, "Hostility on the Rise on Facebook and Other Social Media," *Adweek*, April 10, 2013; http://www.adweek.com/socialtimes/ study-hostility-joseph-grenny/418228.

[48] Zachary Crockett, "What I Learned Analyzing 7 Months of Donald Trump's Tweets," Vox.com, May 16, 2016; http://www.vox.com/2016/5/16/11603854/ donald-trump-twitter.

[49] Felix Richter, "Americans Use Electronic Media 11+ Hours a Day," *Statista*, March 13, 2015; https://www.statista.com/chart/1971/electronic-media-use/.

[50] Haidt, *The Happiness Hypothesis*, 94.

[51] Haidt, *The Happiness Hypothesis*, 167.

[52] Haidt, *The Happiness Hypothesis*, 167.

[53] Erik Parens, *Shaping Our Selves: On Technology, Flourishing, and a Habit of Thinking* (New York: Oxford University Press, 2015), 13.

[54] Parens, *Shaping Our Selves*, 13.

[55] Sharon L. Bracci and Clifford G. Christians, *Moral Engagement in Public Life: Theorists for Contemporary Ethics* (New York: Peter Lang Publishing, 2002), 25.

[56] Kenan Malik, *The Quest for a Moral Compass: A Global History of Ethics* (Brooklyn, NY: Melville House, 2014), 3.

[57] Malik, *The Quest for a Moral Compass*, 78.

[58] Carolyn Marvin, *When Old Technologies Were New* (New York: Oxford University Press, 1988), 69.

[59] Marvin, *When Old Technologies Were New*, 76.

[60] Wendy Shalit, *A Return to Modesty: Discovering the Lost Virtue* (New York: Free Press, 2014), 147.

[61] Jonathan Haidt, *The Righteous Mind: Why Good People Are Divided by Politics and Religion* (New York: Vintage Books, 2013), 116–17.

[62] James G. Webster, *The Marketplace of Attention: How Audience Takes Shape in a Digital Age* (Cambridge, MA: MIT Press, 2014), 1.

[63] Mark Andrejevic, "Social Network Exploitation," in *A Networked Self*, ed. by Zizi Papacharissi (New York: Routledge, 2011), 96.

[64] George Ritzer, *The Globalization of Nothing 2* (Thousand Oaks, CA: Pine Forge Press, 2007), 165.

[65] Vicki Rideout, "Common Sense Census: Media Use by Tweens and Teens," Common Sense report, San Francisco, 2015, 15; https://www.commonsensemedia .org/sites/default/files/uploads/research/census_executivesummary.pdf.

[66] Sean Grover, "3 Mistakes Parents Make with Technology," *Psychology Today*, April 3, 2016; https://www.psychologytoday.com/blog/when-kids-call-the -shots/201604/3-mistakes-parents-make-technology.

[67] Jim Taylor, "Is Technology Creating a Family Divide?" *Psychology Today*, March 13, 2013; https://www.psychologytoday.com/blog/the-power-prime/201303/ is-technology-creating-family-divide.

[68] Sherry Turkle, *Life on the Screen: Identity in the Age of the Internet* (New York: Simon and Schuster, 1995), 83.

Chapter Five

[1] Daniel Goleman, *Emotional Intelligence* (New York: Bantam Books, 1995).

[2] Meridee Duddleston, "Graduation and Elgar's 'Pomp and Circumstance'— What's the Connection," WRTI, May 23, 2016; http://wrti.org/post/ graduation-and-elgars-pomp-and-circumstance-whats-connection#stream/0.

[3] Ellen Wexler, "Chancellor Criticized for Using Phone at Commencement," *Inside Higher Ed*, May 25, 2016; https://www.insidehighered.com/ quicktakes/2016/05/25/chancellor-criticized-using-phone-commencement

4 "Non-apology Apology," Wikipedia; https://en.wikipedia.org/wiki/
Non-apology_apology.

5 Kelly Wallace, "Half of Teens Think They're Addicted to Their Smartphones,"
CNN, May 3, 2016; http://www.cnn.com/2016/05/03/health/teens-cell-phone
-addiction-parents/index.html

6 Wallace, "Half of Teens."

7 Lee Rainie and Kathryn Zickuhr, "Americans' Views on Mobile Etiquette," Pew
Research Center, Aug. 26, 2015; http://www.pewinternet.org/2015/08/26/
americans-views-on-mobile-etiquette/.

8 Sherry Turkle, "Stop Googling. Let's Talk," *New York Times*, Sept. 26, 2015; http://
www.nytimes.com/2015/09/27/opinion/sunday/stop-googling-lets-talk.html?_r=0.

9 See A. V. Laskin and J. Avena, "Introduction of Mobile Media Into Formal
Classroom Learning Environments," *Journalism & Mass Communication
Educator* 70, no. 3 (2015), 276–85.

10 Carl Straumsheim, "Leave It in the Bag," *Inside Higher Ed*, May
13, 2016; https://www.insidehighered.com/news/2016/05/13/
allowing-devices-classroom-hurts-academic-performance-study-finds.

11 Stephenie Petit, "5 Things to Know About America's Got Talent Winner Grace
Vanderwaal," People Magazine, Sept. 15, 2016; http://www.people.com/article/
grace-vanderwaal-americas-got-talent-winner-5-things-to-know.

12 Anna Kuchment, "Teens Who Won Google Science Fair Took a Leap of
Imagination," *Scientific American*, Sept. 23, 2015; http://blogs
.scientificamerican.com/budding-scientist/teens-who-won-google-science-
fair-took-a-leap-of-imagination/.

13 Sunil Iyengar, "To Read or Not to Read: A Question of National Consequence,"
National Endowment for the Arts, available via the Library of Congress, May 8,
2008, at http://www.loc.gov/today/cyberlc/feature_wdesc.php?rec=4319.

14 Juana Summers, "Kids and Screen Time: What Does the Research Say?" NPR,
Aug. 28, 2014; http://www.npr.org/sections/ed/2014/08/28/343735856/
kids-and-screen-time-what-does-the-research-say.

15 No author, "Bullying," Center for Emotional Intelligence, Yale University, no
date; http://ei.yale.edu/what-we-do/bullying-2/.

16 Carrie James, *Disconnected: Youth, New Media, and the Ethics Gap* (Cambridge,
MA: MIT Press, 2014), 30.

17 James, *Disconnected*, 103.

18 Eric Holder Jr., "Child Pornography," National Strategy Conference on
Combating Child Exploitation in San Jose, California, May 19, 2011; https://
www.justice.gov/criminal-ceos/child-pornography.

19 Bruce Drushel and Kathleen M. German, *The Ethics of Emerging Media: Information,
Social Norms, and New Media Technology* (New York: Continuum, 2011) 100–101.

20 Drushel and German, *Ethics of Emerging Media*, 155, 157.

21 Clive Thompson, *Smarter Than You Think: How Technology Is Changing Our
Minds for the Better* (New York: Penguin Books, 2014), 211.

22 Thompson, *Smarter Than You Think*, 195.

23 See Dan Brown, "Teaching Computer Coding in K–12," HomeRoom, March 2013; http://blog.ed.gov/2013/03/teaching-computer-coding-in-k-12/.

24 Jason Kolb and Jeremy Kolb, *Secrets of the Big Data Revolution* (Chicago: Applied Data Labs, 2013), 59.

25 Kolb and Kolb, *Secrets of the Big Data Revolution*, p. 59.

26 See "Culture," Rio Salado College at http://www.riosalado.edu/about/research-planning/Pages/culture.aspx.

27 See "How Has Technology Changed Education," Purdue University, http://online.purdue.edu/ldt/learning-design-technology/resources/how-has-technology-changed-education.

28 Merrill Perlman, "How Truthful Is Your 'Truthiness,'" *Columbia Journalism Review*, Aug. 11, 2015; http://www.cjr.org/analysis/how_truthful_is_your_truthiness.php.

29 Jill Lepore, "After the Fact: In the History of Truth, a New Chapter Begins," *New Yorker*, March 21, 2016; http://www.newyorker.com/magazine/2016/03/21/the-internet-of-us-and-the-end-of-facts.

30 Millie Ferrer and Anne Fugate, "The Importance of Friendship for School-Age Children," University of Florida Extension, June 2014; http://edis.ifas.ufl.edu/fy545.

31 Suren Ramasubbu, "Friendship in the Time of Technology," *Huffington Post*, Aug. 13, 2015; http://www.huffingtonpost.com/suren-ramasubbu/friendship-in-the-time-of_b_7974934.html.

32 Amanda Lenhart, "Teens, Technology, and Friendship," Pew Research Center, Aug. 6, 2015; http://www.pewinternet.org/2015/08/06/teens-technology-and-friendships/.

33 Lenhart, "Teens, Technology, and Friendship."

34 Ilana Gershon, *Breakup 2.0: Disconnecting over New Media* (New York: Cornell University Press, 2010), 37–38.

35 Amanda Lenhart, Monica Anderson, and Aaron Smith, "After the Relationship: Technology and Breakups," Pew Research Center, Oct. 1, 2015; http://www.pewinternet.org/2015/10/01/after-the-relationship-technology-and-breakups/.

36 Andrew Keen, *The Internet Is Not the Answer* (New York: Atlantic Monthly Press, 2015), x.

37 John Palfrey and Urs Gasser, *Born Digital: Understanding the First Generation of Digital Natives* (New York: Perseus, 2008), 91.

38 Mitch van Geel, Paul Vedder and Jenny Tanilon, "Relationship Between Peer Victimization, Cyberbullying, and Suicide in Children and Adolescents," *JAMA Pediatrics* 168, no. 5 (May 2014); http://archpedi.jamanetwork.com/article.aspx?articleid=1840250.

39 David D. Luxton, Jennifer D. June, and Jonathan M. Fairall, "Social Media and Suicide: A Public Health Perspective," *American Journal of Public Health* 102 (May 2012); https://www.ncbi.nlm.nih.gov/pmc/articles/PMC3477910/.

40 Sherry Turkle, *The Second Self: 20th Anniversary Edition* (Cambridge, MA: MIT Press, 2005), 81.

[41] Lee Rainie and Andrew Perrin, "Slightly Fewer Americans Are Reading Print Books, New Survey Finds," Pew Research Center, Oct. 19, 2015; http://www.pewresearch.org/fact-tank/2015/10/19/slightly-fewer-americans-are-reading-print-books-new-survey-finds/

[42] David Denby, "Do Teens Read Seriously Anymore?," *New Yorker*, Feb. 23, 2016; http://www.newyorker.com/culture/cultural-comment/books-smell-like-old-people-the-decline-of-teen-reading.

[43] Denby, "Do Teens Read?"

[44] Nicholas Carr, "The Bookless Library," in *Is the Internet Changing the Way You Think?* ed. John Brockman (New York: Harper-Perennial, 2011), 2.

[45] Eric Fischl and April Gornik, "Replacing Experience with Facsimile," in Brockman, *Is the Internet Changing the Way You Think?*, 146.

[46] Roger Schank, "Everyone Is an Expert," in Brockman, *Is the Internet Changing the Way You Think?*, 356.

[47] Lee Crockett, Ian Jukes, and Andrew Churches, *Literacy Is Not Enough: 21st-Century Fluencies for the Digital Age* (Kelowna, BC: 21st Century Fluency Project, 2011), 79.

[48] Crockett et. al, *Literacy Is Not Enough*, 89.

[49] R. S. Peters, *Ethics and Education* (London: Allen and Unwin, 1970), 46.

[50] Jeremy Rifkin, *The Empathic Civilization: The Race to Global Consciousness in a World in Crisis* (New York: Penguin, 2009), 153

[51] Rifkin, *The Empathic Civilization*, 335.

[52] Rifkin, *The Empathic Civilization*, 154.

Chapter Six

[1] See transcript, *Meet the Press*, Oct. 23, 2016; http://www.nbcnews.com/meet-the-press/meet-press-october-23-2016-n671406.

[2] Nicholas Carr, *The Big Switch: Rewiring the World from Edison to Google* (New York: W. W. Norton, 2013), 143.

[3] Jane Wakefield, "Foxconn Replaces '60,000 Workers with Robots,'" BBC, May 25, 2016; http://www.bbc.com/news/technology-36376966.

[4] Aaron Smith, "Public Predictions for the Future of Workforce Automation," Pew Research Center, March 10, 2016; http://www.pewinternet.org/2016/03/10/public-predictions-for-the-future-of-workforce-automation/.

[5] "Digital America: A Tale of the Haves and Have-Mores," James Manyika, Sree Ramaswamy, Somesh Khanna, et. al., the McKinsey Global Institute, December 2015; http://www.mckinsey.com/industries/high-tech/our-insights/digital-america-a-tale-of-the-haves-and-have-mores.

[6] "Millennials: A Portrait of Generation Next," ed. Paul Taylor and Scott Keeter, Pew Research Center, February 2010; http://www.pewsocialtrends.org/files/2010/10/millennials-confident-connected-open-to-change.pdf.

[7] Eric Chester, *Reviving Work Ethic: A Leader's Guide to Ending Entitlement and Restoring Pride in the Emerging Workforce* (Austin, TX: Greenleaf Book Group Press, 2012), 11–12.

[8] Chester, *Reviving Work Ethic*, 13.

[9] See David Essex, "HR Analytics Tools Bring Increased Employee Privacy Concerns," techtarget.com, February 2016; http://searchfinancialapplications.techtarget.com/feature/HR-analytics-tools-bring-increased-employee-privacy-concerns.

[10] Tony Bush, Les Bell, and David Middlewood, *The Principles of Educational Leadership and Management* (Los Angeles: SAGE, 2010), p. 137.

[11] Carol Kinset Goman, *The Truth About Lies in the Workplace* (San Francisco: Berrett-Koehler, 2013), 28–29.

[12] Goman, *The Truth About Lies*, 51–52.

[13] Tim Raynor, "Foucault and Social Media: Life in a Virtual Panopticon," *Philosophy for Change*, June 21, 2012; https://philosophyforchange .wordpress.com/2012/06/21/foucault-and-social-media-life-in-a-virtual -panopticon/.

[14] Simon Head, *Mindless: Why Smarter Machines Are Making Dumber Humans* (New York: Basic Books, 2014), 45.

[15] Douglas Rushkoff, *Life Inc: How Corporatism Conquered the World, and How We Can Take It Back* (New York: Random House, 2011), 99–100.

[16] Quentin Hardy, "A Talk With Simon Head, Author of 'Mindless: Smarter Machines Are Making Dumber Humans,'" *New York Times* blog, April 12, 2014; http://bits.blogs.nytimes.com/2014/04/12/a-talk-with-simon-head-author-of -mindless-smarter-machines-are-making-dumber-humans/?_r=0

[17] Rushkoff, *Life Inc*, 205.

[18] Rushkoff, *Life Inc*, 242.

[19] William Powers, *Hamlet's BlackBerry: A Practical Philosophy for Building a Good Life in the Digital Age* (New York: Harper, 2010), 15.

[20] Sophie McBain, "Head in the Cloud," *New Statesman*, Feb. 23, 2016; http://www .newstatesman.com/politics/education/2016/02/head-cloud.

[21] Sherry Turkle, *The Second Self: 20th Anniversary Edition* (Cambridge, MA: MIT Press, 2005), 14.

[22] Sherry Turkle, *Alone Together: Why We Expect More from Technology and Less from Each Other* (New York: Basic Books, 2011), 13.

[23] Howard A. Doughty, "Surveillance, Big Data Analytics, and the Death of Privacy," *College Quarterly* 17, no. 3 (May 2014); http://collegequarterly .ca/2014-vol17-num03-summer/doughty1.html.

[24] David Autor and David Dorn, "How Technology Wrecks the Middle Class," *New York Times*, Aug. 24, 2013; http://opinionator.blogs.nytimes.com/2013/08/24/ how-technology-wrecks-the-middle-class/?_r=0.

[25] Noah Smith, "The End of Labor: How to Protect Workers From the Rise of Robots," *Atlantic*, Jan. 14, 2013; https://www.theatlantic.com/business/ archive/2013/01/the-end-of-labor-how-to-protect-workers-from-the-rise-of -robots/267135/.

[26] Tony Schwartz, Jean Gomes, and Catherine McCarthy, *The Way We're Working Isn't Working: The Four Keys to Transforming the Way We Work and Live* (New York: Free Press, 2010), 4.

[27] Schwartz et al., *The Way We're Working*, 50.

[28] Clifford G. Christians and Michael Traber, eds., *Communication Ethics and Universal Values* (Thousand Oaks, CA: Sage, 1997), 6–8.

[29] See "Integrity," vocabulary.com; https://www.vocabulary.com/dictionary/integrity.

[30] Boris Groysberg and Robin Abrahams, "Manage Your Work, Manage Your Life," *Harvard Business Review*, March 2014; https://hbr.org/2014/03/manage-your-work-manage-your-life.

[31] See Jan Currie and Joan Eveline, "E-Technology and Work/Life Balance for Academics with Young Children," *Higher Education* 62, no. 4 (2010), 533–50.

[32] Thomas de Zengotita, *Mediated: How the Media Shapes Your World and the Way You Live In It* (New York: Bloomsbury Publishing, 2005), 190.

[33] Robert Jackall, *Moral Mazes: The World of Corporate Managers* (Oxford: Oxford University Press, 2010), 55).

[34] See "Distracted Driving," Foundation for Public Safety; https://www.aaafoundation.org/distracted-driving.

[35] Robert Glattner, "Texting While Parenting: What Effect Can It Have on Your Children?," *Forbes*, Sept. 30, 2012; http://www.forbes.com/sites/robertglatter/2012/09/30/texting-while-parenting-what-effect-can-it-have-on-your-children/#590f7a83555d.

[36] De Zengotita, *Mediated*, 213.

[37] Jodi Kanter and David Streitfeld, "Inside Amazon: Wrestling Big Ideas in a Brutal Workplace," *New York Times*, Aug. 15, 2015; http://www.nytimes.com/2015/08/16/technology/inside-amazon-wrestling-big-ideas-in-a-bruising-workplace.html?_r=0.

[38] Catherine Clifford, "Why Amazon and Other Companies Are Trying 30-Hour Work Weeks," CNBC, Sept. 16, 2016; http://www.cnbc.com/2016/09/16/why-amazon-and-other-companies-are-trying-30-hour-workweeks.html.

[39] Bunmi Laditan, "What's Wrong with Using Tech to Distract Kids?," CNN, July 3, 2013; http://www.cnn.com/2013/07/03/living/cnn-parents-technology-children/.

[40] Amanda Lenhart, "Couples, the Internet and Social Media," Pew Research Center, Feb. 20, 2014; http://www.pewinternet.org/2014/02/20/couples-the-internet-and-social-media-2/.

[41] William J. Byron, *The Power of Principles: Ethics for the New Corporate Culture* (Maryknoll, NY: Orbis Books, 2006), 19.

[42] Byron, *The Power of Principles*, 20.

[43] Byron, *The Power of Principles*, 24.

[44] Philip J. Vergragt, *How Technology Could Contribute to a Sustainable World*, GTI Paper Series (Boston: Tellus Institute, 2006), 2.

[45] Jeremy Rifkin, *The Empathic Civilization: The Race to Global Consciousness in a World in Crisis* (New York: Penguin, 2009), 546.

Chapter Seven

[1] Nicholas Carr, *The Shallows: What the Internet is Doing to Our Brains* (New York: W. W. Norton, 2011), 5.

[2] No Author, "Do We Need Asimov's Laws?," *MIT Technology Review*, May 16, 2014; https://www.technologyreview.com/s/527336/do-we-need-asimovs-laws/.

[3] Sherry Turkle, *Life on the Screen: Identity in the Age of the Internet* (New York: Simon and Schuster, 1995), 86.

[4] Matthew Dickerson, *The Mind and the Machine: What It Means to Be Human and Why It Matters* (Grand Rapids, MI: Brazos Press, 2011), 18.

[5] Sherry Turkle, *The Second Self: 20th Anniversary Edition* (Cambridge, MA: MIT Press, 2005), 243.

[6] Will Knight, "Tougher Turing Test Exposes Chatbots' Stupidity," *MIT Technology Review*, July 11, 2016; https://www.technologyreview.com/s/601897/tougher-turing-test-exposes-chatbots-stupidity/.

[7] Knight, "Tougher Turing Test."

[8] Nicholas Carr, *The Glass Cage: Automation and Us* (New York: W. W. Norton, 2014), 11.

[9] Wiebe E. Bijker and John Law, *Shaping Technology/Building Society* (Boston: MIT Press, 1992), 205.

[10] Bijker and Law, *Shaping Technology*, 205.

[11] Alison Motluk, "How the Brain Detects the Emotions of Others," *New Scientist*, May 12, 2008; https://www.newscientist.com/article/dn13874-how-the-brain-detects-the-emotions-of-others/.

[12] Motluk, "How the Brain Detects the Emotions of Others."

[13] Joelle Renstron, "Artificial Intelligence, Real Emotions," *Slate*, April 9, 2015; http://www.slate.com/articles/technology/future_tense/2015/04/ex_machina_can_robots_artificial_intelligence_have_emotions.html.

[14] Sherry Turkle, *Alone Together: Why We Expect More from Technology and Less from Each Other* (New York: Basic Books, 2011), 45.

[15] Turkle, *Alone Together*, 45.

[16] John Markoff, *Machines of Loving Grace: The Quest for Common Ground Between Humans and Robots* (New York: HarperCollins, 2015), 2.

[17] Markoff, *Machines*, 329.

[18] Augustine of Hippo, *On Grace and Free Will*, Chapter 7, "Grace Is Necessary, Along with Free Will, to Lead a Good Life," A.D. 426; http://www.newadvent.org/fathers/1510.htm.

[19] Lawrence Pasternack and Philip Rossi, "Kant's Philosophy of Religion," *Stanford Encyclopedia of Philosophy* (Fall 2014 edition); http://plato.stanford.edu/archives/fall2014/entries/kant-religion.

[20] Victor Hugo, *Les Miserables*, tr. Isabel F. Hapgood (New York: Crowell, 1887).

[21] Donald Rutherford, "Descartes' Ethics," *Stanford Encyclopedia of Philosophy* (Spring 2013 Edition), ed. Edward N. Zalta, http://plato.stanford.edu/archives/spr2013/entries/descartes-ethics.

[22] Lex Newman, "Descartes' Epistemology," *Stanford Encyclopedia of Philosophy* (Winter 2014 edition), Edward N. Zalta (ed.), http://plato.stanford.edu/archives/win2014/entries/descartes-epistemology.

[23] Rutherford, "Descartes' Ethics."

[24] Sandra Shapshay, "Schopenhauer's Aesthetics," *Stanford Encyclopedia of Philosophy* (Summer 2012 edition), ed. Edward N. Zalta, http://plato.stanford.edu/archives/sum2012/entries/schopenhauer-aesthetics.

[25] Bruce Weber, "Hilary Putnam, Giant of Modern Philosophy, Dies at 89," *New York Times*, March 20, 2016, 20.

[26] Weber, "Hilary Putnam," 20.

[27] Jill Lepore, "After the Fact: In the History of Truth, a New Chapter Begins," *New Yorker*, March 21, 2016; http://www.newyorker.com/magazine/2016/03/21/the-internet-of-us-and-the-end-of-facts.

[28] Lepore, "After the Fact."

[29] Raffi Khatchadourian, "The Doomsday Invention: Will Artificial Intelligence Bring Us Utopia or Destruction?" *New Yorker*, Nov. 23, 2015; http://www.newyorker.com/magazine/2015/11/23/doomsday-invention-artificial-intelligence-nick-bostrom.

[30] David Von Drehle, "Encounters with the Archgenius," *Time*, March 7, 2016, 46.

[31] Drehle, "Encounters," 46.

[32] Drehle, "Encounters," 49.

[33] Nicholas Carr, *The Glass Cage: Automation and Us* (New York: Norton, 2014), 149.

[34] Andrew Keen, *Digital Vertigo: How Today's Online Social Revolution Is Dividing, Diminishing, and Disorienting Us* (New York: St. Martin's Press, 2012), 12.

[35] Keen, *Digital Vertigo*, 16.

[36] Keen, *Digital Vertigo*, 65.

[37] Jaron Lanier, *You Are Not a Gadget: A Manifesto* (New York: Vintage, 2011), 4.

[38] Lanier, *You Are Not a Gadget*, 19.

[39] Lanier, *You Are Not a Gadget*, 27.

[40] Carolyn Marvin, *When Old Technologies Were New* (New York: Oxford University Press, 1988), 125.

[41] Marvin, *When Old Technologies Were New*, 125.

[42] Marvin, *When Old Technologies Were New*, 141.

[43] See Ray Kurzweil's *The Singularity Is Near: When Humans Transcend Biology* (New York: Penguin Books, 2005).

[44] Robert Jay Lifton, *The Protean Self: Human Resilience in an Age of Fragmentation* (New York, NY: Basic Books, 1993), 120.

[45] Lifton, *The Protean Self*, 123.

[46] Langdon Winner, *The Whale and the Reactor: A Search for Limits in an Age of High Technology* (Chicago: University of Chicago Press, 1986), 114.

[47] Winner, *The Whale and the Reactor*, 114.

[48] Winner, *The Whale and the Reactor*, 117.

[49] Yochai Benkler, *The Wealth of Networks: How Social Production Transforms Markets and Freedom* (New Haven, CT: Yale University Press, 2006), 25.

[50] Benkler, *The Wealth of Networks*, 27–28.

[51] James Carey, *Communication as Culture: Essays on Media and Society* (New York: Routledge, 1992), 114.

[52] Carey, *Communication as Culture*, 115.

[53] Carey, *Communication as Culture*, 116.

[54] Evgeny Morozov, *The Net Delusion: The Dark Side of Internet Freedom* (New York: Public Affairs Books, 2011), 284.

[55] Morozov, *The Net Delusion*, 283.

[56] Bruce Drushel and Kathleen M. German, *The Ethics of Emerging Media: Information, Social Norms, and New Media Technology* (New York: Continuum, 2011), 172.

[57] J. D. R. de Raadt and Veronica D. de Raadt, *From Multi-Modal Systems Thinking to Community Development: Regaining Our Humanity Through Community* (Australia: Melbourne Centre for Community Development, 2014), 113–14.

[58] De Raadt, *From Multi-Modal Systems Thinking*, 189.

[59] De Raadt, *From Multi-Modal Systems Thinking*, 277.

[60] Carr, *The Glass Cage*, 123.

[61] Carr, *The Glass Cage*, 123.

[62] Carr, *The Glass Cage*, 193.

[63] Turkle, *Life on the Screen*, 21.

[64] Deni Eliott, "Universal Values and Moral Development Theories," in *Communication Ethics and Universal Values*, ed. Clifford G. Christians and Michael Traber (Thousand Oaks, CA: Sage, 1997), 71.

[65] Christina Hoff-Sommers, "Teaching the Virtues," *Chicago Tribune*, Sept. 12, 1993, 16.

[66] Clifford Christians, "The Ethics of Being in a Communications Context" in Christians and Traber, *Communication Ethics*, 12–13.

[67] Matthew Dickerson, *The Mind and the Machine: What It Means to Be Human and Why It Matters* (Grand Rapids, MI: Brazos Press, 2011), xi.

[68] Dickerson, *The Mind and the Machine*, xi.

[69] Dickerson, *The Mind and the Machine*, 71.

[70] Dickerson, *The Mind and the Machine*, 73.

[71] James Barrat, *Our Final Invention: Artificial Intelligence and the End of the Human Era* (New York: Thomas Dunn Books, 2013), 5.

[72] Barrat, *Our Final Invention*, 18.

[73] Barrat, *Our Final Invention*, 97.

[74] Roger Penrose, *The Large, the Small, and the Human Mind* (New York: Cambridge University Press, 1997), 101.

[75] Hannah Arendt, *The Human Condition* (Chicago: University of Chicago Press, 1958), 19.

[76] Arendt, *The Human Condition*, 151.

[77] Jeremy Rifkin, *The Empathic Civilization: The Race to Global Consciousness in a World in Crisis* (New York: Penguin, 2009), 163.

SELECTED BIBLIOGRAPHY

....

Aboujaoude, Elias. *Virtually You: The Dangerous Powers of the E-Personality.* New York: W. W. Norton, 2011.

Albarran, Alan B., ed. *The Social Media Industries.* New York: Routledge, 2013.

Arendt, Hannah. *The Human Condition.* Chicago: University of Chicago Press, 1958.

Asimov, Isaac. *The Bicentennial Man.* New York: Ballantine Books, 1976.

Baesens, Bart. *Analytics in a Big Data World: The Essential Guide to Data Science and Its Applications.* New York: Wiley, 2014.

Bagdikian, Ben H. *The Information Machines: Their Impact on Men and the Media.* New York: Harper & Row, 1971.

Baldwin, John R. et al., eds. *Redefining Culture: Perspectives Across the Disciplines.* Mahwah, NJ: Lawrence Erlbaum, 2008.

Barrat, James. *Our Final Invention: Artificial Intelligence and the End of the Human Era.* New York: Thomas Dunn Books, 2013.

Baym, Nancy K. *Personal Connections in the Digital Age.* Cambridge, UK: Polity Press, 2011.

Benkler, Yochai. *The Wealth of Networks: How Social Production Transforms Markets and Freedom.* New Haven, CT: Yale University Press, 2006.

Bertrand, Claude-Jean. *Media Ethics & Accountability Systems.* New Brunswick, NJ: Transaction Publishers, 2000.

Bijker, Wiebe E. *Of Bicycles, Bakelites, and Bulbs: Toward a Theory of Sociotechnical Change.* Cambridge, MA: MIT Press, 1997.

Bijker, Wiebe E. and John Law. *Shaping Technology/Building Society.* Boston: MIT Press, 1992.

Boyd, Danah. *It's Complicated: The Social Lives of Networked Teens.* New Haven, CT: Yale University Press, 2014.

Bracci, Sharon L. and Clifford G. Christians. *Moral Engagement in Public Life: Theorists for Contemporary Ethics.* New York: Peter Lang Publishing, 2002.

Brockman, John, ed. *Is the Internet Changing the Way You Think? The Net's Impact on Our Minds and Future.* New York: Harper Perennial, 2011.

Bugeja, Michael and Daniela Dimitrova. *Vanishing Act: The Erosion of Online Footnotes and Implications for Scholarship in the Digital Age.* Minneapolis: Litwin Books, 2010.

Byron, William J. *The Power of Principles: Ethics for the New Corporate Culture.* Maryknoll, NY: Orbis Books, 2006.

Carey, James. *Communication as Culture: Essays on Media and Society.* New York: Routledge, 1992.

Carr, Nicholas. *The Glass Cage: Automation and Us.* New York: W. W. Norton, 2014.

Carr, Nicholas. *The Big Switch: Rewiring the World, from Edison to Google.* New York: W. W. Norton, 2013.

Carr, Nicholas. *The Shallows: What the Internet is Doing to Our Brains.* New York, W. W. Norton & Company, 2011.

Castells, Manuel. *The Power of Identity.* Oxford, UK: Blackwell, 1997.

Chester, Eric. *Reviving Work Ethic: A Leader's Guide to Ending Entitlement and Restoring Pride in the Emerging Workforce.* Austin, TX: Greenleaf Book Group Press, 2012.

Christians, Clifford, G. and Michael Traber, eds. *Communication Ethics and Universal Values.* Thousand Oaks, CA: Sage, 1997.

Christians, Clifford G. and Jay M. Van Hook, eds. *Jacques Ellul: Interpretive Essays.* Urbana: University of Illinois Press, 1981.

Colvin, Geoff. *Humans Are Underrated: What High Achievers Know That Brilliant Machines Never Will.* New York: Penguin, 2015.

Crockett, Lee, Ian Jukes, and Andrew Churches. *Literacy Is Not Enough: 21st-Century Fluencies for the Digital Age.* Kelowna, BC: 21st Century Fluency Project, 2011.

D'Souza, Dinesh. *The Virtue of Prosperity: Finding Values in an Age of Techno-Affluence.* New York: Free Press, 2000.

De Zengotita, Thomas. *Mediated: How the Media Shapes Your World and the Way You Live in It.* New York: Bloomsbury, 2005.

Dennis, Everette E. and John C. Merrill. *Media Debates: Great Issues for the Digital Age.* Belmont, CA: Wadsworth, 2002.

Dickerson, Matthew. *The Mind and the Machine: What It Means to Be Human and Why It Matters.* Grand Rapids, MI: Brazos Press, 2011.

Drushel, Bruce and Kathleen M. German. *The Ethics of Emerging Media: Information, Social Norms, and New Media Technology.* New York: Continuum, 2011.

Ess, Charles. *Digital Media Ethics.* Malden, MA: Polity, 2014.

Feenberg, Andrew. *Questioning Technology.* London: Routledge, 1999.

Fortner, Robert S. and Mark Fackler, eds. *The Handbook of Global Communication and Media Ethics.* Malden, MA: Wiley-Blackwell, 2011.

Frankl, Viktor. *Man's Search For Meaning.* Boston: Beacon Press, 2006.

Gans, Herbert J. *Popular Culture & High Culture: An Analysis and Evaluation of Taste.* New York: Basic Books, 1999.

Gershon, Ilana. *Breakup 2.0: Disconnecting over New Media.* New York: Cornell University Press, 2010.

Goleman, Daniel. *Emotional Intelligence: Why It Can Matter More Than IQ.* New York: Bantam Books, 1995.

Goman, Carol Kinsey. *The Truth About Lies in the Workplace: How to Spot Liars and What to Do About Them.* San Francisco: Berrett-Koehler, 2013.

Green, Lelia. *Communication, Technology, and Society.* Thousand Oaks, CA: Sage, 2002.

Gurak, Laura J. *Cyberliteracy: Navigating the Internet with Awareness.* New Haven, CT: Yale University Press, 2001.

Haidt, Jonathan. *The Happiness Hypothesis: Finding Modern Truth in Ancient Wisdom.* New York: Basic Books, 2006.

Haidt, Jonathan. *The Righteous Mind: Why Good People Are Divided by Politics and Religion.* New York: Vintage Books, 2013.

Head, Simon. *Mindless: Why Smarter Machines Are Making Dumber Humans.* New York: Basic Books, 2014.

Ihde, Don. *Philosophy of Technology.* New York: Paragon, 1993.

Jackall, Robert. *Moral Mazes: The World of Corporate Managers.* New York: Oxford University Press, 2010.

James, Carrie. *Disconnected: Youth, New Media, and the Ethics Gap.* Cambridge, MA: MIT Press, 2014.

Keen, Andrew. *Digital Vertigo: How Today's Online Social Revolution Is Dividing, Diminishing, and Disorienting Us.* New York: St. Martin's Press, 2012.

Keen, Andrew. *The Internet Is Not the Answer.* New York: Atlantic Monthly Press, 2015.

Kelly, Kevin. *What Technology Wants: Technology Is a Living Force That Can Expand Our Individual Potential—If We Listen to What It Wants.* New York: Penguin, 2010.

Kolb, Jason, and Jeremy Kolb. *Secrets of the Big Data Revolution.* Chicago: Applied Data Labs, 2013.

Kunstler, James Howard. *Home from Nowhere: Remaking Our Everyday World for the 21st Century.* New York: Simon & Schuster, 1996.

Kurzweil, Ray. *The Singularity is Near: When Humans Transcend Biology.* New York: Penguin Books, 2005.

Lanier, Jaron. *Who Owns the Future?* New York: Simon and Schuster, 2013.

Lanier, Jaron. *You Are Not a Gadget: A Manifesto.* New York: Vintage, 2011.

Lifton, Robert Jay. *The Protean Self: Human Resilience in an Age of Fragmentation.* New York: Basic Books, 1993.

Lindstrom, Martin. *Clicks, Bricks & Brands.* London: Kogan Page, 2001.

Malik, Kenan. *The Quest for a Moral Compass: A Global History of Ethics.* Brooklyn, NY: Melville House, 2014.

Marchand, Phillip. *Marshall McLuhan: The Medium and the Messenger*. New York: Ticknor & Fields, 1989.

Markoff, John. *Machines of Loving Grace: The Quest for Common Ground Between Humans and Robots*. New York: HarperCollins, 2015.

Marvin, Carolyn. *When Old Technologies Were New: Thinking About Electric Communication in the Late Nineteenth Century*. New York: Oxford University Press, 1988.

Mayer-Schönberger, Viktor, and Kenneth Cukier. *Big Data: A Revolution That Will Transform How We Live, Work, and Think*. New York: First Mariner, 2014.

McLuhan, Marshall. *Understanding Media: The Extensions of Man*. Cambridge, MA: MIT Press, 2002.

McLuhan, Marshall, and Quentin Fiore. *The Medium is the Massage: An Inventory of Effects*. San Francisco: HardWired, 1996 reprint.

Mercer, David. *The Telephone: The Life Story of a Technology*. Westport, Conn.: Greenwood Press, 2006.

Morozov, Evgeny. *The Net Delusion: The Dark Side of Internet Freedom*. New York: Public Affairs Books, 2011.

Negroponte, Nicholas. *Being Digital*. New York: Knopf, 1995.

Noble, David F. *The Religion of Technology: The Divinity of Man and the Spirit of Invention*. New York: Penguin, 1997.

Norris, Pippa. *Digital Divide: Civic Engagement, Information Poverty, and the Internet Worldwide*. Cambridge, UK: Cambridge University Press, 2001.

Nye, David E. *Technology Matters: Questions to Live With*. Boston: MIT Press, 2007.

Palfrey, John, and Urs Gasser. *Born Digital: Understanding the First Generation of Digital Natives*. New York: Perseus, 2008.

Palmer, Parker J. *The Company of Strangers: Christians and the Renewal of America's Public Life*. New York: Crossroad, 1981.

Papacharissi, Zizi, ed. *A Networked Self: Identity, Community, and Culture on Social Network Sites*. New York: Routledge, 2011.

Parens, Erik. *Shaping Our Selves: On Technology, Flourishing, and a Habit of Thinking*. New York: Oxford University Press, 2015.

Penrose, Roger. *The Large, the Small, and the Human Mind*. New York: Cambridge University Press, 1997.

Peters, R. S. *Ethics and Education*. London: Allen and Unwin, 1970.

Postman, Neil. *Technopoly: The Surrender of Culture to Technology*. New York: Vintage, 1993.

Powers, William. *Hamlet's BlackBerry: A Practical Philosophy for Building a Good Life in the Digital Age*. New York: Harper, 2010.

Preston, Paschal. *Reshaping Communications: Technology, Information, and Social Change*. Thousand Oaks, CA: Sage, 2001.

Putnam, Robert D. *Bowling Alone: The Collapse and Revival of American Community*. New York: Simon & Schuster, 2000.

Qualman, Erik. *Socialnomics: How Social Media Transforms the Way We Live and Do Business*. New York: Wiley, 2011.

Rheingold, Howard. *Smart Mobs: The Next Social Revolution*. New York: Perseus, 2002.

Rheingold, Howard. *The Virtual Community: Homesteading on the Electronic Frontier.* Cambridge, MA: MIT, 2000.

Rifkin, Jeremy. *The Empathic Civilization: The Race to Global Consciousness in a World in Crisis*. New York: Penguin, 2009.

Ritzer, George. *The Globalization of Nothing 2*. Thousand Oaks, CA: Pine Forge Press, 2007.

Roszak, Theodore. *The Cult of Information*. Berkeley: University of California Press, 1994.

Rushkoff, Douglas. *Life Inc: How Corporatism Conquered the World, and How We Can Take It Back*. New York: Random House, 2011.

Sathi, Arvind. *Big Data Analytics*. Boise, ID: MC Press, 2012.

Scharff, Robert and V. Dusek, eds. *Philosophy of Technology: The Technological Condition*. Malden, MA: Blackwell, 2003.

Schmarzo, Bill. *Big Data: Understanding How Data Powers Big Business*. New York: Wiley, 2013.

Schneier, Bruce. *Data and Goliath: The Hidden Battles to Collect Your Data and Control Your World*. New York: W. W. Norton, 2015.

Schwartz, Tony, Jean Gomes, and Catherine McCarthy. *The Way We're Working Isn't Working: The Four Keys to Transforming the Way We Work and Live*. New York: Free Press, 2010.

Seabrook, John. *Nobrow: The Culture of Marketing, the Marketing of Culture*. New York: Vintage, 2001.

Shalit, Wendy. *A Return to Modesty: Discovering the Lost Virtue*. New York: Free Press, 2014.

Silverstone, Roger. *Media and Morality: On the Rise of the Mediapolis*. Malden, MA: Polity, 2007.

Smolan, Rick and Jennifer Erwitt, eds. *The Human Face of Big Data*. Sausalito, CA: Against All Odds Productions, 2012.

Standage, Tom. *The Victorian Internet: The Remarkable Story of the Telegraph and the Nineteenth Century's On-line Pioneers*. New York: Berkeley, 1999.

Stryker, Eve Munson, and Catherine A. Warren, eds. *James Carey: A Critical Reader*. Minneapolis: University of Minnesota Press, 1997.

Sunstein, Cass R. *Republic.com 2.0*. Princeton, NJ: Princeton University Press, 2007.

Thompson, Clive. *Smarter Than You Think: How Technology Is Changing Our Minds for the Better*. New York: Penguin Books, 2014.

Turkle, Sherry. *Alone Together: Why We Expect More from Technology and Less from Each Other*. New York: Basic Books, 2011.

Turkle, Sherry. *Life on the Screen: Identity in the Age of the Internet*. New York: Simon and Schuster, 1995.

Turkle, Sherry. *The Second Self: 20th Anniversary Edition*. Cambridge, MA: MIT Press, 2005.

Webster, James G. *The Marketplace of Attention: How Audience Takes Shape in a Digital Age.* Cambridge, MA: MIT Press, 2014.

Wilkins, Lee. and Clifford G. Christians, eds. *The Handbook of Mass Media Ethics.* New York: Routledge, 2009.

Winn, Marie. *The Plug-in Drug: Television, Computers, and Family Life.* New York: Penguin, 2002.

Winner, Langdon. *The Whale and the Reactor: A Search for Limits in an Age of High Technology.* Chicago: University of Chicago Press, 1986.

INDEX

....